The Gulf CRISIS
Reshaping Alliances in the Middle East

Contributors

Mohammed Al-Rumaihi
Gerald Feierstein
Kristian Coates Ulrichsen
David B. Des Roches
Courtney Freer
Giorgio Cafiero

Editors

Khalid Al-Jaber
Sigurd Neubauer

منتدى الخليج الدولي
Gulf International Forum

Gulf International Forum
1000 Potomac Street NW, 5th Floor
Washington, DC 20007
GULFIF.com
info@gulfii.com

Ordering Information:
Contact Gulf International Forum, at the address above for additional copies or for quantity ordering by corporations, associations, and others.

Printed in the United States of America
An electronic copy of this publication is available online at
GULFIF.com

First Edition
ISBN: 978-1-7328043-0-2
Gulf International Forum does not take institutional positions on public policy issues; the views represented herein are the authors' own and do not necessarily reflect the views of GIF, its staff, or board members.

Table Of Contents

PART II
International Stakes and the GCC Dispute

Map of the Region

Foreword

On behalf of Gulf International Forum (GIF), I am pleased to present to you *The Gulf Crisis: Reshaping Alliances in the Middle East*. As GIF's first work to be published in book format, we are thrilled at what this occasion means for our organization and we look forward to publishing more books on the Gulf region. In this volume you will find eight chapters from eight esteemed scholars on the region, each of which deals with a specific aspect of the ongoing Gulf Crisis.

GIF is an independent think-tank located in Washington D.C. Our region of focus is the Gulf, a region we define as including the Gulf Cooperation Council in addition to Iran, Iraq and Yemen. Our vision is to share knowledge of the Gulf region with policymakers, academics, students, and the public, in the East and West alike. Through the open proliferation of ideas, we aspire to enhance peace, security, and stability in the Gulf and the greater Middle East region. We serve as a platform of publication for both in-region and out-of-region scholars. GIF is committed to allowing informed opinions from across the spectrum of a given policy debate to have a voice. Although this book may be one small addition to scholarship on the Gulf, it is one step towards fulfilling our mission.

This book would not have been possible without our team members' hard work. Specifically I would like to thank Anas Al-Qaed, who worked with authors to organize the effort; Ali N, whose design can be seen throughout this volume; Jesse Schatz, who did several rounds of edits on these chapters; and Nabeel Al-Nowairah, whose intensive Arabic to English translation work allows the oft-ignored voices of Gulf-based scholars to be read by an English-speaking audience. This is our first book of a series of publications that we endeavor to produce for audiences interested in the Gulf region.

Dania Thafer
Executive Director, GIF

Introduction

In the decades since the end of foreign domination, much of the greater Middle East has witnessed numerous ethnic, religious, and territorial conflicts. While the Arab Gulf region has remained during this period an oasis of relative stability, the Gulf region too has seen its share of violence, with the Iran-Iraq War (1980), the Invasion of Kuwait (1990), the invasion of Iraq (2003), the events of the Arab Spring (2011), and the war in Yemen (2015) representing the most notable examples.

The Arab Spring in particular exacerbated the differences among the GCC States, sequestering Qatar and a bloc consisting of Saudi Arabia, the UAE and Bahrain. The former supported the revolutions that swept a number of Arab countries, including GCC States, while the latter camp opposed bottom-up regime change, fearing that the ripple effect may endanger GCC leadership and the security and balance of power in the region. Qatar's independent policy in the region, which received widespread supportive media coverage by Al Jazeera, has angered the Kingdom of Saudi Arabia, an important regional power, in addition to the other GCC States. Such differences have resulted in clear tensions and a rift among the GCC States that in June 2017 prominently coalesced in the GCC Crisis that is seen today. This has developed into a shocking rift that has severely damaged any sense of common Arab Gulf security and economic solidarity.

The current row appears so deep that even if the GCC is reunited, Gulf economic and military unity may never be the same. GCC official media has been negatively used to attack other GCC States and their leaders at an unprecedented level. An official green light to target opponent GCC States, and in some cases legislatively criminalizing expressions of sympathy with such states, has allowed the GCC public to indulge in exchanges of accusations

1

and insults that have disintegrated a GCC society that previously shared common traditions, tribal roots and marital ties.

To say that the GCC Crisis of 2017 has been complicated for the nations in and around the Arabian Peninsula would be a grand understatement. Years of internal disagreement within the Gulf Cooperation Council finally boiled over as Saudi Arabia, Bahrain, and the United Arab Emirates, severed all ties with Qatar and instituted a land, sea and air blockade of that nation (a move Egypt enthusiastically endorsed). This "Gulf Crisis" certainly has disrupted what up until this point was viewed as the most stable bloc of nations within the greater Middle East. With few hopes of actual reconciliation, actors on all sides of the schism are now adjusting to new networks of regional alliances.

Historically, the GCC States have relied on wealth from natural resources to make possible the rapid modernization that gives the region its luster. Changing economic realties have spurred the realization among rulers of these nations that diversification represents the only safeguard available to protect their ailing economies.

As a hedge against declining oil and gas revenues, GCC governments have tried to steer their way towards "knowledge economies" capable of developing a citizenry and reducing reliance on foreign innovation. Such economic change must be accompanied by social change that frees dynamism and encourages innovation by their peoples. One important consideration would be a sincere desire to relax restrictions on free expression, women's roles and other facets of modernization. However, tensions arise in that what may be a welcome development for many youths is simultaneously an uncomfortable change for those who fear the old ways may be slipping away.

Certainly, the Gulf does not exist in isolation and its internal conflicts cannot be viewed independent of the wider world. The resultant tensions led to internal conflict that has empowered Iran and led to tragic proxy conflicts in Syria, Yemen and Bahrain as Tehran's traditional rivals in Riyadh and Abu Dhabi compete with it for supremacy. This is not to speak of the near-disintegration of Iraq, which only three decades ago had the strength to launch a full-scale invasion of Gulf territory.

Meanwhile, Russia and the growing and newly assertive Asian economies of China and India have recognized the chaos facing Gulf monarchs and have looked to extend their influence by taking advantage of these regional shifts and engaging the Gulf states as new partners. The decision by the Obama administration to break with traditional policies and reach out to Iran did much to fray GCC confidence in the US relationship. By negotiating a diplomatic end to the Iranian nuclear program through the Joint Comprehensive Plan of Action (JCPOA) signed in November 2013, the US appeared to end Iran's isolation. President Trump delighted some GCC regimes by pulling out of the JCPOA. By reinstituting Iranian sanctions, he allowed some regional leaders to once again consolidate power internally by elevating Iran as the regional boogeyman. Now, the Europeans, Russia, the UN and China are trying to reassure Iran of the agreement's viability and to prevent a new nuclear threat, but their success will depend on the US's willingness (or lack thereof) to add secondary and tertiary sanctions to its trade war against Europe.

What were once small British protectorates, that after independence (mostly in the 1960s-1970s) remained dependent on Western support to maintain sovereignty, have now become global players in their own right. The region's path forward is certainly fraught with challenges, both internal and external. However the future of the Gulf is certainly one that goes beyond mere "Crisis."

This volume has been divided into two parts, the first examining the Crisis through the lenses of Qatar and other Gulf region states. Part Two examines how the Crisis involves nations in the West.

Part I begins with a chapter by Dr. Mohammed Al-Rumaihi within which he provides brief background on the history of the GCC as an institution, going on to categorize and outline the litany of threats currently facing the region. He concludes with a call for greater cohesion amongst the Gulf countries.

Chapter 2 by Mr. Giorgio Cafiero looks at an alliance between Saudi Arabia and the United Arab Emirates that began to emerge prior to and only continued to grow in strength since the isolating of Qatar. He goes on to show how this alliance is perceived by the excluded GCC states. Ultimately, he concludes that, although a reality that must be contended with, Saudi-Emirati cooperation faces its own unique set of challenges due to distinctions between the two Arabian powerhouses.

The following chapter by Professor David Des Roches takes a conceptual approach to the idea of the so-called "Small State." Using Qatar as an example, Des Roches looks at the steps the embattled emirate has taken to quickly build a military capable of standing up to neighboring pressures. Additionally, his analysis looks at historical precedents of how small states have successfully challenged the whims of powerful neighbors. In the end, while Des Roches argues that Qatar does have reasons to feel secure, the small nation still faces many challenges and is a long-way from being considered a military powerhouse comparable to the UAE or Saudi Arabia.

Chapter 4 by Dr. Kristian Coates Ulrichsen examines the ways in which the Qatari economy has been affected by the regional blockade. Although the blockade took many observers by surprise, Dr. Ulrichsen argues that Qatar had actually been preparing for such a scenario and was thus able to quickly attain security within the new status quo. Whether this security is sustainable in the long-term, according to Ulrichsen, is up for debate.

Chapter 5 by Dr. Khalid Al-Jaber zeroes in on the role of the media in both initiating and escalating the ongoing crisis. Dr. Al-Jaber argues that media institutions in the GCC have yet to catch-up with the modernity suggested by their capitals' skylines. Drawing on Noam Chomsky's theories of "Manufacturing Consent," Dr. Al-Jaber shows how the central authority of the Gulf States has allowed the government to formulate media campaigns akin to those used by warring parties during the World Wars. Subsequently, Dr. Al-Jaber looks at the ways in which social media platforms allowed such vitriol to escalate the crisis among the involved parties.

Part I's final chapter by Ambassador Gerald M. Feierstein looks at how the involvement of various actors in Yemen have placed the various nations on a path towards conflict. Compounded by involvement of all GCC states, in addition to that of Iran, Feierstein seems to believe that each nation's differing agenda has allowed for the proliferation of mistrust on all sides of the conflict.

Part II changes perspective, examining the roles played by nations not holding membership within the Gulf Cooperation Council. Beginning with the United States, Mr. Sigurd Neubauer looks at the steps the Trump administration has taken to (and failed to) solve the schism between Qatar and the Quartet. Mr. Neubauer ultimately concludes that the United States' inability to forge such a rapprochement could signal a decline of American power in the region.

Finally, this volume concludes with a chapter by Dr. Courtney Freer, who looks at the stakes and positions of France, Germany and Britain, in addition to Russia. She draws different conclusions vis-a-vis each nation, from those that want little to do with assisting in the crisis's resolution, to those that are hoping to use the crisis to gain a stronger diplomatic foothold in the Gulf region.

As an independent institute based in Washington D.C., Gulf International Forum aims to educate the public on the Gulf region. GIF's vision is to build a bridge between the East and West. We aspire to enhance peace, security and stability both regionally and globally through the dissemination of knowledge. While it may have a small impact, we hope that this work is but one way in which this mission can been fulfilled.

The Editors

PART I

GCC Crisis and the Greater
Middle East

CHAPTER 1

Lessons from the Gulf Cooperation Council's Institutional History*

MOHAMMED AL-RUMAIHI

Introduction

F ounded amidst the sunset of the Pan-Arab political era, the Gulf Cooperation Council (GCC) has been a unique example of a unitary bloc within the Arab world that has at least partially represented the ideals espoused by those seeking Arab unity. The relationship among the six countries forming the GCC has developed over the past thirty-seven years, establishing cooperation and coordination in many fields. According to Arabists, in the wake of the collapse of Egypt-Syria unity in the 1960's, as well as the failure of a variety of subsequent unity attempts among Arab nations, the GCC remains the most promising model to be followed by those still calling for Arab unification. Despite the romantic connotations of Pan-Arabism, others disagree as to the motives behind the GCC's establishment, arguing that it was simply a pragmatic response in order to confront the ferocity of the 1980-1988 Iran-Iraq War. Still, others contend that the GCC arose out of popular desire due to the region's historical cohesion and extensive ties, both familial and tribal. Ultimately, a single origin story of the GCC may not be agreed upon, however, such mixed opinions only point to the conclusion that a variety of motives, including the Iran-Iraq war, the strategic and social necessities after the withdrawal of Britain from east of Suez, deep historical

*Translated from Arabic by Nabeel Al-Nowairah

joint relationships and interests, and the popular desire for unity in the region each contributed to the institution's birth. Having had the privilege of being assigned to a small group of researchers at Kuwait University to write the first papers highlighting the importance of the GCC, I have become very familiar with the council's history, an awareness that has certainly informed the following analysis.[1]

Beginning with an overview of the debates concerning the GCC's formation and elaborating on a few instances when the institution successfully responded to regional threats, I will then proceed to highlight four major risks currently facing the region. In each of these risks I hope the reader will see how various external threats contributed to fomenting and escalating the third threat: the ongoing Gulf crisis. Subsequently, I will show how the Gulf crisis largely obfuscates the internal threats presented by unaddressed changes to Gulf society. Finally, I will conclude with a few thoughts as to how the Gulf Cooperation Council can successfully move beyond its current stalemate.

1.1. A Brief Institutional History

Those who credit the Iran-Iraq War with spurring the creation of the GCC are not entirely incorrect, as the war was certainly intense. There was indeed a desire from the GCC states to protect the security of the region amidst the nearby conflict. However, it should be noted that notions of "cooperation between the Gulf states" had emerged even earlier when Britain announced in the late 1960s its intention to vacate its colonies and protectorates East of Suez (including the Gulf region), ending almost a century and a half of British presence. Naturally, the new challenge became reaching collective regional security in the vacuum left by the United Kingdom's retreat. The countries bordering the Gulf (the eventual GCC states, as well as Iran and Iraq) met in a conference in Muscat in 1975, but failed to develop an arrangement as Iran and Iraq refused to cede to the other chairmanship of the body.[2] When the two countries went to war, the remaining nations took the opportunity to establish strategic cooperation amongst themselves that did not include the two rival nations.

Iran did not make significant contributions to the GCC's formation, especially after the departure of Shah Mohammad Reza Pahlavi in 1979. However, Iraq was still consulted in the body's development. Interestingly, when the idea for the GCC was presented to Iraqi President Saddam Hussein at the 1981 Arab League Summit in Amman it is reported that Saddam himself proposed "Cooperation Council" as a name for the new body, ensuring that no one could take from him the credit for the idea of Pan-Arab unity.

Observers of the inner workings of the GCC from its establishment through the present day would note a number of unique aspects about the literature detailing the body's development. First, that there is a density of writing about the GCC, as writers (especially from the Gulf) have a tendency to continually remind audiences of the body's necessity. Second, that there exists a canon of reports, policy briefs and editorials by local writers and think-tanks emerging over the last thirty-seven years, most of which tends to argue for the council's further development. However, despite being in large agreement, proposals from these writings have yet to be translated into reality, as many are unable to grasp the idea that exacerbating threats to the Gulf have instituted a period of change for the region and its people. Most notably, the 2014 crisis, followed by the ongoing and tenser 2017 Gulf Crisis, has largely quashed the hopes of those looking for centralized GCC development. Given these shifts, the main concern for many Gulf elites has not been a question of how to further unify the council, but simply a quest to preserve its few notable achievements.[3]

On May 25, 1981, five of the body's founding members gathered in Abu Dhabi to ceremonially proclaim the GCC's birth to the world, an anniversary that is celebrated each December during the GCC's annual summit.[4] However, some say that this "ceremonial stage" has never really ended. At each summit, the Gulf public expects the council to step up the development of this system in order to meet the region's evolving challenges. Some leaders have presented important ideas consistent with the adaptability the general populace desires, such as an initiative of the late King Abdullah Bin Abdul Aziz to develop the structure of the council into a flexible unit capable of responding effectively to the winds of change hitting many Arab countries.[5] His initiative, however, was lost amidst the council's litany of committees and sub-committees. Many plans have similarly evaporated amidst the GCC's bureaucracy, as many fear the development of a more unified system would infringe upon member nations' individual sovereignty. It is clear the adage, "The whole is greater than the sum of its parts," has not yet been instilled in the minds of some Gulf states' decision-makers, even if it has become firmly rooted in the minds of its citizens.

However, challenges facing the region may force all parties to reach a unified conclusion in the future. In order to be an effective political deterrence to the major challenges facing the Gulf countries, officials should develop the council's flexibility, with a high level of coordination between members pooling together material, moral, human, and geographical resources. The challenges facing the Gulf are evident in three key issues. First, the oil revenues the GCC states largely rely on for their budgets are shrinking. Second, the GCC is threatened by the expansionist ambitions of its regional neighbors, especially Iran. Third, the influence and *desire* of traditional international powers *to influence* the goings-on in the Gulf are on the decline, especially in the United States where international relations are now viewed as transactions by President Donald Trump. Additionally, volatile wars, whether in Iraq, Syria, or Yemen, negatively affect the situation in the GCC states. Given that the GCC was formed in response to one war, logically, the institution's structure should be further developed in response to the impact of *three* ongoing ones. In actuality, such a reorganization has yet to happen.

Perhaps the most prominent success of the GCC has been its ability to forge political cooperation and policy coordination in times of crisis and common interest. The first of these successes evidenced itself amidst the 1990 occupation of Kuwait. In what was a difficult political moment, the Gulf states did not hesitate to denounce the occupation and work in all possible ways with the international community in forcing Iraq into retreat. At that critical time, due to GCC's regional solidarity, the people of Kuwait found a safe haven and a warm welcome within other GCC states until they were able to return to their country. The GCC also has stood united in the face of other territorial concerns, including the right of the United Arab Emirates to regain sovereignty over islands that have been occupied by Iran since 1970, demanding in repeated declarations that Iran must accept international arbitration.[6] The council remains cohesive amidst domestic issues that pose a significant risk to any of its member states, as happened to Bahrain in 2011 when Saudi Arabia and the UAE sent forces supporting the protection of vital installations on the island.[7] The GCC countries stood firm with Iraq after the fall of the former Saddam regime in order to diplomatically rehabilitate and allow Iraq to reenter the Arab League. The Gulf Initiative in Yemen after the uprising of the Yemeni people against Saleh's rule was also a unified position in which all GCC members participated, at least initially, in the military intervention.[8]

2.1. Major Risks Facing the GCC

The GCC (arguably sharing a similar path and destiny with other Arab countries) acts as a counter current to the ongoing disintegration of Arab hegemony–regional or worldwide. Such a task has required Arab support outside of those with membership in the organization, a development that started with Moroccan participation in a April 2016 GCC Summit in Riyadh.[9] The Maghreb nation's inclusion was in order to build a supposed "coalition of the capable," able to minimize risks and maximize gains within the Arab world. However, even with the inclusion of Morocco, such a new beginning was not built on the involvement of other Arab countries, and afterwards, decisionmakers in Tangier decided not to continue Morocco down this path, leaving the GCC regionally isolated in facing the surrounding chaos. The risks encroaching upon the GCC countries reduce the effectiveness of the GCC in responding to the regional reality. Here, we will attempt to review the risks surrounding the GCC countries as well as their motives, contexts, and role in leading to a disruption of the GCC on as evidenced by the ongoing Gulf Crisis.

The major risks facing the region can be organized into two primary groups: external *non*-Arab risks (ie. Iran and the United States) and external Arab risks (ie. civil wars raging in the neighborhood. These two categories have arguably contributed to the formation of two internal risks to the GCC, namely, intra-Arab risks (ie the Gulf Crisis) and internal societal risks, (ie. the deterioration of the GCC social contract). While each of these categories are interconnected, for analysis purposes, I will deal with each component separately in order to better outline each risks historicity. For each challenge I will propose a few simple and realizable remedies.

2.2. External non-Arab Risks: The US-GCC Relationship

Whether through the GCC collectively, or bilaterally through individual Gulf leaders, observers have noticed a changing tone at US-Gulf meetings. The tension at recent meetings indicates that the relationship between the GCC countries and the United States is going through an unprecedented rough patch. Disagreements in large part boil down to discrepancies between the GCC countries' *expectations* of the US, and the United States' *willingness* (never mind capability) to resolve the Gulf's hot-button issues. This rift will continue until GCC countries are convinced of the need to find internal solutions to their own problems.

As a result of the mostly negative legacy of US administrations in the Middle East, the Obama Administration adopted a different approach than those used in the last six or more decades, executing a "hands-off policy" when it came to political affairs in the region. The Obama presidency preferred to watch the developments in the region remotely, a policy that in general received great support from observing politicians and journalists in the US. In the end, the Obama Administration, from its point of view, believes it achieved many "positive" results through this low-cost observer approach, requiring no additional American boots on the ground or blood sacrifices. These results include reaching an Iranian nuclear deal in July 2015, reinforcing Israel's strategic security, withdrawing chemical weapons from Syria, linking many arms deals and getting cheaper oil from the gradually depleting Gulf.

On the other hand, the crux of strategic disagreements between the GCC and the United States after the Obama Administration have shifted from differences over the status of Israel and its policies, to disputes over how to best counter the threat posed by Iran. This new quagmire saw no theoretical or practical solution between the US and the GCC states until near the end of President Obama's term.

The Gulf states believe that Iranian intervention in the Arab region injects chaos into the area's political scene. Additionally, Tehran is seen as such a threat to national security that some have blamed its ubiquitous presence as a primary contributor to the region's arms build-up, loosely seen in the militarization of some Arab capitals in preparation for possible Iranian aggression. During the Obama era, the US did not earn the trust of the GCC states, despite reassurances that Washington would take necessary steps related to the Iran threat.

With the inauguration of President Donald Trump in 2017, the GCC countries took a sigh of relief, an ease that became even more palpable in May 2018 when President Trump announced the US's withdrawal from the Iranian nuclear deal.[10] Just one component of President Trump's more hawkish policy towards Tehran, his administration also threatened to escalate conflict if Iran does not end its military interventions in Arab countries (Yemen, Iraq, Syria, and Lebanon), or cease its ballistic missile program. However, despite these demands, the threats have yet to crystalize into anything besides bloviating verbal exchanges and accusations between the two parties, an outcome predicted by some Arab writers who have always doubted the seriousness of American intentions.

Given these developments (or lack thereof), the US's Iran portfolio remains a concern for GCC countries. The Gulf states have relied on nothing but the supposed good intentions of the US for the region's external security for quite some time, perhaps dating back to the withdrawal of Britain from the Gulf in the early 1970s. The problem, however, is that some GCC parties have not awoken to the recent structural changes in America's foreign policy stances that have occurred in two key areas.

First, the US has redefined its approach due to changing financial resources and the newly realized limits of its own power. Although not admitted by all, the US is not the same kingmaker of international affairs that existed in the last quarter of the 20th century. The reconsideration of the limits of its power is not related to a specific administration but rather is a long trend in the country's strategic positioning.

Second, influential circles in Washington DC have come to see the Iranian rivalry against the Gulf as exaggerated, obfuscating the GCC's own internal threats. Consequently, certain policy wonks in DC are pushing for GCC monarchies to reevaluate their internal social contracts (as will be elaborated upon) to better prep for the changing expectations of the region's youth bulge. Additionally, some see the ongoing Qatari crisis (a boon to the robustness of US-GCC cooperation in the future) as a more pressing issue to be resolved in the region.

This newfound emphasis on internal reform is likely not an anomaly and for two primary reasons will likely remain an undercurrent in future US administrations. First is the high ethical globalization-driven stance taken by the United States as it relates to human rights, empowerment of women and related buzzwords. Second, although contrary to some views, is America's dwindling power. The current anti-Iran stance taken by President Trump is temporary. Up until this point, this strategy has been limited to channels of soft power, such as the American President's tweets. That being said, the assurance felt by GCC states regarding the intentions of the Trump Administration should be reviewed in light of the alternative paths available to Washington. Perhaps, in the near future the US could soften its approach towards Iran as it has recently done with North Korea. Regardless, the current Trump Administration is undoubtedly changing the global game. Whereas in the past only the players only changed, today it appears that the rules of gameplay are changing as well.

2.3. External non-Arab Risks: The Relationship with Iran

Despite commentators who say otherwise, it can be argued that Iran constitutes a *real* threat to the GCC states. In addition to being a major influence over political decisions in Iraq, Tehran is also intervening militarily in Syria, dominating politics in Lebanon via Hezbollah, maintaining an important presence in Yemeni politics via the Houthis, and occupying a prominent position within the Palestinian question. Iran also counters the Gulf monarchies by touting its superficial periodic changes of some elected rulers, presenting itself as a quasi-democratic counterweight the Gulf's absolute monarchies. Even for some Arabs this argument has proven persuasive.

There are a number of possibilities governing the Gulf's options for its relationship with Iran. I can briefly elaborate on three possible outcomes. First, some argue that Iran and the Gulf will be forced into a pragmatic détente. Belief in such a possibility is due to the realities of Iran's geographic location, military and industrial capability, scientific development, and its direct influence on some national segments of the GCC, particularly its Shi'a citizens. Proponents of such a path believe that if the GCC states work seriously enough across these commonalities, this might convince Iran to back away from certain actions causing GCC security concerns.

The second scenario suggests that Iran really is the "shameful neighbor" that is popularly described, and that the Persian nation is inherently hostile to the Arabs. This scenario is derived from a history, both real and imagined, of Arab-Persian conflicts and concludes that reconciliation between the Persian state and Gulf Arabs is impossible.

The third scenario which I consider to be the most realistic is that Iran will fall short of the influence declared by supporters of its party-line. Despite grand rhetoric, in reality, Iran is a third -world country and suffers from many of the weaknesses that come with such a categorization. Iran contains great inequalities within its borders, and is surrounded by deep political and economic difficulties. Its current policies originate from two issues that can collectively be reduced to mere phobias. The first fear stems from the legacy of British-American interventions in the 1950s that overthrew Mussadiq's rule and crushed Iran's national ambitions. The second issue, which is known but ignored, is the limit of the Iranian theocracy's ability to continue existing in the world. It is a hybrid rule dominated by the clergy, an antiquated mix of government that must adapt if it is to survive, a concern recognized by many of the Iranian elite.

This leads us to the GCC stance on Iran. In the near future the GCC's policy will not see substantial change, and as long as the current generation of Iranians remain in power, the fear of revolution exportation will influence the policies of the Arab Gulf states. For at least the next quarter century, the GCC states must develop ways to *manage* rather than *resolve* ongoing Iranian threats. Steps that could be taken to mitigate these threats include strengthened Gulf cohesion based off both *Khaleeji* and Muslim identities. As it stands today, it seems this is the strategy being pursued by Saudi Arabia. However, even for the Kingdom, this is just a start.

In Iran, there are three main perceptions amongst elites of their neighbors on the Arab side of the Gulf. The first is that Tehran is responsible, both morally and politically for Shiites worldwide, including Arab Shiites in the Gulf. The second is that Tehran sees the Gulf regimes as arrogant and unfair to their people, an opinion seemingly compounded by the GCC's allying with Western powers. Third, there exists the perception that most of the Gulf countries' reforms since 1979 are a result of direct Iranian pressure.[11] To some, these perceptions may be disregarded as "Iranian myth," but, regardless of their historical veracity, the extent to which these assumptions are engrained in the Iranian public imagination necessitates that they are dealt with by Gulf leaders.

2.4. External Arab Risks: Arab Civil Wars

Regional conflicts, regardless of their relative proximity to the Gulf states, constitute a great danger. It is no secret that some Gulf states continue to have an ongoing role in the war in Libya, a conflict well outside the Gulf's immediate geographic position. Also in North Africa, the Gulf states maintain a close eye on Egypt due to fears that it could fall into radical hands. Closer to the Arabian Peninsula, several GCC governments are also active in civil wars in both Yemen and Syria. To the north in Iraq, there is fierce internal conflict amongst some regional powers that for some has resulted in boots on the ground. On top of Iran, Turkey too is in some way involved in both the Syrian and Iraqi theatres. In Syria, the primary concerns are the continuity of the regime, as well as Iran's related support for regional coalitions and their affiliated militias such as Hezbollah and other Iraqi, Afghani, and Pakistani groups. The complexity of the challenges in Syria could potentially put the Gulf states in range of its political, economic, or even military fallout.

The most significant challenge for the GCC remains in Yemen, a nation bordered by the council via Oman and Saudi Arabia. In particular, the national security of Saudi Arabia remains intertwined with the security of Yemen and the Bab al-Mandab Strait. For these national security reasons, the Kingdom was forced to get involved in the armed conflict in Yemen. Years later, and any prospect of stopping, or at least minimizing the conflict remains to be seen. Unless there is a sudden change in Iran's support for Houthi forces, the conflict remains a financial, military and strategic risk.

At this point, the fiery conflicts around the Gulf region are more likely to expand than dwindle. It remains a realistic possibility that in each of these instances, Iraq, Syria and Yemen, could boil over into even more fractured sectarian and ethnic states, increasing the risks to the Gulf states and neighboring countries. In a vicious cycle, increased instability in neighboring nations will necessitate continued regional intervention, thusly exposing the whole region to continued chaos.

Domestically, these military conflicts are a huge drain on the Gulf States' financial and human capital. The funding of these military campaigns comes as an additional burden to the Gulf states, whose already draining resources are being spread thin by efforts to keep neighboring countries out of bankruptcy and providing financial relief to those affected by these conflicts. While speculating on the region's financial future, one must also take into account the negative affect of the Qatar Crisis on the region's resources, as well as the likelihood that the Gulf countries, (willingly or unwillingly), will bear the burden for reconstruction plans in both Syria and Yemen.

2.5. Intra-GCC Risks: The Gulf Crisis

The aforementioned threats, namely discrepancies over regional responses to the threat, (or lack thereof) posed by Iran, boiled over and resulted in the diplomatic stalemate currently dominating Gulf narratives. Those who have been closely observing the ongoing crisis between Qatar and the Quartet of blockading nations are mainly divided into two camps. In the first camp are those toning down the severity of the crisis, characterizing the blockade as no more permanent than a drifting summer cloud, set to disappear and be forgotten. Found in this camp are the optimists who want to preserve the GCC's cohesion. In the opposing camp are those magnifying the severity of the crisis, claiming that unless there is a resolution in the immediate future, the Gulf region will never be the same.

Personally, I view the crisis somewhere between these two more extreme possibilities, however despite this self-described even-handedness, each side must admit that the crisis comes with serious risks. Even if the crisis has been overexaggerated, that does not mean the seriousness of the crisis should be underestimated. After all, as the region's history shows, a crisis can begin so small that parties involved think it possible for its effects to be contained, only for it to quickly snowball out of control. As an example, look no further than the events that preceded the Iraqi invasion of Kuwait. In the first half of 1990, many thought that what the Iraqi regime was doing was nothing more than a distraction, discounting entirely the eventuality that Saddam would mobilize his army to occupy another Arab country. Similarly, there was an impression that this too was a summer cloud slowly drifting by. Through hindsight however, we know today how many Kuwaitis, Iraqis, Arabs and American Coalition forces paid, (and continue to pay) in money, men, blood, and homelands for this underestimation.

Do not fall for misinterpretation. I am *not* implying that the Qatar Crisis and Occupation of Kuwait are identical scenarios. What I simply want to point out are the similar mechanisms that led to the formation of each crises. A most possible scenario for the Qatar crisis is that it will extend to include new players, each with different, and perhaps opposing interests. An additional lesson we might learn from the invasion of Kuwait are the ways in which internal ruptures provide an entrance for those waiting and watching for opportunities to take advantage of a divided country, or in this case, trade bloc. The tensions of the spring and summer of Kuwait in 1990 resulted in wide and serious differences among Kuwait's internal political powers. From the perspective of the Iraqi regime, a divided Kuwait made the invasion of the nation much easier. A similar outcome for the Gulf crisis is certainly not expected, but it shows that if the split of the GCC is prolonged, various regional powers may be tempted to achieve gains by taking advantage of a GCC made vulnerable by internal distractions.

This is clearly already the case for Turkey and Iran. While both nations understand that the GCC states will not be made completely vulnerable by the Qatar crisis, Turkey especially is preparing to make marginal gains during this period of distraction. Although Turkey too is embroiled in its own regional issues, including those involving the Kurdish question, wars in Iraq and Syria, and campaigns of internal repression that left tens of thousands of Turkish citizens in jail, its regime may be looking toward the Gulf in order to divert attention from these problems, all while achieving their political and financial goals. The crisis also provides opportunities for neighboring Iran. Already claiming to have provided assistance to the embargoed Qatar, each additional complexity in the crisis is only good news for Tehran's ears. As division in the Gulf increases, so do opportunities for the expansion of Iranian influence, a dominance that would be symbolically achieved if Iranian forces ever step foot on the Peninsula.

The benefits of hindsight provided by a reexamination of the events that led to the invasion of Kuwait make the conflict a worthy model for those looking to posit potential futures of the Gulf crisis. Just to reiterate, the severity of these crises are not made identical due to shared details, but rather because of what pre-invasion Kuwait an teach us about the potential consequences for a GCC hampered by an internal schism.

Given these lessons, a large part the world is taking the Quartet's blockading of Qatar very seriously. The United States Secretary of State has engaged in extensive shuttle diplomacy between involved nations, in addition to visits by the British, French, and German foreign ministers in the second half of

2017.[12] Each dignitary brought a similar message, urging the GCC to contain the crisis by minimizing the bloc's internal differences in order to preserve the GCC's linchpin role in dealing with more pressing global affairs. After all, the Gulf states supply much of the world's energy, especially to an increasingly oil-hungry East Asia, for which the Gulf is a vital trade corridor. Given the Gulf's vital importance, both as it relates to energy, as well as simply being an oasis of relative stability within a largely chaotic region, the global community will not allow the Gulf to deteriorate. However, given that negotiation and mediation efforts related to the crisis have reached a proverbial "dead-end," one is left to wonder how dire the "undesired consequences," as put by Kuwaiti Emir Sheikh Sabah al-Ahmad, must become before there is more effort to normalize the region's diplomacy.

The Gulf Region is historically unified by its shared history, a reality seen in the region's convergent social fabric and family cohesion extending from the opulent capitals dotting the Arabian littoral to the remote villages of the region's desert quarters. In the face of this reality, the wisest of people are those calling for an end to the diplomatic standoff amongst some GCC states. Given the changing nature of the US's role in the region, relying on the West to resolve the crisis may prove to be a waste of time and an erroneous political calculation. As opposed to the nominally well-intentioned West, the parties actually most prepared to insert themselves into the conflict are the Gulf's neighbors (Turkey and Iran), whose intentions are certainly less than benign. Although many "What Ifs" remain, I believe there is reason to be optimistic about a resolution to the current crisis, if not due to the economic, social and political damages a continuation of the crisis would bring to the region, then due to the stake the community of nations shares in maintaining the Gulf's stability.

As with any other crisis, speculative statements regarding the actions of the various GCC states have been replete with rumors and writings that are fueled by ignorance and meant to do nothing more than incite rage. For those with a hand in solving the crisis, it is prudent to balance the tense emotions brought about by this rhetoric with the long-term interests of the GCC as a whole. It is a dream of this latter goal held by many people in the Gulf to develop the GCC into a more effective institution, gradually integrating and preserving its security and wealth, all while supporting an Arab identity. An outcome such as this would resonate with the wishes of ordinary people in the Gulf who hope for nothing more than stability; the establishment of modern institutions; collaborations for sustainable domestic growth; and capable military cooperation against external threats. In fact, if the Gulf states seek to maximize the positive effects that the resolution of this crisis could bring about, the subsequent energy sparked by a solving of the crisis could spark the development of the very institutions the GCC has yet to effectively build. In such a turbulent era, even seemingly small mistakes can become very costly. The Gulf crisis constitutes a great loss for all Gulf parties and reduces the effectiveness and vulnerability of all actors at the regional and international levels.

As a kind of faux solution, in recent months, some Gulf countries have gone on to finalize intra-GCC bilateral agreements, including those between the UAE and Saudi Arabia, and Kuwait and Saudi-Arabia.[13,14] Some believe that the region's historical precedent of exclusionary intra-GCC bilateral agreements do not hinder the GCC's collective development. Others, however, believe that the bilateral agreements are a sign of danger, which could lead to the dissolution of the Council. However, it is my belief that so long as these bilateral agreements do not result in specific policies, their potential to inflict damage is insignificant.

2.6. Internal Societal Risks: A Fracturing Social Contract

The pressure on the internal social contract in the GCC countries is felt in two areas. The first is the difficulty reconciling the globalization of citizens with the localization of the state. The second area is the impending decline of the welfare state. The unsurprising plummet in oil prices, coupled with the growing reliance on the public budgets of Gulf states to meet the needs of increased development and military spending, have encouraged Gulf states to seriously reconsider the welfare policies that typified the Gulf's so-called "Golden Decades." Given these changes, the foreshadowed rearrangement of the Gulf economic sector must coincide with a serious reassessment of the current social contract.

Knowing that increased globalization amongst Gulf citizens requires institutions develop alongside the expectations amongst their citizens, the requirement of popular participation in legislative and institutional monitoring practices is all the more paramount. Political satisfaction is directly proportional to financial abundance, and vice versa. Indicators that the social contract is changing continue to appear. Most discussed in the media are perhaps those comments by then-President Obama, who in *The Atlantic*'s "Obama Doctrine" profile piece emphasized the importance of creating internal reforms related to education, citizenship, administrative and financial corruption, political participation and gender equality. From the point of view of his administration, these reforms strengthen internal security and help deter external challenges. Reflecting the President's supposed doctrine, there is a growing demand by Gulf elites for reforms, including elevated political participation and the adoption of a modern civil state.

Appearing on social media and in print (two widely influential outlets in the Gulf), calls for a drastic rethink of the political, social and economic policies of the Gulf have come from both citizens, and more importantly, government officials.[15, 16] For proponents of the "Obama Doctrine," and other similar philosophies, the distractions provided by the Gulf Crisis inhibit further collaboration on the internal threats facing the Gulf.

3.1. How to Address Potential Risks?

Viable preparations to confront these dangers cannot be implemented until two conditions are met. The first is the need for a widespread recognition these problems will have a negative impact on the national and regional security of the Gulf. The second, perhaps more difficult condition to be met, is the need for a firm political will to confront these challenges.

An example of this can be seen in the changing policies of Saudi Arabia, where a distinct shift can be seen since the years when the Kingdom functioned as a cautious observer, to the present day when the Saudi leadership's confrontational actions in Yemen, Egypt, and Lebanon have established the once meek nation as a newly dynamic, if contentious, actor. Each of these cases evidences the proactive tendencies of the new Saudi political leadership. Though Saudi policy certainly has not been without its own challenges, their sense of efficacy should be adopted by all dimensions of Gulf leaders, who will be forced to take courageous, and sometimes risky, measures to realize the recent mantra of Gulf elites, *"The whole is greater than the sum of its parts."* Given such a motto, it is for the benefit of the entire GCC that differences over Iran, Syria, Yemen, and the Muslim Brotherhood do not blind regional leaders to the instances where they *need* to collaborate. Until this happens, the current internal issues of each Gulf state will continue to go unaddressed, ultimately strengthening the Gulf's supposed "enemies" in the long-run. This is a call for serious Gulf unity in pooling resources, maximizing opportunities, and deterring dangers. There is an urgent need to discuss the ongoing Qatari crisis and forging a safe exit from this rift, which if prolonged further will not only hinder the journey of the GCC, but will also expose the Gulf region to imminent risks.

Endnotes

1. It was an assignment in the early 1980s by Sheikh Subah Al-Ahmed Al-Subah (current Emir of Kuwait), the then Minister of Foreign Affairs under the request of the then Emir, late Sheikh Jaber Al-Ahmed Al-Subah.

2. Matteo Legrenzi, *The GCC and the International Relations of the Gulf: Diplomacy, Security and Economic Coordination in a Changing Middle East*, p. 24: (New York: I.B. Tauris & Co. Ltd).

3. Habib Toumi, "GCC Endured Its Worst Diplomatic Crisis in 2014," *Gulf News*, December 27, 2014. https://gulfnews.com/news/gulf/saudi-arabia/gcc-endured-its-worst-diplomatic-crisis-in-2014-1.1432568

4. Ola Salem, "1981: The dawn of the GCC," *The National*, November 22, 2011. https://www.thenational.ae/uae/1981-the-dawn-of-the-gcc-1.417681

5. "32nd GCC Summit Final Statement and Riyadh Declaration," *Saudi-US Relations Information Service*, December 21, 2011. http://susris.com/2011/12/21/32nd-gcc-summit-final-statement-and-riyadh-declaration/

6. "Gulf states urge Iran to negotiate in UAE island dispute," *Gulf Business*, September 19, 2016. http://susris.com/2011/12/21/32nd-gcc-summit-final-statement-and-riyadh-declaration/

7. "Saudi soldiers sent into Bahrain," *Al Jazeera*, March 15, 2011. https://www.aljazeera.com/news/middleeast/2011/03/2011314124928850647.html

8. Stacey Phibrick Yadav and Sheila Carapico, "The Breakdown of the GCC Initiative," Middle East Research and Information Project, 2014.

9. Aberrahmane Naji, "Morocco-GCC Summit: Gulf Cooperation Council conscious of its commitments with Morocco," *Wall Street International*, May 17, 2016. https://wsimag.com/economy-and-politics/20318-morocco-gcc-summit

10. Kevin Liptak and Nicole Gaouette, "Trump withdraws from Iran nuclear deal, isolating him further from the world," *CNN*, May 9, 2018. https://www.cnn.com/2018/05/08/politics/donald-trump-iran-deal-announcement-decision/index.html

11. The author heard a number of times in Tehran from Iranian elites that many of the reforms in the Gulf states were because of the impact of the Iranian Revolution.

12. "Qatar dispute: Tillerson starts shuttle diplomacy," *The Strait Times*, July 13, 2017. https://www.straitstimes.com/world/middle-east/qatar-dispute-tillerson-starts-shuttle-diplomacy

13. "20 MoUs Signed in First Meeting of Saudi-Emirati Coordination Council," *Al Sharq Al Awsat*, June 7, 2018. https://aawsat.com/english/home/article/1292926/20-mous-signed-first-meeting-saudi-emirati-coordination-council

14. "Saudi Arabia, Kuwait Sign Deal to Establish Joint Coordination Council," *Al Sharq Al Awsat*, July 18, 2018. https://aawsat.com/english/home/article/1335636/saudi-arabia-kuwait-sign-deal-establish-joint-coordination-council

15. Jeffrey Goldberg, "The Obama Doctrine," *The Atlantic*. April 2016. https://www.theatlantic.com/magazine/archive/2016/04/the-obama-doctrine/471525/

16. Norah O'Donnell "Saudi Arabia's Heir to the Throne Talks to 60 Minutes," *CBS News*, March 19, 2018. https://www.cbsnews.com/news/saudi-crown-prince-talks-to-60-minutes/

CHAPTER 2

The Saudi-Emirati Alliance in a Polarized Middle East

GIORGIO CAFIERO

Introduction

I t goes without saying that the Kingdom of Saudi Arabia and the United Arab Emirates are extremely close allies. The leadership in both these oil-wealthy Arabian monarchies are united in their shared perceptions of regional threats, as well as their joint long-term interests. Riyadh and Abu Dhabi's coordination on regional issues has increased substantially after the 2011 Arab Spring uprisings swept across the Middle East and North Africa. Officials in both capitals largely share a vision for the MENA region's political, environmental and security architecture based on a rejection of Iranian influence and political Islam, both in its moderate forms (i.e. the Muslim Brotherhood) and its more extreme versions (ISIS and al-Qaeda). Leaders in both Saudi Arabia and the UAE seek to create a future geopolitical order based on Arab Gulf hegemony.

Riyadh and Abu Dhabi have generally responded in alignment to the region's upheaval. That both have internally consolidated power in the hands of de facto rulers, escalated the war against Yemen's Houthi rebellion, applied pressure on Lebanon to reject

Iran's influence, blockaded Qatar, and deepened tacit alliances with Israel evidences the moves which the leadership in Riyadh and Abu Dhabi have been making in recent years. Yet I argue that such actions come with major risks and high costs that may undermine Saudi Arabia and the UAE's important national interests in the future, as well as those of their neighbors and others in the MENA region.

This chapter will analyze the regional dynamics that have pushed Saudi Arabia and the UAE closer together as allies, in addition to assessing the implications of Riyadh and Abu Dhabi's foreign policy agendas for the other four monarchies ruling the Arabian Peninsula. First, we will take stock of how the Arab Spring uprisings of 2011 impacted Saudi-Emirati relations and their perceptions of both regional threats and opportunities. Ultimately, while Riyadh and Abu Dhabi saw the tsunami of unrest across the Arab world as directly and indirectly threatening their respective rulers, in specific ways, both Gulf states also saw the regional transformations as occurring at a time that afforded the Saudis and Emiratis a unique set of chances to project greater influence across the Arab world. Riyadh and Abu Dhabi's new strategies for expanding their regional clout marked a new era of Saudi and Emirati foreign policy in which both Gulf states began playing more active roles in the region by directly involving themselves in politics and military interventions, rather than through traditional "petrodollar diplomacy."[1]

1.1. Regional Context of the post-Arab Spring Environment

In 2011, the fall of Saudi and UAE-backed autocratic leaders in Egypt, Tunisia, and Yemen plus Arab Spring unrest in Jordan, Bahrain, and Oman significantly frightened Riyadh and Abu Dhabi. The status quo of the Arab world order that both Saudi Arabia and the UAE had vested interests in preserving came under assault in 2011, when revolutionary forces had various degrees of success across different MENA countries in removing authoritarian heads of state. Moreover, Iran's exploitation of regional unrest, especially in Syria and Bahrain, combined with mainly

Muslim Brotherhood Islamist groups gaining various degrees of power in post-revolutionary Arab states, represented major challenges and ideational threats to the legitimacy of the conservative Gulf monarchies.

At the heart of the fearful perceptions that political gains secured by grassroots movements and anti-status quo actors were anxieties that such revolutions would inspire citizens of the Kingdom and the Emirates to challenge their rulers' legitimacy. For decades, the wealthy Gulf monarchies saw their regimes and countries as largely fortressed from the instability present in poorer parts of the Arab world where social contracts between states and citizens have been more challenging to broker, due to larger populations and governments with significantly less natural resource wealth. Although anti-regime protests occurred in the Gulf states prior to 2011, the Arab Spring uprisings spread into the Arabian Peninsula's petro-states in truly unprecedented fashion, due in no small part to social media's role in mobilizing and organizing public demonstrators. Although the MENA region's monarchs survived the Arab Spring's initial phases, street protests in Bahrain, Oman, and Saudi Arabia in 2011 shattered the perception that the Arab world's hydrocarbon-rich monarchies were immune from the type of grassroots movements that closely paralleled those of Arab protestors demanding reforms in North Africa.

Under pressure from demands for political and economic reforms from their own citizens, all Gulf regimes felt a need in 2011 to ease the simmering tensions in their countries. Each of the six Gulf monarchies—where no Arab Spring protests occurred—responded to the unrest with hand-outs of cash, the creation of public sector jobs, and/or the increasing of wages and benefits for workers. In Saudi Arabia's case, the government quickly announced two welfare packages worth USD 130 billion for its own citizens and pledged USD 15 billion to Bahrain, Egypt, Jordan, and Oman to help those governments cope with their internal Arab Springs. Abu Dhabi focused on addressing socio-economic grievances in the poorer Northern Emirates and proceeded with infrastructure and welfare spending.[2]

Yet, amid such Arab Spring turmoil the wealthy Gulf regimes' perspectives on the region's rapid changes were not solely informed by concerns about their own legitimacy coming under challenge from the Gulf's citizenry. Rulers in Saudi Arabia, the UAE, and Qatar also saw the Arab Spring as offering their respective countries an invaluable opportunity to play a leading role in shaping the course of such unprecedented events to suit their own national interests. Amid the backdrop of a decline in US influence, the internal problems of the Arab world's traditional heavyweights—Egypt, Iraq, and Syria—prevented Cairo, Baghdad, and Damascus from taking a leading role in reshaping of MENA's regional political environment. Consequently, the wealthy and relatively stable Gulf states saw the unrest of 2011 as creating an opening to assert their clout throughout the greater Middle East. Nonetheless, there was much division among the Gulf states with respect to their responses to the Arab Spring, as underscored by the ongoing Qatar crisis and its preceding 2014 standoff, both of which largely resulted from the Saudi/UAE alliance's strong disapproval of Doha's independent foreign policy and national media coverage throughout the post-2011 period. Such different perspectives on the part of the Gulf monarchies were most evident in Egypt and Libya, where the Emiratis/Saudis and Qataris supported opposing sides.

Although currently aligned extremely closely, Saudi Arabia and the UAE have not always acted in tandem regarding regional issues in the post-Arab Spring period. When King Abdullah sat on throne and Muhammad bin Nayef (MbN) was the Crown Prince, Saudi Arabia focused on establishing a pan-Sunni alliance of state and non-state actors to push back against the expansion and consolidation of Iranian/Shia influence in the Arab world. The Kingdom invested in ties to a host of Sunni Islamist actors, such as Sunni rebels in Syria and anti-Iranian/anti-Shia forces in Yemen. Despite joining the UAE and Bahrain in recalling its ambassador from Qatar from March to November 2014, Saudi Arabia coordinated with Qatar and Turkey on a host of regional files, especially Syria and (at least in Qatar's case) Yemen's Houthi rebellion.

The UAE, with its staunchly anti-Islamist foreign policy and deep-rooted grievances with Qatar and the Turkish Justice and Development Party (AKP), disapproved of Riyadh's coordination with such Islamist groups. It also rejected the foreign policies of Doha and Ankara, seen in Abu Dhabi as being pro-Muslim Brotherhood. Consequently, Syria's civil war became an area of disagreement between the Kingdom and the Emirates. Whereas the Saudis were keen to back Sunni Islamists fighting the Damascus regime, Abu Dhabi took a more centrist position; it opposed Syria's Iranian-backed Ba'athist government and the Islamist opposition, seeing both as a threat to the region.

However, the ascension of Saudi Crown Prince Mohammed bin Salman (MbS), who maintains a special relationship with the Crown Prince of Abu Dhabi Sheikh Mohammed bin Zayed (MbZ), has been key to Riyadh and Abu Dhabi's growing alignment.[3] Indeed, the rise of MbS to Deputy Crown Prince and then Crown Prince in 2015 and 2017, respectively, offered MbZ a valuable opportunity. MbZ, who is 24 years older than MbS, views himself as the Arab leader who can most easily impact key decisions made by the Kingdom's de facto ruler. Since MbS' rise, MbZ has been correct about this point. By working with the new Saudi leader, who he has described as a "Younger version of himself," MbZ has managed to influence the Kingdom's foreign policy in numerous domains, making Riyadh's agenda more suitable to Abu Dhabi's perceived interests within a chaotic regional environment.[4]

The two nations' handling of Qatar and the Muslim Brotherhood is a case in point. Like MbZ, MbS sees the Muslim Brotherhood as being, "forces of evil."[5] This perception markedly contrasts with the views of other Saudi royals and elites who view the Sunni movement as a "natural ally" in the struggle to curtail Tehran's ascendancy in the Middle East by ejecting Iranian influence from Arab lands.[6] In contrast to MbN, who favored a strong Saudi-Qatari alliance (especially vis-à-vis Iran, Syria, and Yemen), MbS has seen Doha through an Emirati lens. MbS's perspectives on Qatar as a threat to Gulf security have served Abu Dhabi's interests in terms of coordinating with Saudi Arabia in efforts to pressure Qatar into returning to the foreign policy conducted by Doha prior to the mid-1990s as will be discussed below.

2.1. The Trump Factor

Growing Saudi-Emirati coordination with MbS and MbZ at the helm must be analyzed within the context of US President Donald Trump winning the 2016 election and entering the Oval Office in January 2017. The crown princes of Saudi Arabia and Abu Dhabi both saw the Trump presidency as providing the Kingdom and the Emirates a special opportunity to create a new regional security architecture in both the Gulf and the greater Arab world. Having staunchly opposed US President Barack Obama's responses to the Arab Spring uprisings and his diplomatic policies toward Iran (evidenced by the 2015 JCPOA), MbS and MbZ have welcomed the Trump administration's more aggressive countering of Tehran's regional ascendancy.

Establishing contact and warming ties with an unpredictable White House was a high priority for Saudi Arabia during the early days of the Trump presidency. After Trump won the 2016 presidential election, the Saudis and Emiratis took advantage of his inexperience in the world of politics—especially at the international level—and worked to push the administration's foreign policy in a direction that most suited Abu Dhabi and Riyadh's interests. From the beginning of Trump's term, Saudi Arabia and the UAE quickly observed signs that the president would reject traditional American foreign policy norms by making decisions that were mainly transactional in nature and not based on values or a coherent plan.

To solidify close relations with the Trump White House, MbS utilized his special ties with Abu Dhabi's ambassador to the United States, Yousef al-Otaiba, who is said to have arranged Trump's lunch with MbS in March 2017, making Saudi Arabia's de facto ruler the first Gulf royal to visit the Trump White House.[7] Two months later, MbZ came to the White House to help the 45th American president prepare for his historic visit to the Arab Islamic summit in Riyadh; there, it seemed as if both MbS and MbZ's efforts to invest in a close relationship with the Trump administration appeared, at least at first, to have paid off.[8]

Four days after the Quartet's blockade went into effect in 2017, Trump tweeted allegations against high-ranking officials in Doha, accusing Qatar of sponsoring terrorism while hailing the Saudi/UAE-led bloc's actions against Qatar as proof of his administration's ability to influence Washington's Arab allies into taking effective action against Sunni extremist groups and Iran. Riyadh and Abu Dhabi interpreted the American president's tweets as a signal of Washington's support for the blockade.[9] Until other branches of the US government warned the Saudis and Emiratis against taking military action against Qatar, the Qataris, and probably the Saudis and Emiratis too, interpreted Trump's tweets as "a green light for the Saudis and Emiratis to launch further action" against Doha.[10]

3.1. Qatar

With MbS and MbZ at the helm, the Saudi/UAE-led siege of Qatar has been a defining characteristic of both Riyadh and Abu Dhabi's regional foreign policies. Evidenced by the thirteen demands of the Quartet, the blockading countries' interests in Qatar are oriented around Doha returning to the role which the emirate played in the Arabian Peninsula's pre-1995 geopolitical order. In other words, the Saudi/UAE bloc besieged Qatar with the aim of returning it to Riyadh's orbit of influence and ending the independent foreign policy that Doha began conducting after Hamad bin Khalifa Al Thani ascended to power in 1995. In practice, this would mean cooling Qatar's relatively cordial relationship with Tehran, cutting off support for the Muslim Brotherhood's regional branches, extraditing dissidents and alleged "terrorists" from various Arab states to their home countries, and shutting down media outlets that covered Saudi Arabia, the UAE, and other Gulf regimes unfavorably.[11]

Yet over a year later, as David Roberts puts it, "It's difficult to see how the blockade succeeded... Qatar didn't capitulate, and no important international states joined in."[12] The campaign against Qatar has highlighted Riyadh and Abu Dhabi's limited capacity to shape the order of the Arabian Peninsula on their terms, let alone that of the greater Arab world. The outcome of the blockade has been precisely what the Saudis and Emiratis feared most from Doha—an increasingly autonomous and assertive Qatar that not only survives independently but also prospers outside of the Saudi shadow.

Moreover, by turning to organs of international law and strengthening its alliances, partnerships, and friendships with the West, Asia, Russia, Turkey, Iran, and Oman, Qatar has dealt with the Gulf crisis in ways that prevented it from suffering in isolation. Exemplified by the International Court of Justice's July 25, 2018 ruling, which decided that aspects of the UAE's actions against Qatar violated Abu Dhabi's obligations under the International Convention on the Elimination of All Forms of Racial Discrimination, both Riyadh and Abu Dhabi face growing threat of isolation as a consequence of the blockade.[13]

Of course, if or how the Gulf crisis eventually ends is unclear and the impasse could last for many years, if not decades. Nonetheless, with Qatari leadership calling its sovereignty a "red line" and proving resilient in the face of the blockade, Doha's capitulation to Saudi Arabia and the UAE's demands for a restoration of relations is unlikely. By the same token, it is difficult to imagine either Saudi Arabia or the UAE lifting the blockade without significant concessions from Doha, as doing so would be humiliating to both Riyadh and Abu Dhabi. Within this context, an institutionalization of the Qatar crisis may well be an outcome of the new regional climate.

The Kingdom and the Emirates are likely betting on waging a bloodless war of attrition with Qatar, hoping that the emirate's policies for remaining resilient throughout the blockade prove unsustainable. Yet, several factors may contribute to the relative resiliency of an isolated Qatar. First, reserves from Qatar's sovereign wealth fund have enabled Doha to gain credibility and legitimacy in countries worldwide. Second, Qatar's gas exports continue to reach buyers worldwide, including increasingly dependent developing nations in Asia. Finally, a pragmatic and carefully constructed foreign policy has secured Doha's close alliances with major powers. Among others, these factors may be why Qatar has succeeded and continues to succeed in preventing the Saudi/UAE-led bloc from weakening its economy to the point where the Al Thani rulers lose their legitimacy—or worse, chaotic conditions arise which could be used as a pretext for launching a Saudi/Emirati invasion of the blockaded emirate.

Ultimately, the Saudi/UAE-led bloc's siege of Qatar effectively ended the Gulf Cooperation Council's relevance as a regional institution. The blockade itself was contrary to the fundamental principles of the GCC, as the GCC charter requires all six members to agree on all substantive issues. That the blockade did not go to the Supreme Council or receive Kuwaiti, Omani, and of course Qatari support, raises major questions about whether the governments and citizens of GCC countries will ever be able to trust the rule-based institution to protect the sovereignty and security of its members. Now that the GCC has essentially died as sub-regional organization, the prospects for Arab Gulf solidarity replete with financial, cultural, and economic integration among GCC members have been severely damaged.

MbS and MbZ's tactics for pressuring Qatar into abandoning its independent foreign policy and relinquishing its sovereignty have had major implications for the states of Kuwait and Oman. These two states, which have remained officially neutral in the Gulf crisis, have long favored a strong GCC and deeper integration between the council's six members. Thus, the Saudi/UAE-led bloc's initiation of a zero-sum conflict with Doha has left Kuwait City and Muscat unsettled by the Gulf's new environment of greater polarization in what looks like the emergence of a post-GCC era.

4.1. Kuwait

The growing Saudi-UAE alliance, evidenced by MbS and MbZ's shared approach to confronting Iran and Qatar, has created an increasingly polarized regional environment in which Kuwait finds its autonomy shrinking. Against the backdrop of an increasingly aggressive US foreign policy vis-à-vis Iran, Kuwait's efforts to ease tensions in Saudi-Iranian relations and end the Qatar crisis diplomatically have left the emirate seeing itself as increasingly vulnerable to regional trends that threaten Kuwait's interests in the northern Gulf and the MENA at large, not to mention the country's internal stability and cohesion among its citizens.

Whereas Kuwait has sought to mediate between Riyadh and Tehran, Saudi Arabia's advocacy of regime change in Iran underscores a fundamental difference between the two Arab Gulf states' approaches for addressing Iranian conduct in the region. Although solidly committed to maintaining its historic and special alliances with Saudi Arabia and the United States, Kuwait is not on the verge of joining Riyadh and Abu Dhabi on the anti-Iran bandwagon, nor can the emirate be expected to support the Trump administration's most aggressive policies against Tehran.

A host of historical, security, demographic, geographic, energy, economic, and geopolitical factors inform Kuwait's stances on Iran. As the Iran-Iraq war raged, Kuwait suffered from the tanker wars and Iranian-sponsored terror attacks in the emirate. Such memories heavily factor into Kuwaitis' calculations about the risks of conducting a foreign policy that is excessively anti-Iranian and too closely aligned with Riyadh and Abu Dhabi against its Persian neighbor.

That Kuwait's leadership did not join MbS and MbZ in welcoming the US administration's decision to pull out of the JCPOA underscores the country's more pragmatic outlook toward the Islamic Republic. Additionally, Kuwait City remains concerned that the JCPOA's unravelling could leave the northern Gulf states more vulnerable to the destabilizing impact of any war involving Iran.

Even if war never breaks out, the rise in sectarian tensions as Tehran responds to Washington, Riyadh, and Abu Dhabi's moves against the Islamic Republic's exertion of influence in the Arab World could threaten Kuwait's larger goals. With roughly 30% of Kuwaitis being Shia, the government must consider Shia sensitivities when determining how Kuwait should react to potentially polarizing developments in the region that, if handled incorrectly, could divide the country along sectarian lines.[14] Indeed, a key pillar of the regime's strategy for ensuring domestic stability has been an alliance between the royal Al Sabah family and the emirate's urban Shia, including prominent Shia merchant families with deep ancestral, business, and religious links to Iran. Undoubtedly, as tension builds up between the US, Saudi Arabia, and UAE on one side and Iran on the other, the Al Sabah rulers are forced to conduct a balanced foreign policy that can preserve Kuwait City's close alliances with Washington, Riyadh, and Abu Dhabi without triggering anger from the country's Shia minority.

Kuwait's leadership has skillfully maintained pragmatic policies in response to rising sectarian temperatures in the Arab world that have left other societies, as well as Kuwait's, deeply divided along sectarian and ideological lines. When the Arab Spring erupted in Bahrain in 2011, Kuwait demonstrated its solidarity with the Al Khalifa rulers in Manama and their allies in Riyadh and Abu Dhabi by deploying a naval presence to Bahraini waters. However, to avoid any backlash from Kuwaiti Shia, the Kuwaiti monarch avoided sending ground forces to the island nation to help the Bahraini regime quell a Shia-dominated uprising.[15]

In Yemen, Kuwait joined the 2015 Saudi-led military coalition against the Iran-allied Houthi rebellion. However, Kuwaiti forces have never participated in operations inside Yemen. Additionally, despite having yet to see any success, the emirate has taken a lead in the Gulf by promoting dialogue between the different state and non-state actors fighting within the impoverished Arab country.[16,17] Similarly, in 2016 Kuwait withdrew its ambassador to Iran. But unlike Saudi Arabia and Bahrain, it maintained relations with Tehran following the violence waged against Riyadh's diplomatic outposts in response to the execution of Saudi Arabia's Shia cleric Sheikh Nimr Baqir al-Nimr.[18] In each of these cases, domestic politics and social cohesion among Kuwait's different communities heavily factored into the Al Sabah rulers' decision-making.

Energy factors also influence gas-thirsty Kuwait's pragmatic approach toward Iran. Kuwait, as Iran's neighbor, has maintained relatively warm and cooperative ties with Tehran, leaving the door open for Iranian gas importation. Although Kuwait has not started importing Iranian natural gas (largely due to Saudi pressure), officials in Kuwait City and Tehran have been discussing the prospect for years. The emirate's quickly growing demand for foreign natural gas supplies as a result of Kuwait's seeking to meet rising domestic demands for electricity, water desalination, petrochemicals, and enhanced oil recovery techniques means that the country's need to find a new source of energy may outweigh its need to appease Saudi Arabia.[19]

In particular, Iran's Khuzestan province—where civil unrest has resulted from years of Tehran's ignoring locals' grievances over poor living conditions and public health crises stemming from environmental degradation—is a source of concern for Kuwait. Situated next to Khuzestan, Kuwait is unsettled by the prospects that instability in the oil-rich Iranian province could spill across the borders of the northern Gulf states and severely damage Kuwait's ability to establish itself as a logistics, finance, and tourism hub in the northern Gulf. As this vision depends on peace between Kuwait's neighbors, the Kuwaiti leadership is clearly at odds with the aggressive Saudi posturing against Tehran that aims to internally and externally weaken the Islamic Republic.

Regarding the Qatar crisis, Kuwait's response illustrates the emirate's grand strategy of relying on regional and international institutions to empower itself as an influential actor in the region. As put by scholar Kristen Diwan, "The Kuwaitis are also personally invested in the survival of the GCC due to the personal role played by the emir in its creation, and his over 40 years as a senior diplomatic voice within the Gulf." She continues: "The bypassing of the GCC by Gulf powers Saudi Arabia and the UAE in favor of their own strategic bilateral relationship removes the institutional leverage Kuwait has cultivated and leaves Kuwait more isolated. Kuwait's unease at its exclusion from UAE-Saudi decision making is palpable."[20]

Although with less autonomy than in past years, today Kuwait is attempting to thwart any escalation in regional tensions that would risk military confrontation. As a promoter of pan-Arabism, Kuwait's efforts to preserve the GCC by mediating between the Qatar crisis' involved parties will remain a priority. The Kuwaitis understand that with the current leadership in Abu Dhabi, Riyadh, and Doha, achieving success on this front will be difficult. Nonetheless, Kuwait believes that only diplomacy can resolve not only the GCC's Qatar rift but also the war raging in Yemen.[21]

Kuwaitis will also look to their recent history to inform their views of current regional security dilemmas that are at odds with MbS and MbZ's visions. Lessons from the three nearby wars since Iran's 1979 revolution, Iran-Iraq (1980-1988), Kuwait (1990-1991), and Iraq (2003), influence the decisions made by Kuwait's ruler, Emir Al Sabah, who served during these conflicts as foreign minister (1963-2003). An understanding among Kuwaitis is that when powers, such as Kuwait, Iraq or Iran, are invaded, their actions backfired in ways that resulted in instability and turmoil across the region. Kuwait is therefore inclined to caution against Saudi Arabia and the UAE's combative actions in the region, instead working with all parties in the Gulf to foster a greater dialogue, even if such calls sometimes fall on deaf ears in other Gulf capitals. Since the Iraqi invasion and occupation of 1990/1991, Kuwaitis have carefully balanced their relationships with all three of their larger neighbors (Iran, Iraq, and Saudi Arabia), rather than solely aligning with Riyadh against Tehran. This approach, based on playing larger actors against each other in the northern Gulf, has enabled the emirate to empower itself and preserve its sovereignty and independence.

With Kuwait leading the GCC's "in-house" efforts to diplomatically settle the Gulf dispute, Oman is strongly backing Kuwait City's role as an interlocutor between Doha and the blockading states. Sharing a conviction that restoring relations between all six Gulf monarchies would advance the interest of long-term stability and economic integration in the Arabian Peninsula, Kuwait is closely aligned with Oman in terms of opening channels of communication in the increasingly polarized region.

5.1. Oman

Like Kuwait, Oman is not aligned with Riyadh and Abu Dhabi when it comes to Iran or Qatar. For years, the Saudis and Emiratis have taken issue with Muscat's warm and cooperative relationship with Iran. Oman's accommodation of Iran's foreign policy and the Sultanate's plans to begin importing Iranian gas via a planned subsea pipeline against the backdrop of Muscat and Tehran's military cooperation in the Gulf, have left some in the GCC questioning the Sultanate's commitment to the council of Gulf monarchies.[22, 23] Yet Oman's views of the Qatar crisis do much to dispel this notion that Muscat was not in favor of a strong GCC. To the contrary, the opposite has always been true. Indeed, it is the Sultanate's support for a strong and healthy GCC that has largely contributed to Muscat's unease with MbS and MbZ orchestrating Saudi and Emirati foreign policies.

As Oman's secretary-general of the Ministry of Foreign Affairs Sayyid Badr bin Hamad al-Busaidi put it,

> We have long been a supporter of the idea that the GCC should be expanded and its security dimensions strengthened... We want to see the organization enhanced and strengthened. This is after all the Gulf Cooperation Council and without dialogue there cannot be cooperation. Indeed, the current crisis within the GCC is unprecedented because it undermines the very logic upon which the organization was first founded.[24]

Much like Kuwait, the Sultanate's stance on the Gulf dispute has not been at all surprising, given Muscat's historic neutrality in regional conflicts as evidenced by its role as interlocutor between a host of actors in regional conflicts from Yemen to Syria to Libya.[25, 26, 27] Oman could not have seriously considered severing ties with Qatar in June 2017 because Muscat values fruitful and highly cooperative relations with all Gulf states including Qatar and Iran. The Sultanate's leadership prioritizes maintaining channels of dialogue with as many parties as possible while avoiding threats, confrontations, and petty spats during times of disagreement. Had Muscat taken the uncharacteristic action of severing its ties with Qatar, it would have marked the first time that Oman ended diplomatic relations with a foreign government since His Majesty Sultan Qaboos's rise to power in 1970.

As a neutral state in the Gulf crisis, Muscat has pushed for both sides to reach a peaceful settlement. On June 5, Oman's foreign minister His Excellency Yousuf bin Alawi bin Abdullah, took a private trip to Qatar, planned prior to the eruption of the Gulf crisis. During the days that followed, Qatari officials reportedly looked to the Sultanate for mediation, which Muscat agreed to give.[28] Although Omani officials have disagreed with their counterparts in Doha on several issues concerning the post-Arab Spring environment, the Sultanate, in contrast to the blockading countries, has never perceived Qatar as such a major threat to its interests.

Unquestionably, the Gulf dispute has afforded the Sultanate economic opportunities. This may be particularly beneficial for Oman, which has seen its budget deficit grow over the past several years. As the Qatar crisis prevented Qatar and the UAE's national carriers from using certain routes that violated airspace restrictions, Oman Air has enjoyed major advantages since the blockade has gone into effect. Muscat International Airport and Oman's Sohar International Airport have been the hubs for Qatar Airways' flights. As a consequence of Qatar losing access to Dubai's Jebel Ali and other ports in the Emirates and Saudi Arabia, the Qataris have become increasingly reliant on two Omani ports, Sohar and Salalah, for their trade with the rest of the world. Between April and July 2017, Omani-Qatari bilateral trade increased 2,000 percent and the Sultanate appears likely to receive significantly more investment from Doha, an extremely important development for Oman given its set of economic challenges.[29]

Although Oman has benefited from growing trade with Qatar since the start of the blockade, there is a bigger picture in play concerning the decreased potential for the GCC to achieve its economic and security objectives that Muscat finds deeply unsettling. In scholar Abdullah Baabood's words, "Such economic gains have not obscured Oman's vision that regional integration and cooperation offer more long-lasting stability and economic prosperity than the quick and short-term opportunities presented by this crisis."[30]

A key factor in play has been MbS and MbZ's efforts to influence all Arabian Peninsula states' foreign policies into aligning with Riyadh and Abu Dhabi's to create a united Arab front in the Gulf that confronts regional threats on the terms of these two young leaders. According to numerous sources, the Omanis had genuine concerns that after the ATQ blockaded Qatar, the quartet would impose pressure on the Sultanate to realign with the Saudi-led fold and place substantial distance between Muscat and Tehran.

In May 2018, Camille Lons explained:

> Saudi Arabia and the UAE take a dim view of the cordial relationship that Oman enjoys with Iran. Both have criticised the sultanate as dismissive of GCC security concerns. The fact that Oman did not inform them of the 2013 US-Iranian talks remains a particularly bitter pill. They even accuse Oman of not doing enough to interdict arms smuggling from Iran through its territory to the Houthis in Yemen.

Lons continues:

> As regional tensions have escalated, Saudi Arabia and the UAE have increased the political pressure on Oman to fall into line. King Salman's decision in December 2016 to skip Oman during his tour of the GCC countries demonstrated Saudi discontent. But with the exception of this episode, Oman's two neighbours have been careful to keep their grievances and diplomatic pressures private. But on my recent visit to Oman, the talk was all about Saudi/UAE economic pressure, including delayed deals and increased bureaucratic burdens placed on trade and border crossing between the UAE and Oman.[31]

In July 2018, Abu Dhabi's embassy in Lebanon denied a report published by Al Akhbar (a pro-Hezbollah Lebanese newspaper) concerning an "Emirates Leaks" report which stated that the Emirates were pressuring Oman to take their side in the Arab states' Qatar rift. Emirati officials dismissed the reports as "fabricated" by Qatar, yet the Lebanese media outlet attributed the sources to the UAE's embassies in Oman, Iraq, Morocco, and Sudan.[32] Of course, within the regional "information war" being waged over the Qatar crisis, what constitutes fact and fiction in such cases is often difficult to determine.

Nonetheless, some Omanis' perception of the UAE as a menace to the Sultanate's independence and sovereignty is partially informed by claims made by officials in Muscat in 2011 about uncovering an Emirati spy network targeting the Omani government and military. According to Oman's state-run news agency, "Security services uncovered a spying network belonging to the state security apparatus of the United Arab Emirates, targeting ... Oman and the way its government and military work."[33]

It is possible that Abu Dhabi's interest in obtaining more information about the Omani-Iranian relationship, especially in the military and security domains, drove the UAE to carry out such alleged activities in the Sultanate.

From Oman's perspective, the current foreign policies of Saudi Arabia and the UAE pose challenges to the Sultanate's sovereignty, autonomy, and stability, particularly in the south near Yemen. Since MbS and MbZ have been at the helms of their respective countries' foreign policies, officials in Muscat have clearly indicated their dissatisfaction with Saudi and Emirati strategies for fending regional security threats, from threatening Iran to waging the military campaign against Yemen's Houthi rebellion and blockading Qatar.

Oman's foreign minister defended Muscat's decision to be the only GCC member in March 2015 to opt out of the Saudi-led military coalition in Yemen. "Oman is a nation of peace," he said. "We cannot work on peace efforts at the same time we would be part of a military campaign." A senior member of Oman's Shura council explained that the Sultanate "couldn't have participated in this coalition. It's in our constitution. We don't send troops or artillery anywhere, unless requested by the United Nations."[35]

As previously mentioned, officials in Riyadh and Abu Dhabi are not all sympathetic to Oman's neutrality on regional issues. A former high-ranking GCC official told me that Muscat's neutrality is, at times, perceived in other Arab Gulf states as "negative neutrality." Perceptions of Oman as undermining the Gulf monarchies' collective security by maintaining a close relationship with Tehran has led Muscat to cautiously balance its relationship with Iran on one side and the Saudi/UAE-led bloc on the other. Now, the Qatar crisis has created yet another fissure that the Sultanate's foreign policy must carefully navigate.

While Oman has engaged in joint military drills with Iran in waters separating their two countries, in December 2016 Oman became the forty-first member of Saudi Arabia's Islamic Military Alliance to Fight Terrorism (IMAFT)—later renamed the Islamic Military Counter Terrorism Coalition (IMCTC).[36] As Oman, since Sultan Qaboos' ascendancy, has skillfully balanced regional and international powers against each other, positioning Muscat as a "friend of all," the Omanis have had to make difficult decisions to preserve a balanced and neutral foreign policy. There is every reason to expect Muscat to continue pragmatically communicating with all in the Gulf region and coordinating across a host of domains to advance mutual interests.

In the Gulf's evolving security architecture, the Sultanate is increasingly concerned about how Saudi Arabia and the UAE's young leaders are creating greater polarization and initiating zero-sum conflicts that afford Oman, as well as Kuwait, less autonomy and room for maneuverability. From Muscat's perspective, such foreign policies pursued by MbS and MbZ have left the Sultanate increasingly vulnerable to their destabilizing impacts. The Yemeni crisis, which represents the gravest threat to Omani national security, is a salient example. Sharing a 187-mile with Yemen, Oman's view is that the menace of potential spillover of violence from Yemen into the Sultanate has been greatly exacerbated by the Saudi-led campaign against the Houthis, which has led to a humanitarian crisis and power vacuums filled by extremists such as ISIS and AQAP.

A report published on August 6, 2017 further confirmed that Arab states involved in the Riyadh-led coalition worked rather directly with AQAP, at times paying off their militants with "weapons, equipment, and wads of looted cash," even recruiting hundreds of them.[37] Within this complicated arena of battle, a tactical partnership between Saudi Arabia, the UAE, and their allies on one side and extremists such as AQAP on the other has been established in a greater quest to eject Iranian influence from Yemen. Oman has seen both Saudi Arabia and the UAE's actions in Yemen as highly destabilizing for not only the Sultanate but also a host of countries in the region and worldwide.

There is much speculation that in the future, perhaps after Sultan Qaboos passes away and a new Omani monarch ascends to the throne, MbS and MbZ will seek to put more pressure on Muscat to distance itself from Tehran and align more closely with the Saudi/UAE-led fold. Yet Omanis are highly sensitive about outside pressures on the Sultanate's internal and external policymaking. Keen to avoid falling into the Saudi/Emirati sphere of influence that would limit Oman's maneuverability as a neutral state, Muscat will likely react to MbS and MbZ's combative foreign policies in the region by further diversifying the Sultanate's foreign alliances and hedging Muscat's bets in a post-GCC period. The extent to which Bahrain has relinquished its sovereignty as a price for its special relationship with Saudi Arabia informs all the smaller states of the Arabian Peninsula of the need to protect their independence from Riyadh's vision of Saudi hegemony in the region.

6.1. Bahrain

The Gulf's conservative Sunni monarchies have long perceived Shia activism in Bahrain as the GCC's gravest source of weakness. Although many elements of Bahrain's Shia opposition have gone to pains to distance themselves from Iran, their activism is understood in Riyadh and Abu Dhabi as evidence of Iranian meddling in the archipelago sheikdom. As the GCC's only Shia-majority member, many analysts have concluded that Bahrain's Al Khalifa royals have been the only ruling Arab Gulf family truly vulnerable to the prospects of a Khomeinist revolution. The failed coup attempt of December 1981, which the newly established Islamic Republic supported, heavily shapes Bahraini and other Arab Gulf rulers' views of the alleged threat that Tehran poses to the archipelago state.

Despite no evidence that Iran was behind Bahrain's Arab Spring uprising of 2011, or that the Pearl Roundabout protestors had a pro-Iranian or a sectarian agenda, Riyadh and Abu Dhabi saw the island sheikdom's Shia-dominated demonstrations as a sign of Iran flexing its muscles.[38] Tehran's response to Bahrain's Arab Spring confirmed the worst of Riyadh and Abu Dhabi's concerns about Iranian interference in a GCC member. Iran's then-foreign minister Ali Akbar Salehi sought to mobilize the UN, the Organization of the Islamic Conference, the Arab League, and Turkey to pressure Manama into ending its crackdown on Shia protestors. Hardline elements within the Tehran regime such as the paramilitary group Ansar-e Hezbollah "announced plans for a jihad in Bahrain" and Iranian clerics called on the Islamic Republic to take a more assertive position against Bahrain's Sunni monarchy.

Lebanese Hezbollah's solidarity with Bahrain's Shia protestors contributed to Saudi and Emirati anxiety about Iran's "sectarian orientation" vis-à-vis the Shia-majority GCC state.[39]

Riyadh and Abu Dhabi acted quickly to counter Iran's perceived use of its political and religious influence to stir unrest in Bahrain, separated from Saudi Arabia's Shia-majority Eastern Province by a 15-mile causeway. To help Bahraini security forces quell the uprising, on March 14, 2011 Saudi and Emirati tanks, troops, soldiers, and police were deployed under the auspices of the GCC's Peninsula Shield force across the causeway.[40] US President Barack Obama's call on Egyptian President Hosni Mubarak to step down in February 2011, which Riyadh understood as a sign of the American administration's willingness to casually discard an Arab ally of Washington and Riyadh, contributed to Saudi Arabia and the UAE's decision to back the Bahraini regime independently from Washington.[41]

Since the GCC Peninsula Shield's intervention in Bahrain, Saudi Arabia and the UAE have remained in lock-step unity in their support for the royal Al Khalifa family. To keep the Bahraini economy afloat since the Arab Spring, the Saudis and Emiratis have pumped billions into the island kingdom. Such economic and security assistance from Riyadh and Abu Dhabi has enabled Bahrain's Sunni monarchy to remain in power without making substantial concessions to the Shia opposition. Yet a loss of Bahraini sovereignty is a price that Manama has paid for this external support from its Gulf allies.

Saudi and Emirati visions for Gulf security rest on the Al Khalifa family maintaining its rule in Bahrain and preventing Iran from exploiting Bahrain's sectarian tensions. As Riyadh sees it, concessions made by the Manama regime to Shia oppositionists risk emboldening Shia demands not only in Bahrain but also in Saudi Arabia's Eastern Province. To be sure, from the Saudi and Emirati perspectives, the prospects of a Shia revolution in a Gulf state must be interpreted within the context of Iraq's Sunni-minority regime falling in 2003, which left Bahrain as the last Arab state with a Shia majority under Sunni rule. As an Emirati scholar told me, in light of the post-2003 Shia order in Baghdad heavily oppressing Iraqi Sunnis, many Bahraini Sunnis and their co-religionists in Saudi Arabia and the UAE believe that preserving Sunni rule in Manama is essential for thwarting pro-Iranian Shia from establishing a sectarian regime in the island sheikdom that would deny rights to Bahraini Sunnis. Preventing such a scenario is a deeply shared interest on the part of Saudi Arabia and the UAE, which see a successful Iranian-backed revolution in a GCC state as a red line that must never be crossed.

Saudi Arabia and the UAE's military coordination in 2011 against perceived threats posed by Bahrain's Shia demonstrators, whom Riyadh and Abu Dhabi accused of receiving support from Iran and Lebanese Hezbollah, marked a watershed in terms of the Kingdom and the Emirates' quest to maintain the status quo in the Gulf without requiring a green light from Washington. This new approach to regional security, in which Gulf states would act without consulting their US ally, has created new dynamics in the MENA region far beyond the Gulf. In Libya too, the UAE has flexed its muscles, taking unilateral actions to combat perceived menaces.

7.1. Libya

With MbS and MbZ in the driver seats, Saudi Arabia and the UAE have aligned quite closely vis-à-vis the chaotic Libyan crisis. Soon after the Maghrebi country's ongoing civil war erupted in mid-2014, the UAE in tandem with Egypt has played a highly active role in Libya. The Emiratis and Egyptians, with Saudi support, have waged direct military interventions to combat various Islamist militias fighting the Abu Dhabi- and Cairo-backed Libyan National Army (LNA), which fights for the secular-leaning Tobruk-based House of Representatives (HoR). From Abu Dhabi's perspective, Libya has been a hotspot where efforts are required to counter the expansion of Qatari and Turkish influence via Doha and Ankara's support for Islamist factions in the bifurcated North African state.

The Kingdom and the Emirates have sponsored the LNA and HoR. Viewing Libya's new strongman, Field Marshal Khalifa Haftar, who heads the LNA, as a bulwark against Muslim Brotherhood fighters and other Islamists, Abu Dhabi has a vision for Libya following the post-2013 Egyptian model of being ruled by an anti-Islamist military order that keeps Libya aligned with the UAE and does not permit Muslim Brotherhood figures to use Libya as a platform for encouraging Islamists in the Emirates to further challenge the UAE's royal families' legitimacy.

Despite not waging any military interventions in Libya, either multilaterally or unilaterally, Saudi Arabia has been supportive of the HoR/LNA in religious domains. By endorsing certain "quietist" Salafists in Benghazi and elsewhere in eastern Libya, who support Haftar and oppose challenging any Muslim leader on religious or political grounds, Riyadh has sought to strengthen the mercurial field marshal's legitimacy from an Islamic standpoint. Libyan Salafist delegations' movement between Libya and Saudi Arabia has led to a high-ranking religious figure in the Kingdom issuing a fatwa endorsing Operation Dignity, the campaign that Haftar launched in mid-2014 to forcefully defeat Islamist militants in Libya.[42, 43]

At the heart of Saudi Arabia and the UAE's fears of Libya, where Iran is essentially an absent foreign actor, are the prospects for Islamists shaping the Maghrebi country's post-2011 political and social arenas. Given Libya's large size, geographical location, and natural resource wealth, the Muslim Brotherhood's role as a powerful player in the Maghrebi country's domestic political and social arenas would bode poorly for the Quartet's determination to eradicate Islamist influence from the greater Arab world. Emirati threat perceptions of Libya are informed by a view of the local Muslim Brotherhood branch and other Islamist groups using the energy-rich North African country as a base to promote Islamist mobilization throughout the MENA region, including within the UAE where officials in Abu Dhabi have banned formal Islamist networks and perceive informal ones as internal enemies of the state that pose an existential threat to the federation's rulers.

Yet the UAE, and to a lesser extent Saudi Arabia, becoming further involved in Libya's affairs subjects the Emiratis to risks, given problems that certain segments of Libya—chiefly the Islamists—have had with Abu Dhabi's role in the North African country's complicated post-revolutionary state of affairs. For over five years, the UAE has faced dangerous blowback in Libya. On July 25, 2013, militants attacked Abu Dhabi's embassy compound in Tripoli's Siahia neighborhood with a rocket-propelled grenade.

On November 13, 2014, bombs exploded near the UAE and Egypt's embassies, clearly targeting both Arab countries for their opposition to Islamist militias in the Libyan capital.[45]

8.1. Yemen

Nowhere has the Saudi-Emirati alliance's drive to redefine the Arab world's security architecture been so bold as in Yemen. Fearful that the Houthi rebellion, which took over Yemen's capital, Sana'a, in September 2014, would lead to the birth of an Iranian-allied proto-state in northern Yemen along Saudi Arabia's southern border, Riyadh led an unprecedented intervention in concert with a handful of Sunni Arab allies along with US support to defeat the Tehran-backed Houthi fighters. Plans for establishing IMAFT (or perhaps a so-called "Arab NATO") as an effectual force capable of reshaping the Arab/Islamic world's geopolitical order have counted on Yemen as an important test for such ambitions.

Yet the disastrous outcomes of the Saudi-led campaign in Yemen raise major questions about the Gulf monarchies' capacities to emerge as independent and powerful military forces in the chaotic region, let alone to lead a pan-Sunni Islamic military alliance. The war effort in Yemen has resulted in growing international condemnation of Saudi Arabia and the UAE from voices who have harshly criticized Riyadh and Abu Dhabi on human rights and international law grounds against the backdrop of Yemen's humanitarian crises exacerbating daily. The campaign in Yemen has also proven costly in terms of Saudi Arabia and the UAE's blood and treasure, as well as both countries' security, most recently underscored by the Houthi rebel's claimed drone attack on Abu Dhabi's airport on July 26, 2018—which Emirati officials denied—following years of Houthi rockets and missiles being fired into Saudi Arabia from Yemen.[46]

Additionally, Abu Dhabi and Riyadh's conflicting interests in Yemen have also fueled a degree of tension in the alliance. Saudi and Emirati plans for Yemen have diverged most notably in the southern governorates, where Yemen's internationally-recognized President Abdrabbuh Mansur Hadi's legitimacy has suffered and southern separatists have gained momentum. The ongoing conflict has enabled southern separatists to strengthen their argument that only a restoration of South Yemen as a political entity can improve the lives of Aden and other southern cities' inhabitants. Saudi Arabia, which played a key role in supporting Yemen's 1990 reunification, opposes the division of Yemen. Such a development, entailing a Saudi-backed Yemeni president losing two capitals since 2014, would be humiliating for Riyadh.

Yet the UAE would likely view the return of South Yemen as advantageous to Abu Dhabi's interests, explaining why the Emiratis have supported southern separatists who at times fly the UAE's flag next to the one of South Yemen in Aden and elsewhere in southern Yemen. An independent state in southern Yemen could potentially provide the UAE with a foothold along the Gulf of Aden and strategically prized Bab-al-Mandab that would enable the Emiratis to take further advantage of new economic opportunities and compliment the establishment of the UAE's footholds in the Horn of Africa.

This issue of southern Yemen's future is likely the gravest source of contention between MbS and MbZ, as well as the Saudi Arabia-UAE alliance in general. Notwithstanding this one dimension of the Yemeni crisis that pits Riyadh against Abu Dhabi, the Saudis and Emiratis have enough common interests in Yemen and elsewhere to likely guarantee that MbS and MbZ will continue conducting closely aligned foreign policies. "Each country has its own interests in Yemen, but they don't currently diverge enough to result in a parting of ways," said scholar Joost Hiltermann. "The UAE and KSA have been able to settle their differences in Yemen amicably and diplomatically."[47]

9.1. The Future of Saudi Arabia and the UAE's Alliance

Predicting how the Saudi-Emirati alliance evolves in the future requires taking stock of how the Kingdom and the UAE have changed internally with MbS and MbZ at the helm. Just as MbZ has consolidated much power in his hands since he became Abu Dhabi's crown prince in 2004, and especially so following Abu Dhabi's bailing out of Dubai after the 2008 financial crash, MbS has transformed Saudi Arabia's decision-making structure away from what was once a consensus-building format toward a new arrangement in which power is increasingly placed in the hands of the Kingdom's de facto ruler.[48, 49]

With much power concentrated in MbS and MbZ's hands, Saudi and Emirati foreign policy is increasingly defined by these crown princes' visions for the region. Given MbS and MbZ's relative youth, which suggests that both could be the Kingdom and the Emirates' de facto rulers for decades to come, the implications of their foreign policy decision making for the greater region will be significant.

Looking ahead, it is highly possible that the Saudis and Emiratis will come to see MbS and MbZ's reliance on support from the Trump administration as a poor strategy for advancing the long-term interests of both Gulf states. "Policy-making under the Trump Administration is clearly going to be highly transactional at the best of times," said scholar Kristian Coates Ulrichsen. "Although a bilateral relationship stripped of 'values,' such as concerns for good governance or human rights, undoubtedly removes points of friction, the corollary is that President Trump is so unpredictable that he could one day turn against the Saudis or Emiratis just as he turned against the Qataris" in June 2017.[50]

Regardless of the risks, MbS and MbZ have counted on strong support from the Trump administration for their regional initiatives aimed at pushing back Iranian influence and weakening the forces of political Islam across the MENA region. Despite the unpredictability of Riyadh and Abu Dhabi's foreign policies, there are no indicators that either of the crown princes will dramatically alter their strategies for achieving regional objectives. A consequence will likely be greater instability in the MENA region, due to MbS and MbZ's increasingly personalized and unpredictable approaches to foreign affairs against the backdrop of a US role in the region which has also become increasingly personalized and unpredictable during the Trump presidency.

Ultimately, as discussed in this chapter, Riyadh and Abu Dhabi have done much to create new enemies in the region and embolden old ones through their combative foreign policies. Now entering a period in which the GCC is no longer an effectual institution (an outcome of MbS and MbZ's Qatar policies), Saudi Arabia and the UAE will have to fend off an increasingly assertive Iran at a time in which Arab solidarity in the Gulf is at an all-time low. It remains to be seen whether Saudi Arabia and the UAE's leaders will realize how adventurist policies are unrealistic and dangerous strategies to achieve Saudi and Emirati goals. The lack of positive results vis-à-vis Qatar and Yemen call into question the potential of Riyadh and Abu Dhabi to form a bloc in the Arab world that is more successful than past efforts to establish a unified Arab coalition.

Endnotes

1. Kristian Coates Ulrichsen eds., *The Changing Security Dynamics of the Persian Gulf*, (Oxford: Oxford University Press, 2018).

2. Kristian Coates Ulrichsen, *The Gulf States in International Political Economy*, (Basingstoke: Palgrave Macmillan, 2016).

3. Margherita Stancati, "Saudi Crown Prince and U.A.E Heir Forge Pivotal Ties," *The Wall Street Journal*, August 6, 2017, https://www.wsj.com/articles/saudi-crown-prince-and-u-a-e-heir-forge-pivotal-ties-1502017202

4. Dexter Filkins, "A Saudi Prince's Quest to Remake the Middle East," *The New Yorker*, April 9, 2018, https://www.newyorker.com/magazine/2018/04/09/a-saudi-princes-quest-to-remake-the-middle-east

5. Ibid.

6. Rori Donaghy, "Saudi Arabia Shift Closer to Change in Policy Toward Muslim Brotherhood," *Middle East Eye*, February 13, 2015, https://www.middleeasteye.net/news/saudi-arabia-shift-closer-change-policy-toward-muslim-brotherhood-994741112

7. Simon Henderson, "Meet the Two Princes Reshaping the Middle East," *Politico*, June 13, 2017, https://www.politico.com/magazine/story/2017/06/13/saudi-arabia-middle-east-donald-trump-215254

8. "US and UAE Hold Talks on Security and Iran," *The New Arab*, May 17, 2017, https://www.alaraby.co.uk/english/news/2017/5/17/us-and-uae-hold-talks-on-security-and-iran

9. Mark Landler, "Trump Takes Credit for Saudi Move Against Qatar, a U.S Military Partner," *The New York Times*, June 6, 2017, https://www.nytimes.com/2017/06/06/world/middleeast/trump-qatar-saudi-arabia.html

10. Kristian Coates Ulrichsen, "The Needless Crisis in the Arabian Gulf," *Arab Center Washington DC*, June 5, 2018, http://arabcenterdc.org/policy_analyses/the-needless-crisis-in-the-arabian-gulf/.

11. "Arab States Issue 13 Demands to End Qatar-Gulf Crisis," *Aljazeera*, July 12, 2017, https://www.aljazeera.com/news/2017/06/arab-states-issue-list-demands-qatar-crisis-170623022133024.html

12. Mohammed Sergie, "Embattled Qatar is Rich Enough to Get By for Another 100 Years," *Bloomberg Businessweek*, June 6, 2018, https://www.bloomberg.com/news/articles/2018-06-06/a-year-later-iran-is-the-big-winner-of-the-qatar-embargo

13. "Top UN Court Rules UAE Blockade Violated Qataris' Rights," *Aljazeera*, July 23, 2018, https://www.aljazeera.com/news/2018/07/top-court-rules-uae-blockade-violated-qataris-rights-180723131444047.html

14. Gregory Aftandilian, "The Future of Iraq-Kuwait Relations: Overcoming a Troubled History," *Arab Center Washington DC*, July 10, 2018, http://arabcenterdc.org/policy_analyses/the-future-of-iraqi-kuwaiti-relations-overcoming-a-troubled-history/

15. Mohammad Al-Enezi "Bahrain Welcomes Kuwaiti Naval Forces," *Kuwait News Agency*, March 21, 2011, https://www.kuna.net.kw/ArticlePrintPage.aspx?id=2154115&language=en.

16. "Kuwait to Send Troops to Saudi Arabia to Fight Yemen Rebels – Newspaper," *Reuters*, December 29, 2015, https://uk.reuters.com/article/uk-kuwait-yemen-security-idUKKBN0UC0I520151229

17. "Yemen Peace Talks in Kuwait End Amid Fighting," *Aljazeera*, August 7, 2016, https://www.aljazeera.com/news/2016/08/yemen-peace-talks-collapse-fighting-intensifies-160807042106210.html

18. "Kuwait Recalls Ambassador to Iran as Row Escalates," *Aljazeera*, January 5 2016 https://www.aljazeera.com/news/2016/01/kuwait-recalls-ambassador-iran-rising-tensions-160105090603667.html

19. Giorgio Cafiero and Cinzia Miotto, "Kuwaiti-Iranian Relations: The Energy Angle," *Atlantic Council*, September 29, 2016, http://www.atlanticcouncil.org/blogs/menasource/kuwaiti-iranian-relations-the-energy-angle

20. Kristin Diwan, "Kuwait: Finding Balance in a Maximalist Gulf," (Report by The Arab Gulf States Institute in Washington), June 29, 2018. http://www.agsiw.org/wp-content/uploads/2018/06/Diwan_Kuwait_ONLINE.pdf

21. "No Military Solution to Yemen Crisis," *Kuwait News Agency*, March 8, 2018, https://www.kuna.net.kw/ArticleDetails.aspx?id=2739796&language=en

22. "Final Deal on Oman, Iran Gas Pipeline Soon," *Oman Observer*, April 21, 2018, http://www.omanobserver.om/final-deal-on-oman-iran-gas-pipeline-soon/

23. Camille Lons, "Oman: Between Iran and a Hard Place," *European Council on Foreign Relations*, May 3, 2018, https://www.ecfr.eu/article/commentary_oman_between_iran_and_a_hard_place1

24. "Oman's Role in a Turbulent Region," (Presented at Middle East Institute Event, Washington D.C, April 30, 2018), http://www.mei.edu/events/oman-s-role-turbulent-region

25. "Yemen, Houthis and Saudi Arabia in Secret Talks to End War – Sources," *Reuters*, March 15, 2018, https://www.reuters.com/article/yemen-security-saudi-talks/yemens-houthis-and-saudi-arabia-in-secret-talks-to-end-war-sources-idUSL8N1QX1FK

26. "Syria's Top Diplomat Visits Oman on Rare Gulf Mission," *Yahoo!*, March 26, 2018, https://www.yahoo.com/news/syrias-top-diplomat-visits-oman-rare-gulf-mission-174311992.html

27. Hadi Fornaji, "Faiez Serraj Arrives in Muscat For Two-Day Visit to Oman," *Libya Herald*, November 8, 2017, https://www.libyaherald.com/2017/11/08/faiez-serraj-arrives-in-muscat-for-two-day-visit-to-oman/

28. Saleh al Shaibany and Taimur Khan, "Kuwait Emir and King Salman Meet Over Qatar Crisis as Trump Backs UAE and Saudi," *The National*, June 6, 2017, https://www.thenational.ae/world/kuwaiti-emir-and-king-salman-meet-over-qatar-crisis-as-trump-backs-uae-and-saudi-1.82485.

29. "Qatar-Oman Trade Volume Increases," *The Peninsula Qatar*, September 20, 2017, https://www.thepeninsulaqatar.com/article/10/09/2017/Qatar-Oman-trade-volume-increases

30. Abdullah Baabood, "Oman and the Gulf Diplomatic Crisis," OXGAPS, Autumn 2017, https://www.oxgaps.org/files/commentary_-_baabood.pdf

31 Lons.

32. "UAE Denies Pro-Hezbollah Newspaper Claims Of Oman Pressure," *The National*, July 23, 2018, https://www.thenational.ae/world/mena/uae-denies-pro-hezbollah-newspaper-claims-of-oman-pressure-1.753249

33. "Oman Says Busts UAE Spy Network, UAE Denies Role," *Reuters*, January 30, 2011, https://www.reuters.com/article/us-oman-emirates-spying/oman-says-uncovers-uae-spy-network-idUSTRE70T11R20110130

34. Noah Browning, "Yemen Combatants Not Ready for Talks, Says Neighbor Oman," *Reuters*, April 2, 2015, https://www.reuters.com/article/us-yemen-security-oman/yemen-combatants-not-ready-for-talks-says-neighbor-oman-idUSKBN0MT22Q20150402

35. Baba Umar, "Yemen's War Wounded Find Comfort in 'Brotherly' Oman," *Aljazeera*, December 16, 2018, https://www.aljazeera.com/news/2016/11/yemen-war-wounded-find-comfort-brotherly-oman-161120065419274.html

36. "Oman Joins Saudi-Led Islamic Alliance: Gulf Sources," *Reuters*, December 28, 2016, https://www.reuters.com/article/us-saudi-oman-coalition-idUSKBN14H1L4

37. "Report: Saudi-UAE Coalition 'Cut Deals' With Al-Qaeda in Yemen," *Aljazeera*, August 6, 2018, https://www.aljazeera.com/news/2018/08/report-saudi-uae-coalition-cut-deals-al-qaeda-yemen-180806074659521.html

38. "Bahrain Independent Commission of Inquiry Excerpts," *BBC*, November 23, 2011, https://www.bbc.com/news/world-middle-east-15861353

39. Frederic M. Wehrey, *Sectarian Politics in the Gulf: From the Iraq War To the Arab Uprisings*, (New York: Columbia University Press, 2016).

40. "Saudi Soldiers Sent Into Bahrain," *Aljazeera*, March 15, 2011, https://www.aljazeera.com/news/middleeast/2011/03/2011314124928850647.html

41. March Lynch, *The Arab Uprising: The Unfinished Revolutions of the New Middle East*, (New York City: Public Affairs Books, 2013).

42. Abdullah Ben Ibrahim, "Khalifa Haftar's War on Opponents Gets Religious Boost From Radical Salafists," *The Libya Observer*, February 5, 2018, https://www.libyaobserver.ly/news/khalifa-haftar%E2%80%99s-war-opponents-gets-religious-boost-radical-salafists

43. Frederic Wehrey, "Quiet No More?" *Carnegie Middle East Center*, October 13, 2016, http://carnegie-mec.org/diwan/64846

44. Ghaith Shennib and Marie-Louise Gumuchian, "UAE Embassy Compound Attacked in Libyan Capital," *Reuters*, July 25, 2013, https://www.reuters.com/article/us-libya-uae-attack/uae-embassy-compound-attacked-in-libyan-capital-idUSBRE96O04J20130725

45. "Bombs Explode Near Egyptian and UAE Embassies in Libyan Capital," *Reuters*, November 13, 2014, https://www.reuters.com/article/us-libya-security/bombs-explode-near-egyptian-and-uae-embassies-in-libyan-capital-idUSKCN0IX0CO20141113?feedType=RSS&feedName=worldNews&rpc=69

46. "Yemen's Rebels 'Attack' Abu Dhabi Airport Using a Drone," *Reuters*, July 27, 2018, https://www.aljazeera.com/news/2018/07/yemen-rebels-attack-abu-dhabi-airport-drone-180726155103669.html

47. Jonathan-Fenton Harvey, "Saudi Arabia and UAE's Dangerous Rivalry Over Yemen," *The New Arab*, May 31, 2018, https://www.alaraby.co.uk/english/indepth/2018/5/31/saudi-arabia-and-uaes-dangerous-rivalry-over-yemen

48. Matthias Sailer, "UAE Foreign Policy and the Crown Prince of Abu Dhabi: Hardly a Ruler in Waiting," *Qantara*, March 23, 2018, https://en.qantara.de/content/uae-foreign-policy-and-the-crown-prince-of-abu-dhabi-hardly-a-ruler-in-waiting

49. Kristian Coates Ulrichsen, "Crown Prince of Disorder," *Foreign Policy*, March 21, 2018, https://foreignpolicy.com/2018/03/21/crown-prince-of-disorder/

50. Kristian Coates Ulrichsen, "Trump's Transactional Relationship with Saudi Arabia," Arab Center Washington DC, March 22, 2018, http://arabcenterdc.org/viewpoint/trumps-transactional-relationship-with-saudi-arabia/

CHAPTER 3

Gulf Dispute: Military Security in Small States

DAVID B. DES ROCHES

Introduction

Small states face a variety of security dilemmas. If they have large neighbors, they are at risk of assimilation or conquest. If a small state sits between two large states, it may become either a battlefield or a pawn. The larger neighbors of small states often expect their smaller counterpart to comply with the larger states' policies, either as a matter of shared interest or shared security, even if the smaller state demurs.[1] Of course, many larger states often assume the mantle of regional security leader (however self-appointed this title may be) and subsequently impose an obligation on their small neighbors to act as faithful followers.

These problems are not new, nor are they unique. Many of these problems do, however, apply to Qatar, particularly in the wake of the breach with Saudi Arabia, the United Arab Emirates, and Bahrain, among others. In this paper I will briefly examine the military challenges faced by small states, and look at how, in response, Qatar has sought to rapidly increase its military power.

1.1. The Challenge of a Large Neighboring State
The Case of the United States

The first challenge a small state faces is how best to accommodate the desire of the larger state to be seen and followed as the leader of the smaller state's security policies. Large states, particularly large states which have made a significant investment in security, often seek to build coalitions among their neighbors with themselves in the lead. For example, the United States, upon declaration of the Monroe Doctrine in 1823,[2] was one of the first modern states to declare itself as a regional security leader (announcing that European powers were not welcome in the Western Hemisphere). Subsequently, over the better part of the next two centuries, the US conducted a series of interventions into other weaker, mostly failing countries within their self-imposed domain. Notable among these interventions were the decades-long occupations of Haiti,[3] the forced recession of Panama from Colombia[4] (followed by a prolonged occupation of the Panama Canal Zone),[5] and repeated brief incursions into Nicaragua and the Dominican Republic.[6] In the post-World War II era, the United States managed to develop a hemispheric organization of states to validate its regional leadership and solicit the involvement of its smaller neighbors in security operations. For example, the Organization of American States (based in Washington DC) has provided the mandate and troops for recent occupations of both Haiti and the Dominican Republic.[7]

Inevitably, there are small states which view it as their best course of action to enlist an extra-regional power as its sponsor, bucking the role of the dominant neighboring state in the process. In the western hemisphere, this role has been played by Cuba, which for decades acted as a virtual satellite state of the Soviet Union, going on to adopt anti-Americanism as both a defining element of national identity and Cuban foreign policy.[8]

2.1. Small State Status in the Gulf

Applying this example to Qatar, we can see Saudi Arabia (and lately the UAE, which is much smaller but plays an outsized role in security affairs), positioning itself as a leader of the Gulf Arab states. As such the Kingdom appears to be seeking unity of policy and action among the smaller states of the Gulf, including Qatar. Like the case of the USA's Organization of American States, the Gulf Cooperation Council is the logical vehicle for coordinating political and security policy among within the Gulf, a metaphor made even more apt by the GCC's headquartering in Riyadh.

Qatar's deviations from the behavior desired by Saudi Arabia, the UAE, and Bahrain have been publicized for some time. A litany of complaints, Qatar's policy towards the Muslim Brotherhood, Qatar's cooperation with Iran (which is to at least some extent dictated by the geographical reality of shared gas fields), Qatar's willingness to host critics of the other GCC regimes, and Qatar's patronage of media outlets which criticize other GCC states, each are seen by her bigger neighbors as intolerable provocations. Given these tensions, Qatar has sought to ensure its survival in two main ways: alignment with the United States and accelerated purchasing of large amounts of military hardware. I'll discuss the likely results of these two approaches in this paper.

2.2. Small State Survival Strategy #1: Appeal to a Superpower

One complicating factor in the current Qatar crisis are the varying degrees to which GCC states are dependent upon the United States as the ultimate guarantor of their national survival. The Carter Doctrine– a unilateral statement of support for the Gulf states made without any preconditions[9]– is arguably a more robust commitment than is America's commitment to NATO. Unlike America's "Article V commitment" to intervene in the event of another European conflict, the Carter Doctrine was actually tested when American forces led efforts leading to the liberation of Kuwait in 1991.[10] This message was not lost on the other GCC members: the United States' robust military presence in the region is regarded as the ultimate arbiter of security issues, a fact not lost on the other GCC nations.

In such a situation, perhaps it was inevitable that Saudi and Emirati complaints about Qatar were initially phrased in terms which were designed to resonate in the United States. When the blockade of Qatar was announced, the initial purported grievance was Qatar's supposed funding of terrorism.[11] While this is certainly a legitimate concern, it is not one which was unique to Qatar. In fact, most Americans had long regarded Saudi Arabia as the lead funder of al-Qaeda, and thus have a low opinion of the Kingdom[12] (in spite of the recent Saudi leadership on this issue). The language and the charges the blockading nations chose were not those which would appeal to Qataris or with other Arab gulf states. To the contrary, they were designed to evoke sympathy in the United States. That President Trump initially appeared receptive and in agreement with the Saudi and Emirati charges seems to lend some credence to this strategy.

As the GCC crisis has dragged on, it seems that Qatar has followed suite, also shifting the focus of its counterarguments to the United States. There have been millions of dollars spent on lobbying by the countries since the crisis started. The Qataris have revived what had been a moribund presence in Washington and have sought to counter the vibrant presence of the UAE's extremely effective ambassador to Washington.[13] These efforts have met with some success given that the GCC standoff is now regarded by many in Washington as a local dispute requiring local resolution. In many ways, this represents a victory for Qatar.

A precedent for appealing to an outside superpower can be seen in the Greek-Turkish dispute. During the Cold War and particularly in the wake of the invasion of Cyprus in 1974, both Greece and Turkey were in a state of confrontation close to war. The complexity of the situation was compounded since both nations are NATO members, making each nation reliant upon the United States (and the greater NATO network), as their ultimate security guarantor.[14]

Greece and Turkey also chose to make their case in Washington in terms that would resonate amongst Americans. The Greeks tended to note their commitment to democratic values while the Turks noted their military posture on the borders of the Soviet Union and their commitment to NATO's military structure.

One complicating factor in the feud was the discrepancy between each nation's diaspora within the United States. There was a large Greek and Greco-American population in the United States, with which Turks and Turkish-Americans could not compare.[15] Logically, in any American political forum, the Turkish government was at a huge disadvantage. In the current Gulf dispute, such a factor does not come into play for any of the GCC states as they all lack domestic constituencies in the United States.

Taken in this light, we can assess Qatar's concerted Washington outreach effort to be mostly successful. In the past, the Qatari presence in Washington paled alongside the more aggressive and engaged lobbying efforts of Saudi Arabia and the UAE. Especially after the Dubai Ports World fiasco of 2006, the UAE established its embassy as one of the most influential in Washington. Qatar was not even in the same league. However, due to a more recent focus on organizing a powerful embassy with influential advocates, Qatar has managed to rebuff most of the hostile or potentially hostile legislation in Washington, claiming a second victory by bringing the blockade to a standstill.

Qatar has done more than pay lobbyists– it has engaged Washington in a whole new way. Senior Qatari officials, such as the Minister of Foreign Affairs, have made repeated visits to the USA and have made themselves available to reporters, academics, and think tank analysts on a scale that is rare for the Arab world.[16] In a time of American fiscal austerity, Qatar has announced plans for the expansion of a base that hosts American forces, currying favor among many in Washington. In another effort to appeal to the US government, Qatar even ceded ground on the issue of open skies for American-flagged airlines, previously a key irritant in the two states' bilateral relations.[17] Finally, Qatar has purchased large amounts of American weapons far in excess of what its domestic population will be able to effectively field.[18] Each of these steps have served to cast Qatar in a favorable light, gradually discrediting the Saudi and Emirati portrayal of Qatar as rogue state hostile to American interests.

Militarily, Qatar's main move has been to play up the importance of its joint airbase at al-Udeid, one of the largest American overseas bases in the world and the only base in the GCC capable of conducting B-52 operations.[19] Hosted at this base are the forward headquarters of the United States Central Command, the Combined Air Operations Center, and the forward headquarters of CENTCOM's Special Operations component. Additionally, al-Udeid includes a long, reinforced runway, numerous revetments, a large housing area with amenities for US soldiers, and a great degree of freedom of action for American forces.

The importance of the base has not been lost on Qataris. Indeed, at the onset of the GCC crisis, one of the major objectives of the anti-Qatar coalition seemed to be moving the US headquarters at al-Udeid to al-Dhafra air base in Abu Dhabi.[20] While the Pentagon has been steadfast in opposing this move (due mostly to reasons of cost and military requirements of redundancy), relocating the base has been a constant theme during the crisis.

Amidst this push by some for relocation, the Qataris have responded by announcing plans to implement upgrades and expansions at al-Udeid. In his address at the Heritage Foundation in January 2018, the Qatari Minister of Defense announced that, in addition to developing a US Naval facility in Qatar, he would be adding housing and an American school to the site as well.[21]

While these measures are welcome in Washington, they are not determinative. The United States has, in the past, walked away from bases when it was deemed they were either too limited to support American goals or too expensive to continue to operate.[22] If Qatar were to impose restrictions on American forces operating within the country, the value of the bases would decline irrespective of any physical infrastructure. That does not appear to be the case: the American bases are active, valued, and apparently expanding. One common misconception concerns the possible military use of these bases in repelling any military attack against Qatar. The two major American facilities in Qatar are concerned with command and control, air power, and logistics, not combat. American military facilities in Qatar do not house ground combatant forces. Should Qatar's GCC neighbors take military action, the American reaction would be political, as the forces at these bases are not suitable for defensive action against a ground invader.

Of course, the American–Qatari alliance involves more than just air bases. To be sure, that Qatar hosts these bases is a visible sign of the relationship. However, their importance should not be overstated. If serious security issues develop between the US and Qatar, the mere presence of a base will not be permitted to overshadow other issues. Hosting American military facilities is appreciated, but it does not give the host a blank check to ignore other American security concerns. The United States has, over its recent history, opened and closed numerous bases in response to changing conditions. Qatar's position on this front is strong, but it is not unassailable. Qatar would be well served to continue with steps such as the Defense Minister's announcement of the al-Udeid housing expansion.

3.1. A Potential Military Disaster: Qatar Allies with an Outside Hostile Power

Some small states, faced with demands by bigger neighbors, choose to ally with an outside power hostile to the bigger neighbor. Cuba has used this strategy to maintain its independence from the United States (if not its prosperity). The Cuban alliance with the Soviet Union, while a disaster in terms of economic and political progress, was the key factor in maintaining an independent Cuba able to pursue policies in contravention to the wishes of Washington for over 30 years.[23] Cuba went from being a near-dependency to an independent voice in foreign affairs and a global leader of the non-aligned movement. While Cuba is one of the most oppressive countries in the world, with one of the worst economies in the hemisphere, it is *independent*. Even the collapse of the Soviet Union did not bring Cuba into the United State's orbit, as the island nation instead allied with the like-minded, (and oil rich), Venezuela.[24] How long this arrangement and this hostility towards the United States can last is an open question, but at least as it relates to the short-term maintenance of independence, Cuban policy can be assessed as successful. While this is a low hurdle Cuba remains a sovereign state outside the orbit of American influence.

Arguably, Qatar's growing military, political, and economic ties with Turkey (which the blockading countries view as a semi-hostile power) arguably fills the "Soviet Union/Venezuela" role.[25] While Turkey's military capabilities are often overstated, it has established a small military presence in Qatar and is frequently (if inaccurately) portrayed in the press as a potential guarantor of Qatari independence.

Qatar has also made overtures to Russia.[26] While not as deep or as potentially significant as those made to Turkey, Qatari purchases of Russian combat aircraft are not sensible or justifiable when viewed solely in any military sense. However, when viewed as a political act, it makes perfect sense: it reminds America as well as the other GCC members, that Qatar has options and, if pressed, would exercise them.

One available option that does not seem to have been pursued by Qatar is an alliance with Iran. Although doing so may provide some kind of short term gain, it is a good thing that Qatar's leaders have not established a security relationship with the Islamic Republic. There is no doubt that strengthening ties with Iran as a counterbalance to the blockading GCC powers would do damage Qatar's security in the long term. While Tehran would certainly be eager to position itself as an alternative to cooperation with the Saudis and Emiratis, any enhanced Iranian presence in Qatar would risk alienating the United States and other Western powers. Indeed incorrect reports that Iranian Revolutionary Guardsmen were stationed Doha were circulated to discredit the Qataris.

3.2. Small State Survival Strategy #2: Become a Military Power

Some small states have managed to transform their security environments by becoming far more powerful than their size suggests. Since the genocide of 1994, Rwanda has become the military powerhouse of Central Africa, intervening in the Congo and exerting across much of the African continent. Meanwhile, in Asia, Singapore, a tiny state by any measure, is a major security player in its region and is treated as if it were much larger than a city-state.[27]

Closer to Qatar, the United Arab Emirates is a model of how a small country can rather quickly develop a truly impressive military capacity. The Emirati armed forces have, in just over 30 years, transformed from a loosely organized group of constabulary forces into the most advanced force in the Arab world, conducting opposed amphibious landings and operating bases in Africa and Yemen. Given these developments Emiratis can take justifiable pride in the given honorific "Little Sparta."[28]

Can Qatar emulate its neighbor and become an outsized military power? Recent Qatari arms sales suggest it is indeed attempting to follow this pattern, seeking a broad range of advanced weapons from the French, British, Americans, and the Russians.

Since the beginning of the GCC crisis, Qatar has purchased (or announced the intent to purchase) a multitude of combat aircraft. In December 2017, Qatar signed a $6 billion contract to buy 36 F-15 fighters.[29] Earlier that month, Qatar announced the purchase of 12 more French Rafale fighters (in addition to its 36) with a possible option for another 24 fighters.[30] Earlier in the fall, Qatar announced plans to buy 24 British Eurofighter Typhoons.[31] Taken together, these purchases would expand the Qatari Air Force from 12 fighter aircraft to at least 72. There has been similar growth in the other armed services, including orders for ships, air defense systems, and infantry fighting vehicles. It is tempting to regard Qatar as a budding superpower.

Such a categorization would, however, be deceptive as there are still several problems preventing Qatar's military from truly blossoming. While hardware is a key component of military capacity, it is uncertain if Qatar has the manpower or the expertise to convert its raw numbers of ships, airplanes, and tanks into a truly effective military. Qatar's citizenry hovers only around 330,000 (roughly the size of the London Borough of Ealing and less than Anaheim, California), making it difficult to find enough citizens who are qualified, willing, and available to train to the high level of proficiency required to operate modern military equipment. The diversity of the military equipment also poses another challenge. Again, only looking at fighter aircraft, Qatar will have to maintain three separate supply chains, three separate pilot and weapons officer training establishments and three separate sets of weapons. Some Air Force officers will have to learn French while others will be required to learn English. Given the small manpower pool to draw from, this diversity of equipment is another potential crippling factor.

Finally, none of this equipment will be delivered for years to come. Qatar may indeed become a true "Little Sparta," but only after years of dedicated effort. Right now, the large military equipment orders indicate mere military ambition as opposed to actual military capacity. Qatar simply does not have the luxury of time to build up its military capacity. In spite of what one sees in the Gulf, military capacity is not simply a function of purchasing equipment. Rather, true military capacity requires at least a generation to acquire, educate, train, and promote leaders and integrate them into effective fighting forces. Qatar's lack of defense capacity now reflects the investment decisions made by Qatar's leadership who chose since the 1990s to focus on domestic infrastructure and improving Doha's suitability to host international events rather than on the patient spadework of building military forces. Such changes cannot be quickly remedied.[32]

Conclusion

Security is not a neat or compartmentalized field of study. Implementation of theories and strategies are always much messier than people plan for or expect. Qatar is best served by pursuing multiple tactics for small state survival simultaneously as opposed to a singular strategy, something it indeed appears to be doing. Qatar is well-served by its commitment to constant improvement and expansion of American facilities on its soil. Doha should continue to highlight and develop these facilities, while at the same time recognizing that the bases are a tactical, not strategic, factor in relations with America. A renewed Qatari commitment to a friction-free hosting of American forces will result in a bottom-up recognition of the relationship. Including measures such as reducing customs formalities for troops entering and exiting the base would go a long way to establish a pro-Qatari consensus even within the rank and file of the U.S. military.

Qatar's efforts to rapidly enhance its military capacity are ambitious and welcome. Despite this, Doha will be challenged to translate this new equipment into effective military capability leaving Qatar's manpower situation a key point of concern. In any event, military capacity is never developed quickly, but rather is the result of decisions made over decades. At the very least, in making these recent purchases Qatar has committed itself to moving in the proper direction.

At the end of the day, few countries manage to make themselves secure simply through military measures. The border between the United States and Canada is completely indefensible, as the friendship developed between the two nations was secured through joint trade and culture, not by military means. For Qatar to truly resolve the current crisis and prosper again as it has in the past, Qatar must do more than survive: it also must reconcile with its neighbors. This means that there will have to be compromises made, some of which will come at the expense of a degree of Qatari sovereignty.

While this is unfortunate, it is also inevitable. The state of Qatar can endure as a dynamic, independent, and prosperous state. It can also, over time, become a regional military power. It is certainly on the right track to accomplish both of these goals. First however, Qatar must take a cold and somewhat hard-hearted look at its core interests and develop the strategies through which they can be achieved. The entire Gulf security architecture is being eroded by the current crisis. Only exceptional leadership and some self-sacrifice will resolve it.

Endnotes

1. Lenderking et al, "The GCC Rift: Regional and Global Implications," *Middle East Policy* 24, no. 4 (Winter 2017): 5-28.

2. "A Century of Lawmaking for a New Nation: U.S. Congressional Documents and Debates, 1774-1875," *Annals of Congress,* Senate, 18th Congress, 1st Session, Dec 1823, https://memory.loc.gov/cgi-bin/ampage?collId=llac&fileName=041/llac041.db&recNum=4

3. "US Invasion and Occupation of Haiti, 1915-34," *United States Department of State,* https://history.state.gov/milestones/1914-1920/haiti

4. "Building the Panama Canal, 1903-1914," *United States Department of State*, https://history.state.gov/milestones/1899-1913/panama-canal

5. Suzanne C. Johnston, *An American Legacy in Panama: A Brief History of Department of Defense Installations and Properties in the Former Canal Zone of Panama* (Panama City, Panama: United States Army South, n.d.), https://archive.org/stream/agacyin00suza#page/83/mode/2up/search/date

6. Dionne Sinclair, "US Military Interventions in the Caribbean, 1898-1998," (MA diss., US Army Command and General Staff College, 2012.)

7. "Charter of the Organization of American States," *Organization of American States*, http://www.oas.org/en/sla/dil/inter_american_treaties_A-41_charter_OAS.asp

8. James Suchliki, "Why Cuba Will Still be Anti-American After Castro," *The Atlantic*, March 4, 2013, https://www.theatlantic.com/international/archive/2013/03/why-cuba-will-still-be-anti-american-after-castro/273680/

9. Jimmy Carter, "1980 – The Carter Doctrine Announced." Filmed 1980. YouTube Video, 00:01:05. Posted August 5, 2014, https://www.youtube.com/watch?v=jjcMXKmW28E

10. "Responding to Iraqi Aggression in the Gulf, National Security Directive 54," *The White House*, August 20, 1990, https://nsarchive2.gwu.edu/NSAEBB/NSAEBB39/document4.pdf

11. Adel bin Ahmed al-Jubeir, "Saudi Arabia – Minister for Foreign Affairs Addresses General Debate, 72nd Session," Filmed September 23, 2017, 00:11:00. United Nations Audio/Visual Library. Posted 25 September 2017, https://www.unmultimedia.org/avlibrary/asset/1978/1978089/

12. "Country Ratings," *Gallup,* http://news.gallup.com/poll/1624/perceptions-foreign-countries.aspx

13. Ryan Grim and Akbar Shahid Ahmed, "His Town," *The Huffington Post*, https://highline.huffingtonpost.com/articles/en/his-town/

14. Alan Jangian, "The Cypriot-Turkish Conflict and NATO-EU Cooperation," MA diss., Naval Post Graduate School, 2017): 38-43.

15. "Special Interest Lobbies – Ethnic Lobbies," *Encyclopedia of the New American Nation*, http://www.americanforeignrelations.com/O-W/Special-Interest-Lobbies-Ethnic-lobbies.html

16. "Qatar-U.S Strategic Dialogue Stresses Two Countries Need to Remain Close Allies," *Ministry of Foreign Affairs- Qatar*, February 4, 2018, https://www.mofa.gov.qa/en/all-mofa-news/details/2018/02/04/qatar-us-strategic-

dialogue'-stresses-two-countries'-need-to-remain-close-allies

17. Bart Jansen, "U.S., Qatar Reach Agreement in Long-running Dispute Involving Qatar Airways," *USA Today*, January 30, 2018.

18. Chirine Mountachaf, "A Huge Military Build-up is Underway in Qatar. But Who Will Man The Systems?" *Defense News*, December 15, 2017, https://www.defensenews.com/global/mideast-africa/2017/12/15/a-huge-military-buildup-is-underway-in-qatar-but-who-will-man-the-systems/

19. David Des Roches, "A Base is More Than Buildings," *War on the Rocks*. June 8, 2017.

20. Dr. Robert Gates, "Welcome Remarks by Cliff May with Dr. Robert Gates," 00:50:00, YouTube Video, Published 23 May 2017, https://www.youtube.com/watch?v=bT6ypHHH9JA

21. "U.S.-Qatari Military-to-Military Relations," Filmed, January 29 , 2018, 00:49:13, *The Heritage Foundation*, https://www.heritage.org/defense/event/us-qatari-military-military-relations

22. For example, the United States unilaterally closed its naval air station in Iceland over the objections of the Icelanders in 2006; it was partially re-opened in 2016.

23. Kosmas Tsokhas, "The Political Economy of Cuban Dependence on the Soviet Union," Theory and Society 9, no. 2 (March 1980): 319-362.

24. Will Grant, "Cuba Concerns over Venezuela's Economic Woes," *BBC,* March 11, 2016, http://www.bbc.com/news/world-latin-america-35686683

25. "Turkey Marches Ahead with its Military Plans in Qatar," *Stratfor,* June 16, 2017, https://worldview.stratfor.com/article/turkey-marches-ahead-its-military-plans-qatar

26. "Qatar Mulls Buying Russia's Su-35 Fighter Jets," *Tass*, March 1, 2018, http://tass.com/defense/992351

27. "The Hard Man of the Hills," *The Economist*, July 15, 2017.

28. Rajiv Chandrasekaran, "In the UAE, the United States has a Quiet, Potent Ally Nicknamed 'Little Sparta'," *The Washington Post*, November 9, 2014, https://www.washingtonpost.com/world/national-security/in-the-uae-the-united-states-has-a-quiet-potent-ally-nicknamed-little-sparta/2014/11/08/3f-c6a50c-643a-11e4-836c-83bc4f26eb67_story.html?utm_term=.d0cf389a11da

29. Ryan Browne, "US announces sale of F-15 fighter jets to Qatar," *CNN*, December 22, 2017, https://www.cnn.com/2017/12/22/politics/us-qatar-f-15-fighter-jets-sale/index.html

30. Pierre Tran, "Qatar moves to buy more Rafale jets, order infantry fighting vehicles," *Defense News*, December 7, 2017, https://www.defensenews.com/global/mideast-africa/2017/12/07/qatar-moves-to-buy-more-rafale-jets-order-infantry-fighting-vehicles/

31. Andrew Chuter, "Qatar to buy 24 Typhoon fighters from UK," *Defense News*, September 18, 2017, https://www.defensenews.com/air/2017/09/18/qatar-to-buy-24-typhoon-fighters-from-uk/

32. David Roberts, *Qatar: Securing the Global Ambitions of a City-State*, (London: Oxford University Press, 2017).

CHAPTER 4

The Economic Impact of the Blockade of Qatar

KRISTIAN COATES ULRICHSEN

Introduction

The blockade of Qatar, primarily initiated by four regional states (three of which are members of the Gulf Cooperation Council), has had a range of impacts on Qatar, the GCC as an institution, and the embargoing states. This chapter examines the impact of the blockade on Qatar and assesses its consequences for the GCC as a viable regional entity. While nearly four decades of patient, painstaking work toward regional economic integration is now at grave risk of being squandered, the blockade has consequently accelerated domestic Qatari efforts to diversify its economy and trade patterns. Given Qatar's relative success at resisting pressure from its neighbors, it is difficult to see the GCC reemerging in the immediate future. In its place, it is likely that a two-or-three track economic trajectory will develop as a new regional status quo in the run-up to the 2022 FIFA World Cup.

The announcement that Saudi Arabia, the UAE, Bahrain, and Egypt (in addition to the Comoros, the Maldives, Mauritania, and Yemen), were cutting diplomatic relations with Qatar and imposing an air, land, and sea embargo against the country sent shockwaves across the region and the world. The rift was unprecedented in the GCC's thirty-six-year history, far surpassing in magnitude an earlier 2014 diplomatic spat when Bahrain, Saudi Arabia, and the UAE withdrew their ambassadors from Doha for eight months. Whereas the 2014 crisis brought to a head years of simmering tensions rooted in these nations' very different policy responses following the Arab Spring, the 2017 sequel appears to be more akin to a power play, designed to take advantage of a perception in Riyadh and Abu Dhabi that the new White House in the United States would take their side in the dispute. While President Trump did catch his administration (and Qatari officials) off guard when he initially sided with the so-called "Anti-Terror Quartet," he walked back his support after encountering stiff pushback from key figures in his young presidency.

The standoff in the Gulf has become a stalemate, creating new "facts on the ground," both as a set of careful policy responses by officials in Doha and as the unintended consequences for the blockading nations due to their false belief that the application of such economic pressure would force Qatar into quick submission. It remains unclear what precise endgame the Crown Princes of Saudi Arabia and Abu Dhabi, Mohammed bin Salman and Mohammed bin Zayed respectively, foresaw when they launched the embargo in June 2017.[1]

Rumors of an invasion of Qatar or an attempt to trigger regime change in Doha have swirled for months and have yet to be fully dispelled.[2] However, the immediate ratification of a defense partnership between Qatar and Turkey very considerably raised the cost of potential military intervention, effectively forestalling any aggressive action that may have been in the cards.[3] As it became clear that the blockade would neither be lifted nor serve as the prelude to any further action, this deadlock has gradually become the 'new normal' in the Gulf, while the resulting policy responses have begun to reshape the economic and commercial landscape of the region.

1.1. Qatari Policy Responses

Even if the threat of military intervention did not materialize, the launch of the blockade represented an attempt to squeeze the Qatari economy in hopes that sustained economic pressure might undermine the Al-Thani leadership in the eyes of its citizens and residents. Up to four-fifths of food imports had previously entered

Qatar either directly across its Saudi land border or indirectly via shipping routes that first stopped at Emirati ports.[4] Both the Saudis and Emiratis closed their ports to Qatar-bound shipping (whether Qatari-owned or not), and the UAE banned Qatari vessels from bunkering or refueling at its Fujairah regional hub. These restrictions affected tankers that had previously loaded cargoes of crude oil from Qatar, Saudi Arabia, and the UAE (as well as Kuwait and Oman) before departing the Persian Gulf.[5] Egypt did not, however, block Qatari ships from the Suez Canal, nor did Cairo compel its 300,000 Egyptian residents living in Qatar to leave, as had been done by the Saudis, Emiratis, and Bahrainis. Either move would have caused enormous complications to Qatar's exporting of LNG to key European markets, as well as to the functioning of the Qatari bureaucracy in which many Egyptians work.[6]

In-between the two iterations of the Gulf crisis in 2014 and 2017, Qatar's leadership took actions intended to diversify its regional and international partnerships, especially in the security and economic spheres. In 2014, China sent a delegation to the Doha International Maritime Defense Exhibition, which resulted in the Qatari purchase of nearly US$24 billion worth of Chinese weaponry.[7] Three years later, as the Gulf crisis unfolded, Qatar has acquired an SY-400 short-range ballistic missile system from China, prominently displaying the missiles during the Qatar National Day parade in downtown Doha in December 2017.[8] More important for Qatar in the short-term has been increased military cooperation between Qatar and Turkey. Negotiated in 2014, a Turkey-Qatar Military Cooperation Agreement was approved by the Turkish Parliament in March 2015, subsequently leading to the April 2016 opening of a Turkish military base in Qatar, its first in the Middle East since the Ottoman era.[9] On June 7, 2017, two days after the blockade commenced, the Turkish parliament held an extraordinary session to ratify two agreements allowing Turkish troops to be stationed in Qatar and permitting the Turkish military to train Qatari security forces. As it relates to the latter, Turkish troops were dispatched to Doha within just a few weeks of the start of the crisis for joint training exercises.[10]

Similar initiatives had been underway to bolster Qatar's economic and commercial links with a widened range of partners worldwide. Qatari leaders leveraged the extensive resources available to the Qatar Investment Authority and related entities to ramp up investment across Europe, North America, Asia, and Russia. These included investing in flagship blue-chip companies in Europe, becoming a cornerstone stakeholder in the Agricultural Bank of China, investing in tourism, energy, and infrastructure projects in ASEAN states, as well as joint food security-related business and ventures in India.[11] Such links have facilitated a subsequent restructuring of Qatari trading and shipping routes, including a crucial partnership with India's Ministry of Transportation and Communications that launched the first direct container service connecting Qatar with Indian ports within just ten days of the start of the blockade.[12]

Qatar's enormous natural gas reserves and position as the world's largest exporter of LNG has provided additional points of leverage that Doha has deployed in order to entice a wider array of external partners having a direct stake in Qatar's continued security and stability. Qatar was, by 2017, the second-biggest supplier of LNG to both China and Japan (in both cases finishing behind Australia). LNG shipments to India, South Korea, and the ASEAN states also surged. Meanwhile in Europe, Belgium, France, Italy, and Poland have a track record of purchasing significant volumes of Qatari LNG. The latter's state-owned oil and gas company (PGNiG) agreed to double its Qatari imports in March 2017 in an effort to reduce reliance on Russia as a gas supplier.[13] Perhaps nowhere has Qatari influence been more pronounced than in the United Kingdom, where Qatar not only provided 93% of LNG supplies between 2014 and 2016, but also became the majority shareholder (through Qatar Petroleum's 67.5% holding) of South Hook Gas Company, which operates the LNG terminal at the Milford Haven port in Wales.[14]

The above-mentioned factors rushed into play in 2017. Most obviously, the international energy and investment links Qatar had built meant that—aside from a few African states—the anti-Qatar quartet failed to secure any meaningful international or regional buy-in for its efforts to isolate Qatar. This was significant as it sent a message that Qatar, having drafted measures allowing the nation to adapt to the 'new normal' more swiftly than its detractors seemed to have thought possible, remained open for business. In light of this, trade between Qatar and Oman grew by 144% in 2017 as shipping was rerouted through Omani ports while Qatari trade with Iran, Turkey, and Pakistan all increased significantly in the aftermath of the blockade.[15] In February 2018, Qatar Petroleum announced it would expand LNG production from 77 million tons a year (a plateau it had reached in 2010) to 100 million tons a year by 2024, generating widespread participatory interest from European and North American oil companies and opening the possibility of additional markets for Qatari LNG in the medium- to long-term future.[16]

Domestic food security and industrial strategies also accelerated in 2017 and, in the case of the former, were supported by a reserve that had been formulated by policymakers in response to the 2014 diplomatic crisis. The airlift of cows from the United States to Qatar may have made international headlines, however, other less viral measures to boost domestic self-sufficiency have seen wide success in the midst of the blockade. By spring 2018 domestic production of market consumption chicken reached 98%, while the same measurement for milk and dairy has climbed to 82%.[17] In the first six months of the blockade the number of factories and manufacturing units in Qatar reportedly doubled as the government tapped into patriotic fervor among citizens and residents by throwing its support behind a "Made in Qatar" campaign.[18] Given Doha's plans to boost domestic self-sufficiency in key economic and industrial sectors already existed, the blockade merely provided the impetus to hasten their implementation. The expansion of Qatari food-processing and agricultural capacity led to greater resilience in food security, overcoming a previously-high reliance on Saudi Arabia for imported agricultural products.[19]

The measures detailed above have enabled Qatar to weather the disruptive impact of the diplomatic and trade embargo, emerging relatively unscathed; indeed, upon the first anniversary of the crisis the country had a smaller fiscal deficit, a substantive increase in foreign reserves, an improved trade balance, and a banking sector that had recovered from the initial outflows in the immediate aftermath of the blockade.[20] To be sure, the crisis has not been cost-free, and Qatar Airways in particular reported a substantial (but undisclosed) loss for 2017-18 as the closure of much of the regional airspace around Qatar and subsequent rerouting led to a significant rise in operating costs.[21] While Qatar seems to have found its footing with these immediate solutions, the Gulf Crisis has started to reshape the regional politics and international relations of the greater GCC in ways that will have long-term and far-reaching implications.

2.1. Regional Implications

The GCC, which for 36 years stood as the most durable regional institution in the Middle East, has been damaged, probably beyond repair. In its place has appeared a hyper-hawkish new axis in Gulf politics centered around the Crown Princes of Saudi Arabia and Abu Dhabi. From its foundation in 1981, shortly after the 1979 Islamic Revolution in Iran and the start of the Iran-Iraq War, the GCC functioned best as a loose collection of six states, struggling to reach consensus on 'big-ticket' items that encroached on notions of national sovereignty. By contrast, greater progress typically was made in apolitical technocratic cooperation that, over time, facilitated the growth of a distinctly khaleeji (Gulf) identity throughout the GCC. Neither a political nor a military alliance, the GCC lacks an integrative supra-national decision-making institution akin to the European Commission, has no treaty-based foreign policymaking power, and has member governments bent on retaining responsibility for most aspects of political policy. As the GCC hurriedly came together between February and May 1981, key issues of institutional design were left unaddressed and have remained neglected to this day.[22]

Shortly after the creation of the GCC, the six states signed the Unified Economic Agreement, pledging to harmonize and coordinate oil and industrial policies, design a uniform system of tariffs, and work toward the free flow of labor and capital across their common borders. Progress toward the goals outlined in the Unified Economic Agreement was slow and halting, but a customs union was launched in 2003 and was followed five years later by a common market which became operational on January 1, 2008.[23]

This common market extended equal rights to citizens of GCC states to take up employment and residence, access education and healthcare, and establish companies and buy or sell shares in each member-state. In practice, however, the segmented nature of individual labor markets and comparatively low cross-border trade flows among the six GCC states meant the impact of the common market was less pronounced than might otherwise have been expected. Moreover, GCC financial ministers took more than a decade from the launch of the customs union (in 2003) to reach agreement on the imposition of a common external tariff (in 2014). In November 2016, a Commission of Economic and Developmental Affairs was formed at the GCC Secretariat in Riyadh as a springboard for further integration, but it was overtaken just seven months later by the rupture within the GCC over the standoff with Qatar.[24]

Several examples highlight the GCC's inability to foster greater integration in major policy areas, even before the 2017 rupture with Qatar. At the GCC Summit in November 1989, Qatar proposed a GCC pipeline to export gas from its soon-to-be-developed North Field to the nations of Kuwait, Saudi Arabia, Bahrain, and the UAE. As energy analyst Justin Dargin noted in 2007, Qatari officials "Initially thought the GCC pipeline to be a more pragmatic financial venture than the construction of a capital-intensive LNG facility."[25] Bahrain, however, withdrew from the project due to a then-ongoing territorial dispute with Qatar over the Hawar Islands, while Saudi Arabia backed out to protect its own gas initiatives and withdrew a preliminary grant of transit rights, thusly blocking Kuwait from inclusion in the pipeline.[26] As a result, when the Dolphin Gas Project became operational in 2008 it consisted of only a subsea pipeline from Ras Laffan in Qatar to Taweelah in Abu Dhabi, with overland transmission of gas occurring throughout the UAE and Oman. Even this limited cooperation was a red flag for the Saudi government, which subsequently attempted to halt the construction of the pipeline from Qatar to Abu Dhabi by claiming – as they did with Kuwait – that it crossed Saudi territory and thus required Saudi consent.[27]

Friction between Saudi Arabia and the UAE in the mid-2000s also contributed to the failure of another planned GCC energy initiative. In December 2006, the GCC Supreme Council of leaders passed a resolution to launch a joint-Arab nuclear program that would be implemented by the six GCC states. The then-Secretary General of the GCC, Abdulrahman bin Hamad Al Attiyah, briefed the Director General of the International Atomic Energy Agency, Mohammed El Baradei, on the GCC-led Arab nuclear proposal in early 2007 upon which the GCC and IAEA agreed to cooperate on a feasibility study for a regional nuclear power and desalination program.[28] However, just as the idea was gaining traction, GCC officials were blindsided in April 2008 when the UAE published its own independent policy plan for nuclear energy, establishing the Emirates Nuclear Energy Corporation as an Abu Dhabi-based public entity and invited bids in 2009 for construction of its first nuclear power plant at Ruwais, set to begin operation in 2018.[29]

A more visible instance of intra-GCC geopolitical tension came in 2009 when nearly two decades of work toward a single currency and monetary union floundered in acrimony after less than a year before it was due to launch in 2010, the UAE suddenly withdrew from the project. The UAE had campaigned hard to host the GCC Central Bank in Abu Dhabi and reacted with anger to the May 2009 decision to seat the bank in Riyadh instead. Other GCC-wide plans were affected first by the impact of the post-2014 oil price slump and associated economic slowdown and, of course, by the fracturing of the GCC in 2017. The planned GCC Railway was suspended after declining government revenues made the regionwide rail-link economically unfeasible. The project highlighted the challenge of aligning policy across the six Gulf governments, as each member-state had individually awarded contracts for its own sector of the line while basing project decisions around national, rather than regional GCC, interests.[30] Meanwhile, the Qatar row erupted just as the GCC was preparing to implement a shared Value-Added Tax that was set to come into operation on January 1, 2018.[31]

The GCC's absence from virtually every stage of the current crisis has left it a marginalized institution, irrelevant to the ongoing realignment of centers of gravity in Gulf politics. The body's sidelining is evidenced by the GCC's absence as the mechanism through which the quartet communicated its initial grievances against Qatar, nor was the bloc used as the mode to engage in any form of dialogue or mediation between the disputing parties. Instead, the list of thirteen conditions (which amounted into an ultimatum that would have reduced Qatar to little more than a vassal state, akin to the demands placed on Serbia by Austria-Hungary in July, 1914) was drawn up in Quartet capitals, while Emir Al Sabah of Kuwait took it upon himself to engage in a frenetic round of shuttle diplomacy. The latter's efforts arguably prevented the initial measures against Qatar from escalating into anything more severe, as professed by the Emir during a press conference at the White House with US President Donald Trump in September 2017, saying, "Thank God, now, what is important is that we have stopped any military action."[32]

The potential death knell for the GCC as a fully-functioning organization of six members became visibly pronounced during its annual summit in Kuwait City on December 5, 2017. Qatar was the only state which sent its ruler to attend the summit, which many felt only taking place out of respect to the eighty-eight-year-old Emir Sabah, the elder statesman of the Gulf and a former foreign minister of forty years' standing. A meeting of foreign ministers the day before the summit faltered while the summit itself lasted for less than one session of the planned two-day meeting, as it too descended into recrimination and finger-pointing among representatives of the Gulf nations implicated in the blockade.[33] To compound the situation, officials in Abu Dhabi chose the morning of the GCC Summit to announce details of a far-reaching partnership between the UAE and Saudi Arabia, covering "All military, political, economic, trade, and cultural fields."[34] Launched without warning to the fellow GCC states Kuwait and Oman—and pointedly excluding Bahrain—the Saudi-Emirati initiative formalized the hardline approach to centralize regional politics around the axis of the Crown Princes, MbS and MbZ.

As an institution, the GCC is likely to endure rather than be formally wound up or dissolved, but experience elsewhere in the Gulf suggests that it will grow ever more marginal to the point where it effectively disappears from the policymaking landscape altogether. It is hard to imagine how Qataris could ever again trust an organization that manifestly failed to prevent three of its members from turning against them twice in just three years. Additionally, the GCC has ostensibly done little, if anything, to try and bring the situation under control toward an amicable resolution. Kuwaiti and Omani officials watch on, uneasily aware that they too could be vulnerable to regionally-assertive Saudi and Emirati pressure once they undergo eventual leadership transitions of their own, knowing full well that the Crown Princes of Saudi Arabia and Abu Dhabi have little tolerance for the relative autonomy that has characterized Kuwaiti and Omani (as well as Qatari) foreign policy for decades.[35] Indeed, the new "Saudi-Emirati Coordination Council" that met for the first time in June 2018 was as much exclusionary as the GCC was inclusionary, not even involving Bahrain or the Prime Minister of the UAE, Dubai's ruler, Sheikh Mohammed bin Rashid Al Maktoum, was also conspicuously absent from the gathering.

3.1. Broader Consequences

Far from creating cracks or widening fissures in Qatari society, the blockade has instead uncovered a burgeoning national identity that increasingly seems to be encompassing all residents of Qatar, expatriates as well as citizens. In August 2017, the Qatari government approved a plan to create a pathway toward permanent residency for selected groups of expatriates in a move breaking a GCC consensus that traditionally imposed rigid distinctions between citizens and non-citizens. The blockade has also created human hardships in a region where many who have extended cross-border familial ties are now facing restrictions on visitation, a development roundly criticized by international human rights groups such as Amnesty.[36] Collective memories are being formed on both sides of the divide that will be hard to dislodge, given the sheer intensity of the online and media vilification campaign against Qatar. That the vitriolic nature of the "Quartet" targets Qatar as a whole, rather than any specific group in particular, has damaged the social fabric of Gulf societies.

The wider impact of the blockade of Qatar offered a powerful window into the interconnectedness of Gulf societies at the human level, despite the limitations of GCC integration at the institutional scale as described in this chapter. In Qatar alone, there were more than 6,000 mixed-marriages that involved citizens of Qatar and the three blockading Gulf countries, while many others had extended family living across national boundaries, especially in Saudi Arabia. Instances of family separation occurred as Saudi, Bahraini, and Emirati officials ordered their nationals to leave Qatar within fourteen days of June 5, 2017. Meanwhile, hundreds of students were forced to interrupt their studies and make alternative arrangements. In addition, Qataris made more than 1,900 applications of loss of business or property to a national compensation claims commission after they had been forced to abandon their business interests in blockading nations and return abruptly to Qatar.[37]

For members of the blockading states the decision to sever economic and trading links to Qatar in June 2017 has raised the political risk of doing business in Saudi Arabia and the UAE if or when commercial interests could be subjected to such unpredictable geopolitical buffers. This hit Dubai especially hard as the emirate had built a reputation as a welcoming regional hub for international businesses looking to enter Gulf markets. The Ruler of Dubai has kept a discrete silence over the blockade of Qatar amid suggestions that divisions were emerging among the seven emirates of the UAE in reaction to the hawkish policy positions taken by Mohammed bin Zayed in Abu Dhabi. The apparent defection of a son of the ruler of Fujairah in May 2018 offered a rare snapshot into some of the tensions that may be bubbling underneath the surface of Emirati politics, both over Qatar and the ongoing war in Yemen.[38] In Saudi Arabia, meanwhile, the heavy-handed consolidation of power by Mohammed bin Salman and the lack of due process or application of the rule of law in major decisions (such as the launch of the blockade of Qatar or the subsequent launch of an anti-corruption campaign in the Kingdom) have similarly heightened domestic and international investor concerns about the political risk of doing business at a time of such volatility and uncertainty.

By late-July 2018 the QE Index in Doha had recovered to its pre-blockade, May-2017 level, reversing the 18 percent slump the stock exchange had suffered in 2017 and outperforming its peers in Abu Dhabi and Dubai in the process. Large companies trading on the exchange, such as Industries Qatar and Qatar National Bank, saw significant gains after they increased their foreign ownership limits to take advantage of the emerging market upgrade Qatar had secured a year prior to the blockade.[39] Ahead of the 2022 FIFA World Cup, the abrupt nature of the blockade has provided the impetus to accelerate plans to further open the Qatari economy and to diversify patterns and partners of trade. Ironically, construction costs for the World Cup and related infrastructure may instead decline, rather than increase, as the blockade has freed organizers of commitments they had made to source a proportion of raw materials within the GCC region rather than at prevailing rates on the open market. Moreover, IMF calculations project the Qatari economy will grow at an accelerating rate in 2018 and 2019 (2.6 percent and 2.7 percent respectively) and that the government will reduce its budget deficit to 4.6 percent in 2018, less than half the size of the deficit pre-blockade in 2016.[40] Qatar additionally made a successful return to the international bond market in April 2018 with a triple-tranche US $12 billion offering that attracted strong demand, especially to investors in Asia.[41]

Far from forcing Qatar to make the far-reaching concessions demanded by its four detractors, the blockade has brought to light the regional schisms that have fragmented the GCC and set its members along markedly diverging tracks. For Qataris, the events of 2017 expedited long-term plans to diversify and expand Qatar's political and commercial partnerships and localize industrial and agricultural production. These trends will boost the non-oil economy and may, if handled carefully, provide the building-blocks of a transition toward a post-oil economy. The impact on the blockading states is more uncertain as the political risks of doing business with the Quartet have increased, as has the wariness of international investors as a series of apparent foreign policy missteps that appear to have been taken in haste without full consideration of their longer-term consequences. The Gulf States and their regional and international partners, meanwhile, move unsteadily into a "post-GCC" era in which both the structure of regional architecture and the style of regional policymaking are more uncertain today than at any time since the Gulf War of 1991.

Endnotes

1. At the time the blockade was launched on June 5, 2017, Mohammed bin Salman was still the Deputy Crown Prince of Saudi Arabia, but he was widely considered to be the decision-making authority on all major political and security issues and was elevated to Crown Prince of Saudi Arabia sixteen days later.

2. Alex Emmons, "Saudi Arabia Planned to Invade Qatar Last Summer. Rex Tillerson's Efforts to Stop It May Have Cost Him his Job," *The Intercept*, August 1, 2018.

3. Juan Cole, "David and Goliath: How Qatar Defeated the Saudi and UAE Annexation Plot," *The Nation*, February 16, 2018.

4. Amir Hossein Estebari, "Conflict with Qatar and Unforeseen Consequences for Saudi Arabia – Analysis," *Iran Review*, July 30, 2017.

5. Chris Grieveson and Mads Odeskaug, "What Does the Qatar Embargo Mean for Shipping?," *The Maritime Executive*, July 21, 2017.

6. Nader Kabbani, "The High Cost of High Stakes: Economic Implications of the 2017 Gulf Crisis," *Brookings*, June 15, 2017.

7. Samuel Ramani, "China's Growing Security Relationship with Qatar," *The Diplomat*, November 16, 2017.

8. Theodore Karasik and Giorgio Cafiero, "Why China Sold Qatar the SY-400 Ballistic Missile System," *LobeLog*, December 21, 2017.

9. Paul Cochrane, "Revealed: Secret Details of Turkey's New Military Pact with Qatar," *Middle East Eye*, January 27, 2016.

10. Anon., "Turkey and Qatar: Behind the Strategic Alliance," *Al Jazeera*, February 1, 2018.

11. Julia Hollingsworth, "Why Qatar Matters to China, in Spite of Gulf Isolation," *South China Morning Post*, June 7, 2017; Giorgio Cafiero and Elaine Miao, "India's Role in Qatar's Food Security Crisis," *TRT World*, September 15, 2017.

12. Anon., "New Qatar-India Shipping Line Launched," *Gulf Times*, June 15, 2017.

13. Andrew Torchia, Agnieszka Barteczko, and Oleg Vukmanovic, "Qatargas Agrees to Double LNG Supplies to Poland," *Reuters*, March 14, 2017.

14. Tsvetana Paraskova, "Qatar's LNG Exports to the UK Plunge," *Oilprice.com*, April 12, 2018.; Srivani Venna, "Qatar Petroleum Delivers 500th LNG Cargo to South Hook LNG Terminal in the UK," *Hydrocarbons Technology*, March 27, 2016.

15. Sachin Kumar, "Surge in Qatar-Oman Trade," *The Peninsula*, January 30, 2018; Hafsa Adli, "Turkey, Iran, Pakistan See Big Trade Boost with Qatar," *Al Jazeera*, December 3, 2017.

16. Dmitry Zhdannikov, "Qatar Sees Stampede for Gas Projects to Help Beat Crisis," *Reuters*, January 24, 2018.

17. Anon., "New Mega Projects to Boost Self-Sufficiency in Food Production," *The Peninsula*, April 20, 2018.

18. Mohammad Shoeb, "Number of Factories in Qatar Doubled During Blockade: Minister," *Al Bawaba*, December 18, 2017.

19. Dominic Dudley, "As Qatar Prepares to Mark a Year Under the Saudi Embargo, it Looks Like the Winner in the Dispute," *Forbes.com*, May 17, 2018.

20. Alexander Griffing, "How the Saudi-led Blockade of Qatar Actually Made the Tiny Emirate Stronger," *Ha'aretz*, May 30, 2018.

21. Murad Sezer, "Qatar Airways Confirms 'Substantial' Annual Loss, Blames Regional Row," *Reuters*, April 25, 2018.

22. Christian Koch, "GCC Confronted by Dichotomy," *Gulf News*, December 22, 2012.

23. Dylan Bowman, "GCC Common Market Comes into Effect," *Reuters*, January 1, 2008.

24. Rory Miller, "GCC Meeting in Riyadh Points the Way Forward," *The National*, November 22, 2016.

25. Justin Dargin, "Qatar's Natural Gas: The Foreign-Policy Driver," *Middle East Policy*, 14(3), 2007, p.139.

26. Justin Dargin, "The Dolphin Project: The Development of a Gulf Gas Initiative," Oxford Institute for Energy Studies, NG 22, 2008, pp.23-24.

27. Andy Critchlow, "Saudis Demand Say in Emirates Pipeline," *International Herald Tribune*, July 12, 2006.

28. Newton Howard, "Nuclear Power for the Gulf States," Center for Advanced Defense Studies, Defense Concepts Series, April 2007.

29. Mari Luomi, "Abu Dhabi's Alternative-Energy Initiatives: Seizing Climate-Change Opportunities," *Middle East Policy*, 16(4), 2009, p.109.

30. Anon., "GCC Rail Project Delayed over 'Technical Problems," *Trade Arabia*, March 30, 2017.

31. Anon., "Gulf States Prepare for VAT in Time of Crisis," *AFP*, June 21, 2017.

32. "Remarks by President Trump and Emir Sabah al-Ahmed al-Jaber Al-Sabah of Kuwait in Joint Press Conference," The White House, September 7, 2017.

33. Khalid Al Jaber and Giorgio Cafiero, "The GCC's Worst Summit," *Al Jazeera Online*, December 9, 2017.

34. Simeon Kerr, "UAE and Saudi Arabia Forge Economic and Military Alliance," *Financial Times,* December 5, 2017.

35. Bruce Riedel, "Is the GCC Dead?", *Al-Monitor*, June 18, 2018.

36. Anon., "Gulf Crisis: Six Months On, Families Still Bearing the Brunt of Qatar Political Dispute," *Amnesty International*, December 14, 2017.

37. Ibid.

38. David Kirkpatrick, "Emirati Prince Flees to Qatar, Exposing Tensions in UAE," *New York Times*, July 14, 2018.

39. Filipe Pacheco, "Qatar Stocks Erase Losses Suffered Since Embargo Began Last Year," *Bloomberg*, August 1, 2018.

40. Hassan Jivraj, "Qatar: A Year on From the Boycott," *DebtWire*, July 28, 2018, p.3.

41. Jivraj, p.4.

CHAPTER 5

The War of Manufacturing Consent and Public Mobilization*

KHALID AL-JABER

Introduction

The Quartet of nations (Saudi Arabia, the UAE, Bahrain, and Egypt) imposing the blockade on Qatar have attempted to portray the Gulf crisis as inconsequential, working to minimize its importance on a global scale. The reality, however, appears to show that efforts from the blockading states to downplay the crisis have been unable to fool global, or even regional media. Since June 7, 2017, the goings-on of the Gulf have received coverage in several major media institutions, such as CNN, the New York Times, and the Washington Post, in addition to a large number of British, European, and Arabic newspapers. Emphasizing the global ramifications of the blockade, the severity of the crisis has also been evidenced in the involvement of regional players (such as Turkey and Iran), as well as other members of the international community, particularly Russia.

Amidst this spat has emerged an intense polarization—not limited to the people of the GCC—as well as a severe game of tug-of-war playing out between parties representing opposing nations in the world's major capitals, especially in Washington. It would seem that the crisis has infiltrated nearly every relevant domain,

---

*Translated from Arabic by Nabeel Al-Nowairah

encompassing media, public relations, interest groups, law firms, think-tanks, universities, politicians, and even the minds of ordinary people. Within each of these sectors, politics, money, security, and intelligence remain intertwined, fueling the output received by the public.

1.1. Media as Fuel to the Crisis

As much as the crisis has appeared in the media, it is perhaps ironic that the initial fissures that led to the crisis were caused by the hacking of the Qatar News Agency's (QNA) website, a move that sparked a great wave of political, media, and social controversy.[1] That a number of Gulf satellite channels in the blockading countries (Saudi Arabia, the UAE and Bahrain in particular) seemed all-too-well prepared to quickly cover the incident only sparked further suspicion amongst Gulf audiences about the entity behind the cyberattack.

It soon became clear that the hacking was intentional and had involved extensive preparation. Although beginning with an infiltration of QNA's website, the hack was soon followed by infiltrations into QNA's social media, including the news outlet's YouTube channel. In each of these media, cybercriminals posted unbecoming statements attributed to the Emir of Qatar. It was soon discovered that the content of each statement had also been subject to planning. Some Saudi/UAE-funded Gulf media outlets insisted on accepting these statements at face value (in spite of Qatar's denial and explanation that such statements were implanted by hackers), refusing to publish the denials.[2]

Among those giving the emir's supposed statements airtime were Saudi Arabia's Al-Arabiya and the UAE's Sky News. Both outlets prominently attributed the quotes to the Emir, fomenting both a media crisis as well as establishing the basis for what would eventually become the political positions of the various parties involved in the blockade. Subsequently, a barrage of statements and leaks soon appeared on the TV channels of all concerned parties. These sources began to disclose secret information from files previously sealed to the public, most of which revealed archived records containing unflattering information about the "enemy." A few hours after the media war's commencement, Saudi Arabia, the United Arab Emirates, and Egypt issued similar edicts banning dozens of news websites including, for the first time, all websites related to Qatar's Al Jazeera.[3] Those within Saudi Arabia attempting to access Qatari newspapers, Al Jazeera, or QNA were greeted by a message from the Saudi Ministry of Culture and Information telling the viewer that such access was in violation of the Kingdom's regulations. The UAE and Egypt followed suit, with the latter justifying its actions due to accusing Qatari websites of supporting terrorism and the Muslim Brotherhood.[4] Again, the timing of such censorship decisions raises suspicions as to how surprised the Quartet may have been by the hack, as the shutting down of these websites occurred in less than ten hours.

Trying to avoid a direct clash with Saudi Arabia, Qatar in the beginning instead focused its defenses on the UAE, Bahrain, and Egypt. Even still, the media war has become increasingly aggressive, clearly indicating that the crisis would not be confined to surface-level issues but would cut deeply across national insecurities previously respected as red lines. The crisis has since stalemated; it was not simply the *tempest in a teapot* that some analysts, and some involved countries, had expected it to be.

Those formulating Qatari media were perhaps too late in realizing the endurance of the impending crisis. Many Qatari officials internally viewed the crisis as a passing storm, as had been the case for the diplomatic rift of 2014. The aim of this prior rift was to limit Qatari influence in some of the important issues in the Middle East, particularly the fallout of the Arab Spring in Egypt, Tunisia, and Yemen.

In contrast, in the face of the blockading nation's escalating media attacks, Qatar was nearly forced to use Doha's media arm to match the efforts of the Quartet. Al Jazeera arguably played the biggest role in the confrontation, unsurprising given that shutting down, minimizing, or even targeting Al Jazeera was one of the top grievances of some of leaders in the blockading countries. A leaked Wikileaks document revealed that the Crown Prince of Abu Dhabi, Mohammed bin Zayed Al Nahyan, had even requested that the US bomb Al Jazeera during the American war on Afghanistan in 2001.[5] He also requested that Al Jazeera limit its coverage amidst the invasion of Iraq in 2013.[6] In the years since the 2011 Arab Spring uprisings, the UAE in some form or another has continued escalating its criticisms of Al Jazeera. Disdain for the network has not been limited to UAE, as evidenced in April 2017 in a tweet by the Bahraini Foreign Minister expressed solidarity with its co-blockaders' hostility towards the network by adding the trial of Al Jazeera as a 14th addition to the blockading nations' initial "13 demands."[7]

The barrage of criticism prompted Al Jazeera to adjust the topics its producers were willing to cover, shifting from a focus on the big issues in the Arab world, such as the Israel-Palestine conflict, (a focus which thusly allowed Al Jazeera to avoid discussing internal GCC conflicts) to programming that addressed the Gulf's domestic disputes. Al Jazeera's television news channel has been important for the past two decades, being a large part of what has put tiny Qatar on the map of the world's most prominent countries. Al Jazeera has been a window to the outside world for a country which relies mainly on oil and gas exports. Thanks to Al Jazeera, Qatar was able to play a more influential regional role, culminating in the rights to organize the FIFA World Cup 2022.

Outside the Gulf, paradoxes of the American position on the GCC crisis were evident. Initially, President Donald Trump did not hide his bias towards Saudi Arabia and the Quartet at the expense of Qatar. In response, former US Secretary of State Rex Tillerson and Defense Secretary James Mattis sought to balance the US position amidst a crisis that threatened US interests in an already troubled region.

"During my recent trip to the Middle East, I stated that there can be no funding of radical ideology. Leaders pointed to Qatar," Trump tweeted at the beginning of the GCC crisis. This was a surprise to the international political community, including policy-wonks in Washington DC. President Trump's tweet referenced meetings he held with officials in Riyadh in May 2017.[8] Following the initial tweet the President's knee-jerk support for the Quartet continued, sharing that his visit to Saudi Arabia was, "already paying off" before adding "[The leaders of the Islamic world] said they would take a hard line on funding extremism, and all reference was pointing to Qatar. Perhaps this will be the beginning of the end to the horror of terrorism!"[9]

Thanks to the information given to President Trump by the Departments of State and Defense providing an alternate interpretation of the situation differing from those given by Saudi and Emirati leaders, Trump has since moderated his position on the GCC crisis. Furthermore, the crisis with Iran and the US's withdrawal from the nuclear deal strengthened his willingness to pressure the GCC countries to appreciate GCC mediation efforts and resolve the crisis through dialogue. Western media went further in crediting the American President, quoting informed US officials that Trump personally intervened to curb a Saudi-Emirati plot to take military action against Qatar. His apparent warning to the two nations emphasized that the consequences in taking such a step would likely strengthen the position of Iran in the Middle East.[10] Although President Trump denied the reports during his meeting with Emir Tamim, the statements from Emir Al-Sabah regarding success in avoiding military action in the Gulf indicate that the blockading countries had seriously contemplated pursuing military action against Qatar, only scrapping the option due to the United States' disapproval over the perceived benefits such actions could provide to Turkey and Iran.[11]

Despite President Trump's lack of full comprehension on the subject, it can be said that the combined political, diplomatic, and media forces of the US administration stressed the need to put an end to the blockade against Qatar. The continuation of the Gulf crisis threatens to dismantle one of the most cohesive regional blocs allied to the United States in the region. In addition, this crisis threatens the US war on terror, on which focus from US officials in paramount. Furthermore, the Pentagon seems concerned that its military operations in the Middle East might be affected by the Gulf crisis, especially since Qatar hosts the largest US military base in the Middle East. The Al-Udeid airbase hosts about 11,000 US troops and is home to the US Joint Operations Center for command and control of the US Air Force in Iraq, Syria, and Afghanistan, among others.[12] Al-Udeid Base is an advanced site for the US Central Command and the Joint Air and Space Operations Center. US officials, especially in the Department of Defense, fear that the US privileges in Qatar may be threatened if a diplomatic and media escalation, or President Trump's unruly comments, continue.

2.1. Manufacturing Consent: Carrots and Iron Sticks

The complicated reality of media outlets in the Gulf states is due to a tripartite relationship between the centralized authority, governmental institutions, and naturally, the viewing audience. The former two of this trio have made attempts, whether directly or indirectly, to shape the effectiveness of political communication tools across the Gulf. In a project spanning decades, governments and leaders of the Gulf have drafted restrictive legislations and laws outside the formal political communication channels that exist in most modern democratic societies including independent parliaments, political parties, local councils, civil society organizations, and the fourth estate.

By shaping both the messenger and recipient of a given message, systems and institutions of communication function as a machine aimed at Arabic style of "manufacturing consent," defined here as the successful manipulation of public opinion in a single direction that renders the media apparatus of the state inseparable from the Gulf's highest levels of political leadership. This cyclical process has led to a turbulent situation in the five decades since the Gulf states began achieving independence, hindering the establishment of a valid base for political communication in each of the GCC countries.

The outdated means still used by Gulf leaders to shape and mobilize public opinion differs starkly from the social and economic openness that has developed in the region as a result of generous entitlements and the entry into the age of digitization. Therefore, the institutions that constitute media communication still face many challenges that limit the system's ability to change in terms of form, content, legislation, and the protection of democratic ideals and the rejection of repressive or authoritarian practices.

The hierarchical relationship between the apex and the base of the Gulf's social pyramid (i.e. the rulers and the ruled) has created a Gulf where different power tools are employed to serve the regime's agenda. This process occurs through the promotion of political propaganda aimed at manufacturing consent on specific topics. Given the top-to-bottom, unidirectional control of the media, these tools are designed to serve only the existing regime authority's ability to control public opinion, attack opponents, or even silence otherwise neutral figures who do not espouse the views of the regime.

Prolific contemporary American scholars Edward Herman and Noam Chomsky have addressed the concept of manufacturing consent and as evidence trace the precedent of the administration of former US President Woodrow Wilson.[13]

Like the American people, President Wilson began his political career with a predilection for calm and stability. At the advent of the First World War, President Wilson saw no reason for the United States to get involved in what initially was nominally a European conflict. However, the sinking of US ships by German U-Boats (among other factors) necessitated Wilson's decision to enter World War I. Naturally something had to be done to sway public opinion in support of his decision. Consequently, he established a public information committee, known as the Creel Committee, in order to convince the American populace. Within six months the committee saw success in changing the opinion of the American public from having a general disposition toward nonviolence, to one where so-called "everyday Americans" became hellbent on destroying (or at least tarnishing) anything remotely related to Germany. To achieve this purpose, the Creel Committee used wide and varied means, including fabricating supposed atrocities committed by the German army and accusing Germans—at times falsely—of plans to commit acts of terrorism. Additionally, the Creel Committee organized widespread propaganda campaigns that, at their most grotesque, included images supposedly implying that Germans maimed and tortured children. Today, US history classrooms use these images as relics to evidence the racial attitudes used to propel the United States into war. Such propaganda was indeed an effective and powerful means to sway the opinions of the public, especially in light of the campaign's support from the American intelligentsia.

In the years before WWII, Adolf Hitler wrote in his memoir *Mein Kampf* about the effectiveness of propaganda circulating in WWI, and how it taught him the power of leveraging the media to shape public opinion.[14] As ruler of Germany, Hitler and his

Minister of Propaganda Joseph Goebbels effectively manipulated the media using amplified propaganda techniques to sway the German public into turning a blind eye towards the Reich's tragic genocide against Jews in Europe. While there exists a spectrum of severity concerning how rulers can use media to pursue their ends, the incorporation of "manufacturing consent" within Hitler's atrocities shows that this is not a topic that should be taken lightly.

The process of manufacturing consent is arguably more difficult in democratic countries. In these states, citizens generally believe in the value of viewpoint diversity as opposed to the Arab nations of the Gulf where monarchical regimes control every aspect of society. The absolute power enshrined within Gulf heads of state makes it demonstrably easier to manufacture consent, through either "carrots," or perhaps more effectively the use of "iron sticks."

3.1. Media Dilemmas in the Gulf Region

Although there exists some diversity among Gulf states, it is relatively fair to study Gulf media at the regional level, as the structure of media across the GCC nations is very similar. In many cases various newspapers, TV channels, radio stations, and drama productions are either directly or indirectly linked to the central regime, controlled by members of the royal family or at least their associates. A report published by the Doha Center for Media Freedom suggests that the laws applicable to media and journalism in the Gulf States are a hurdle to freedom of expression due to their attachment to regimes, which necessitates that media institutions receive prior authorization from governments that have monopolized the right to issue and revoke media licenses, thus limiting the media's ability to be impartial.[15] Furthermore, each of the GCC states puts a long list of prohibitions on free speech in their laws and imposes several restrictions on publication topics that are deemed to have the potential to harm the economy or lead to disruption of public order. If not directly imposed by the government, such laws have led to considerable self-censorship among journalists and media professionals.

An analysis of Freedom House reports over time indicates that the level of media freedom in the Gulf states has remained either virtually unchanged, or in a state of regression. Reports from 2009-2017 suggest that the media in each Gulf country remains "not-free" with the exception of Kuwait, which receives a marginally better "partially free" media ranking.[16]

Amidst the Gulf crisis, it has been observed that the blockading countries utilize the media tools at their disposal to foment a general opinion in support of the blockading of Qatar amongst their respective populaces. The subsequent demonization of Qatar has been unprecedented in the Gulf region, even when considering media portrayals of regional boogeyman Iran.

The Gulf media has changed distinctively since the events of June 5, 2017. Prior to the blockade, the media of the six GCC countries generally agreed on most issues. However, such harmony has since been replaced by hostility, aggression, and rivalry. The current divide has led to an exchange of accusations (often distributed via media) between Saudi Arabia, the UAE and Bahrain on one hand and Qatar on the other. Oman and Kuwait took up a neutral position and attempted to deescalate the conflict by calling for cohesion and solidarity. In this call for unity, official Omani and Kuwaiti media outlets made it a point to avoid discussing the details and causes of the crisis so as not to be seen as leaning towards either of the parties. The impartial duo called for the resolution of differences and countered the incitement of hatred by reminding consumers of the Gulf's unity, common land, and shared history. The Kuwaiti media stood by the side of the Kuwaiti emir in his efforts to bridge the Gulf's newly-exposed gap and his attempt to bring the parties to the negotiation table.

While policy gaps between the Quartet and Qatar had been widening for years, such differences were largely excluded from news broadcasts out of respect for ideas of Gulf unity. However, following the onset of the crisis the decorum of years past has been scrapped. Authorities have unleashed the media to cover the opposing side of the crisis in as negative a light as possible, effectively dredging up differences that had been ignored in the past. Moreover, each of these media outlets have taken a single approach in attacking opposing ruling authorities and regimes, each reflecting the eccentric personalities of their respective rulers, such as the Emir of Qatar, the Crown Prince of the UAE, the King of Bahrain, and the Crown Prince of Saudi Arabia. Paradoxically, even amidst this lobbing of insults, each head of state continues to emphasize the unity of Gulf peoples and their mutual love for each other.

Interestingly, despite being on different sides of the GCC's schism the media in each crisis-involved nation has pursued a similar approach—broadcasting news and programs that highlight the supposed violations and corruption of their "opponent" while ignoring that these same problems and violations occur within nations otherwise presented as allies. Additionally, the relevant GCC states have provided impunity to those who attack the "enemy" state, while harshly punishing anyone (whether public opinion leaders, journalists, or ordinary citizens) who criticize the decisions and policies of their own respective nations.

4.1. Social Network Battlefields

Print and broadcast media outlets have not been the only tools used to fuel the crisis. Social media too has played a prominent role in mobilizing the conflict—especially Twitter, which has become a quasi-official platform for community leaders and politicians.

A research study by Northwestern University Qatar published in 2017 revealed that social media is now one of the main sources of news for Arab citizens, with young people assuming a high credibility of the medium that seems to wane as the respondents become older.[17] The study, which was conducted in Qatar, Lebanon, Saudi Arabia, Jordan, Tunisia, and the UAE (encompassing 7,000 respondents), concluded that when countries experience restrictions on traditional media, people tend to compensate by gravitating towards social media for news.[18] According to the study, two-thirds of the respondents receive news daily from social media, with nearly eight out of ten Arab citizens consuming at least some news via social media. Forty percent of respondents received news from Facebook, while the messaging app Whatsapp, used by sixty-seven percent of Arab citizens, functioned as a news source for twenty-eight percent of respondents. Relatively newer to the social media landscape, Snapchat has been increasingly used as a source of news in the Gulf countries (fifty-five percent of citizens in Qatar, fifty-one percent in the UAE and thirty-seven percent in Saudi Arabia).[19]

The Gulf crisis marked a turning point for Gulf officials utilizing new media to influence public opinion. Social media was used as a tool in order to spread rumors and counterfeit information on social media platforms like Facebook and Twitter. Simplistic background research on accounts that espouse such "fake news" reveals that many have real or politically symbolic profile photos, as well as usernames belonging to prominent Gulf families. As it turns out however, purveyors of such information actually have very few followers, and the followers they do retain have names indicating Russian or Ukrainian origins. These accounts, which appear to spread negative hashtags in unison are known as "bots," and have become a source of increased polarization in an already divided region.

"Bots," short for "web-robots," can be loosely described as smart servers that perform repetitive or automated tasks through programs that coordinate to automatically produce "likes" or "retweets" in order to spread a given message quickly on a massive scale. The tasks of these bots are divided through a primary account that instructs other bots to tweet, retweet, and even interact with those participating in the hashtag.

The usage of bots has not been the only source of media-conflict present on Twitter. So-called "electronic committees," known in Arabic as "electronic flies," are real social media accounts (run by real people) that coordinate in trending hashtags to influence public opinion and mislead users by creating the false appearance of widespread popular support for a given media item.

The weaponization of social media platforms, specifically in the Gulf States, was an event horizon amidst the escalation of the crisis. Even a few years ago, people could express their opinions with a large margin of freedom and spontaneity. This lack of inhibition on social media made it possible for social researchers to use the medium as an accurate measure of public opinion on the Arab Street. Since the intensification and complications of the GCC crisis, however, those who may share an opinion contrary to the general trend, (or the angle of the state), must now contend with a vast electronic army. These electronic armies insult and threaten anyone who writes something contrary to the desired opinion with the goal of terrorizing and psychologically pressuring anyone holding an opposing view.

The current Gulf crisis has highlighted the darkest underbelly of the GCC media. Despite initial hopes that it could induce radical, positive change in Gulf politics (and Arab communication in general), social media has instead been used negatively to silence opposition to the party line. The crisis has revealed great dilemmas plaguing the political and media systems in the Gulf states and greater Arab world. It has shown that historical structural imbalances have yet to be eliminated, making the means of communication dependent on and subject to change in accordance to the whim (or intentions) of a given media outlet's state-owner. Given such centralized control, changing state priorities have allowed the media to serve as a primary means of dissemination allowing regimes to switch from allies, to foes and perhaps even back again.

5.1. Weapons of Mass Deception

With reference to the concept of manufacturing consent, Herman and Chomsky addressed ten principles that were employed in the formulation of public opinion. Standing out amongst these ten are the valuing of emotions over critical thinking and the brainwashing of the general public, as was done during WWII by Joseph Goebbels, the Minister of Propaganda in Nazi Germany.[20] This study referred to this model in analyzing the tools employed in the GCC Crisis. The main tools are elaborated upon below:

1) The use of strict laws to prevent sympathy, and empathy with Qatar. Anyone with opposing views could be subject to punishment with the possibility of fifteen years of imprisonment or a fine of no less than Saudi Riyal/UAE Dirham 500,000. [24]

2) The weaponization of religion to market the boycott through the issuing of fatwas by senior religious scholars, the inclusion of crisis-related topics within Friday-sermons, and the statements by Sheikhs to mass media, Twitter or traditional public majlises. The Saudi Grand Mufti stated that the decisions against Qatar are legitimate due to accusations that Qatar has financed terrorism. He insisted that actions taken

by Saudi Arabia are in the interest of Muslims and the future of Qataris themselves, and that Saudi decisions were based on wisdom and are part of a vision that would be good for all.[25]

3) The launch of a systematic media campaign, now considered to be the biggest media scandal ever linked to funding from Gulf States capitals. The extent of the media campaign will require significant study to understand the extent of lies and fabrications deployed amidst the crisis. Also, the unification of messaging across satellite news and official media left viewers unable to be exposed to views divergent from the official state message. These satellite channels have largely abandoned professional standards and have lost the trust and credibility that had distinguished them from governmental media.

4) A blacklisting of media outlets that held opinions concerning the crisis that differed from a given government. Such networks were shunned, while many Qatari or Qatar-allied media such as Al Jazeera were blocked in certain countries altogether.

5) The use of social media as a forum for all sorts of abuses, often at the behest of a given Gulf regime. Electronic flies, supported and financed by influential figures, have contributed to deforming the communication scene, deepening the differences, igniting sedition, tribal tensions and rumors, and accusing others of extremism, racism and terrorism.

6) Conducting systematic arrests targeting Twitter users by referring them to the prosecution and filing complaints and judicial cases against them under the pretext that their vocalization of a differing opinion was a threat to national unity. Many such dissenters were put in jail and were subject to security prosecution without any specific charges. In some cases, jailed individuals within Quartet countries were accusedof fabricated charges, or even had cases filed against them in other GCC countries such as Kuwait.

7) The use of poets, writers, artists, and singers to attack Qatar. Some anti-Qatar songs were made by high officials, such as advisors to Saudi Crown Prince Mohammed bin Salman and Abu Dhabi Crown Prince Mohammed bin Zayed.

8) Attempts to destroy the economy of the opposing side through the spread of fabricated news propaganda within economic and financial circles with the goal to affect currency valuation, scare investors, and influence the stock market to discourage capital investment.

9) The use of Western public relations companies to conduct propaganda media campaigns to sway world public opinion. This was done through the publishing of negative and hostile advertisements that appeared in traditional media, as well as on streets, buses and other public venues.

10) The financing of Western think-tanks and research centers, especially those considered to have hostile or far-right leanings. Even some think-tanks typically viewed as neutral were involved in this process as evidenced by leaks showing that the UAE Ambassador to Washington DC donated $20 million in exchange for support for the Emirati's agenda.[26]

Each of these tools (in addition to other practices) has been used as a weapon of mass deception to garner support for the boycott, legitimize the blockade, and demonize purveyors of opinions that do not resonate with a given regime's party-line.

Therefore, it can be said that the coverage by various audio and visual media in the Gulf States have played a stronger role than during any previous crisis to manufacture the consent of public opinion.

In the current Gulf crisis, no Arab media channel (with rare exceptions) whether in the Gulf or the Arab world, has been able to cover the crisis without exhibiting a clear bias toward either party. In some cases, this has led to public incitement against Arab states and regimes, in addition to the use of language and rhetoric that stands in stark opposition to traditional Arab values.

While we live in an era of open media with established principles independent media around the globe—Arab media officials, perhaps for the first time in the history of modern media, are calling for the oppression of freedom of expression. This has included the shutting down of media outlets such as Al Jazeera on the pretext that this kind of freedom does not fit the Arab peoples and does not further their interests. Such calls have been widely denounced worldwide as a clear aggression against media freedom.

Conclusion

The 2017 Gulf Crisis is arguably the first significant public intra-GCC crisis. The GCC states have managed a number of major military crises successfully, including the Iran-Iraq War as well as the First Gulf war and subsequent liberation of Kuwait. While yet to result in violence, the current Gulf Crisis stands as the third-largest conflict in the history of the GCC.

Since the establishment of the GCC system in 1981, marginal border disputes have erupted between all Gulf states, most of which concerned joint oil wells and coastlines. Minor past conflicts also included Saudi funding for a coup attempt in Qatar in the mid-1990s, and the UAE's attempt to deploy a spy network in Oman in 2009. These differences certainly created tension, but they each ended in détente without impactfully surfacing in the media.

However, unlike these previous crises, the current Gulf row has resulted in prejudiced and biased media with no respect for the codes or ethics of the journalistic profession. The false narratives and counternarratives circulating within the region have nearly irreparably obfuscated the truth, threatening all levels of the homogenous Gulf social fabric.

Despite attempts of reunion and a rapprochement between the parties, the political and media escalation waged by the Quartet and Qatar during the crisis has created a huge cloud of uncertainty over the future of a region that less than a year ago spoke about its intention to issue a single Gulf currency akin to the euro. Today, however, the GCC is on the verge of complete disintegration, with advocacy by some GCC states for regime change within their supposed antagonists.

Gulf media within the region does not appear to be aware of the seriousness of the consequences that will result from the continued publication of falsehoods and fabrications. By their nature, accusations are irreversible, as they will necessarily lead to increasingly muddying counteraccusations. The rhetoric that has been promoted by the Gulf media may turn proof-of-conviction, trapping the entire region in a cycle of endless accusations, thus exposing the Gulf to the threats and ambitions of outsiders.

Unlike domestic Gulf media, the narrative in the international press has not replicated the Saudi-Emirati accusations against Qatar to include the funding of terrorism, unconditional support for the Muslim Brotherhood, Al Jazeera's duplicitous intentions, a purported alliance between Qatar and the Houthis, or a belief that Qatar supports Iranian-backed militants in Bahrain.

In fact, the international media warned that the current Gulf hostility threatens the stability of the greater Middle East, a region already suffering from three civil wars and the spread of jihadist insurgency. American mainstream media and think-tanks have made calls for direct US intervention.[21] The rift also complicates US efforts to mobilize Arab and Muslim leaders to form a united front against Sunni extremists and Shiite Iranian influence.[22] The most dramatic warnings came from Foreign Policy magazine, which cautioned that Washington's failure to defuse the crisis will become historically pivotal if Saudi Arabia and the UAE take spontaneous military action against Qatar.[23] The precarity of the Gulf situation is made all the more clear by the analogy of the pre-WWI environment that set Europe up for disaster in part due the assassination of Archduke Franz Ferdinand in Sarajevo.

By focusing on continuous attacks that weaken the opposing camp while promoting hatred and adopting a policy of mobilization, the Gulf media has turned the region against itself. The crisis is no longer confined to regimes and rulers but has expanded to include ethnic and national considerations. Whereas the relatively young age of individual GCC countries once made a national demonym nothing more than an irrelevant moniker, the attitudes proliferated in the crisis has led to instances of vitriolic hate between Qataris and their Saudi, Emirati and Egyptian blockaders. These deep rifts are by no means a one-way street. On the Saudi side, such tensions reached an unprecedented level when the Kingdom enacted laws criminalizing citizens who express sympathy with Qatar.

Despite pervasive international ramifications, the crisis' gravest effects have been for the institutions that constitute the GCC. The body's precedent of courtesies and protocols (formerly a sign of unity amongst the GCC) have come to an end, allowing the media to expose deep divisions that were once kept out of sight. Also, the spat put an end to the ideas that previously been broadcast enthusiastically, about an EU-style GCC union, potentially including Jordan and Morocco, the adoption of a common foreign and security policy, the issuance of a single currency, the establishment of a Gulf central bank, a single customs area, a unified border and airspace policy, and a string of proposals to further centralize the union. The crisis shows that those ideas were unrealistic, and each country's individual foreign policy interests, in addition to differences in values, ideas, principles and rulers, would have doomed such efforts from the outset.

Once espoused as "brothers," the gulf crisis has divided the rulers of the GCC and brought adversaries and enemies, such as Turkey and Iran, closer to the region on both political and media levels. The schism has highlighted the conflicts of interest among outside parties interested in the Gulf region, with clear support for either side offering its own distinct and irreconcilable "pros" and "cons." Despite the region's importance to the global economy, the general international tendency towards de-escalation within the Gulf has given way to new alliances where old ones once stood. Bottom line: the reality of the Gulf crisis shows that each of the six. nations in the Gulf Cooperation has lost, even though each claims the winner's mantle.

Endnotes

1. "Qatar state news agency 'hacked with fake positive story about Israel and Iran'," *The Telegraph*, May 24, 2017 https://www.telegraph.co.uk/news/2017/05/24/qatar-state-news-agency-hacked-fake-positive-story-israel-iran/

2. "Proof that Qatar News Agency was not hacked," *Al Arabiya English*, May 24, 2017 https://english.alarabiya.net/en/media/digital/2017/05/24/Proof-that-Qatar-News-Agency-was-not-hacked.html

3. "Websites of Al Jazeera, Qatari newspapers blocked in Saudi Arabia and UAE," *Al Arabiya English*, May 24, 2017 https://english.alarabiya.net/en/media/digital/2017/05/24/Websites-of-Al Jazeera-Qatari-newspapers-blocked-in-Saudi-Arabia.html

4. "Egypt blocks 21 websites including Al Jazeera- security sources," *Reuters*, May 24, 2017 https://af.reuters.com/article/egyptNews/idAFL8N1IQ758

5. Caroline Mortimer, "UAE Crown Prince asked US to bomb Al Jazeera during war on terror," *The Independent*, June 29, 2017 https://www.independent.co.uk/news/world/middle-east/uae-crown-prince-us-bomb-Al Jazeera-mohammed-bin-zayed-al-nahyan-wikileaks-qatar-a7814691.html

6. "UAE crown prince asked US to bomb al Jazeera, WikiLeaks claims," *Daily Sabah*, June 29 2017 https://www.dailysabah.com/mideast/2017/06/29/uae-crown-prince-asked-us-to-bomb-Al Jazeera-wikileaks-claims

7. "Bahrain's Foreign Minister Says Putting Al Jazeera on Trial is Gulf Demand," *Bahrain Mirror*, April 23, 2018 http://bahrainmirror.com/en/news/46725.html

8. Donald Trump (@realDonaldTrump), "During my recent trip to the Middle East I stated that there can no longer be funding of Radical Ideology. Leaders pointed to Qatar- look!" June 6, 2017 https://twitter.com/realdonaldtrump/status/872062159789985792?lang=en

9. Donald Trump (@realDonaldTrump), "So good to see the Saudi Arabia visit with the King and 50 countries already paying off. They said they would take a hard line on funding..." June 6, 2017 https://twitter.com/realdonaldtrump/status/872084870620520448?lang=en and "...extremism, and all reference was pointing to Qatar. Perhaps this will be the beginning of the end of the horror of terrorism!" June 6, 2017 https://twitter.com/realdonaldtrump/status/872086906804240384?lang=en

10. Jennifer Jacobs, "Trump Warned Saudis Off Military Move on Qatar," *Bloomberg*, September 19, 2017 https://www.bloomberg.com/news/articles/2017-09-19/trump-is-said-to-have-warned-saudis-off-military-move-on-qatar

11. "War 'stopped' between Qatar, blockading Arab nations," *Al Jazeera*, September 7, 2017 https://www.Al Jazeera.com/news/2017/09/war-stopped-qatar-blockading-arab-nations-170908012658804.html

12. "Blockade against Qatar 'hindering' planning for long-term operation: Pentagon," *Reuters*, June 9, 2017 https://www.reuters.com/article/us-gulf-qatar-usa-military-idUSKBN1902R2

13. Edward Herman and Noam Chomsky, *Manufacturing Consent: The Political Economy of Mass Media* (New York: Pantheon Books, 1988).

14. "Hitler Fought Way to Power Unique in Modern History," *The New York Times*, May 2, 1945 https://archive.nytimes.com/www.nytimes.com/learning/general/onthisday/bday/0420.html

15. Doha Center for Media Freedom, Second Annual Report 2013 http://www.dc4mf.org/wp-content/uploads/2017/12/english_for_web.pdf

16. Freedom House, Freedom in the World 2017 https://freedomhouse.org/sites/default/files/FH_FIW_2017_Report_Final.pdf

17. Mohammed Abdelfattah, "In the Middle East, Two-Thirds Get News on Social Media; Less than Half Trust it," *Northwestern University*, September 17, 2017 https://news.northwestern.edu/stories/2017/september/middle-east-news-social-media-trust/

18. Abdelfattah.

19. Abdelfattah.

20. Edward Herman and Noam Chomsky, *Manufacturing Consent: The Political Economy of Mass Media* (New York: Pantheon Books, 1988).

21. Jordan Cohen, "America Must Actively Seek an End to the Qatar Crisis," *The National Interest*, November 26, 2017 https://nationalinterest.org/feature/america-must-actively-seek-end-the-qatar-crisis-23353

22. Joe Gould, "Qatar rift sets back Trump's Arab NATO'," *Defense News*, June 6, 2017 https://www.defensenews.com/global/2017/06/06/qatar-rift-sets-back-trump-s-arab-nato/

23. John Hannah, "It's Time for the Trump Administration to Step Up in the Qatar Crisis," *Foreign Policy*, June 27, 2017 https://foreignpolicy.com/2017/06/27/its-time-for-the-trump-administration-to-step-up-in-the-qatar-crisis/

24. Tamara Qiblawi, "UAE social media users 'showing sympathy' for Qatar could face jail time," *CNN*, July 27, 2017 https://www.cnn.com/2017/06/07/middleeast/uae-social-media-qatar/index.html

25. Habib Toumi, "Saudi Grand Mufti rejects Brotherhood accusations," *The Gulf News*, June 15, 2017 https://gulfnews.com/news/gulf/qatar/sau-di-grand-mufti-rejects-brotherhood-accusations-1.2044068

26. Ryan Grim, "Gulf government gave secret $20 million gift to D.C. think tank," *The Intercept*, August 9, 2017 https://theintercept.com/2017/08/09/gulf-government-gave-secret-20-million-gift-to-d-c-think-tank/

CHAPTER 6

Yemen and the GCC Crisis

AMBASSADOR GERALD M. FEIERSTEIN

Introduction

Decades of weak governance and internal conflicts have necessitated repeated outside interventions in Yemen. While these interventions have included powers as disparate as Turkey, Britain, and Egypt, the most persistent involvement has come from Yemen's closest neighbors in the region—the other states of the Arabian Peninsula. Over the years, each of Yemen's fellow Arabian nations has generally pursued policies based on their own set of interests and preferences, with an anomaly occurring in 2011 when the GCC states largely coordinated their approaches to Yemen's internal Arab Spring upheaval. This cooperation notwithstanding, differing perspectives on overtures into Yemen and their consequences for the national interests of the GCC states have often been a source of tension within the region. As outliers, Oman and Qatar have long gone against the current of the regional organization's approach to Yemen. As a result, both have been accused of developing policies that reflect sympathies towards Iran, the Muslim Brotherhood, or the Houthis. The outbreak of civil conflict in Yemen and the Saudi decision to intervene on the side of the Hadi government sharpened the intra-GCC conflict over these issues, forming part of the basis for accusations leveled against Qatar by the blockading Quartet in early 2017. Perhaps the most significant policy divergence over Yemen within the GCC lies between Saudi Arabia and the UAE, the region's putative allies. While the Emiratis see Yemen as a stepping stone to building a more dominant position in the Red Sea, the Saudis instead see this UAE build-up as a potential challenge to the Kingdom's core national security interests and regional hegemony.

1.1. Yemen's Conflicts are Internal...

The origins of Yemen's litany of civil wars are almost entirely domestic in nature. In fact, the political crisis that emerged in mid-2014 and metastasized into the current war is only the latest eruption in a cycle of violence that has shaken Yemen repeatedly for nearly sixty years, nor is the current conflict the most violent or longest lasting of these upheavals.[1] There has yet to be a ten-year period in Yemen's history since the 1960s that has not witnessed a violent conflict, coup, or civil insurrection within the nation. Beginning with the 1962 uprising against the Imamate, Yemenis have yet to find a means to build the necessary institutions for a state and society that can successfully address the grievances concerning political and economic marginalization, alienation of populations disadvantaged by governing institutions, and victims of ethnic and sectarian discrimination. That the countries of North and South Yemen were only united in 1990 adds an additional layer of complexity to Yemen's historical divides.

1.2...But Invite External Intervention

Regardless of which party holds responsibility for their origins, Yemen's internal challenges have provoked cyclical outsider intervention. In the 1960s, Egypt and Saudi Arabia backed competing forces in the conflict between the Zaydi Shi'ite Imamate that had ruled in the north for millennia and the republican elements largely drawn from the predominantly Sunni midlands. Since 2014, the Saudi-Iranian regional rivalry has further complicated efforts to find solutions to this internal conflict. The UAE has also been a significant player in the current conflict, initially supporting the Saudis but increasingly pursuing objectives independent of Saudi policy. While there are some who maintain that Iranian intervention in the Yemen conflict was provoked by Saudi involvement, the reverse is actually more likely: Saudi intervention in March 2015 was a direct result of the perceived threat to Saudi security posed by the growing Houthi-Iranian alliance in Yemen.

2.1. Yemen's Problems Have Long Been a Source of Conflict for its Neighbors

Naturally, Yemen's regional history has been most closely intertwined with that of its immediate neighbors but these involvements in internal affairs have never been a one-way street. In the late 1960s to early 1970s, the newly independent South Yemen, first as the People's Republic of South Yemen (PRSY), and later its successor the People's Democratic Republic of Yemen (PDRY), actively supported the Dhofar Liberation Front in Oman (DFL) and the People's Front for the Liberation of Oman (PFLO). PDRY support for the Dhofar rebels did not end until Saudi Arabia offered aid and recognition to Aden in exchange for an end to its assistance to the Omani rebels. In March 1976, Saudi Arabia established relations with PDRY and the authorities there ordered an end to PDRY-Omani cross-border activities, effectively bringing the rebellion to a conclusion.[2]

Still, Saudi Arabia's involvement in Yemen is long-standing and more extensive than that of any of Yemen's neighbors, giving Saudi interests primacy among GCC positions towards Yemen. Saudi-Yemeni engagement dates back to the 1930s, when the Kingdom fought a war with the Yemeni Imamate. Saudi victory in the war led to the transfer of Jizan, Najran, and Asir (sometimes referred to by Yemenis as the three "lost" provinces) to Saudi Arabia. The establishment of a border between the two countries was demarcated by the Treaty of Jeddah in 2000.

Saudi Arabia's objectives in Yemen have generally focused on ensuring the security of its southern border and preventing instability in Yemen from undermining Saudi interests. Tellingly, as one Saudi analyst noted to Ginny Hill and Gerd Nonneman, "Yemen is not about foreign policy, it's about national security–it's about intelligence, security, tribalism and informal contact."[3] Perhaps surprisingly, sectarian distinctions too have not played a particularly large role in determining Saudi interests vis-à-vis its neighbor. In 1962, Yemeni republican elements predominantly drawn from the Shafai'i-majority areas of Yemen's midlands mounted a coup against the Zaydi Shi'a Imamate. Despite their general aversion to Shi'ism, the Saudis supported the Imamate primarily because they saw the republican revolution, backed by Egypt, as a potential threat to their domestic interests. Once the civil war ended in 1970, however, the Saudis reconciled with the Yemen Arab Republic. The Kingdom collaborated with Yemeni authorities by building their own patronage system, particularly for northern tribes under the leadership of the paramount sheikh of the Hashid tribal confederation, Sheikh Abdullah al-Ahmar. Saudi patronage was a major pillar of financial support for Saleh's regime when he came to power in 1978. In addition, by the late 1970s and 1980s, millions of Yemeni workers had crossed the border to find jobs in Saudi Arabia, providing family remittances critical to Yemen's economic survival.

However, Saudi support has not always necessarily translated to Yemeni cooperation. In 1989, Yemen joined the Iraq-initiated Arab Coordination Council (along with Egypt and Jordan), viewed as especially threatening by the Saudis who saw the group as a potentially hostile encirclement of the Gulf states meant to counterbalance the influence of the GCC. Yemen's continued support for Iraq amidst the 1990-91 Gulf War crisis led to the expulsion of as many as one million Yemeni expatriates from Saudi Arabia and a subsequent severing of diplomatic relations between the two nations. Continued frustration with Saleh may also have factored into the Saudis' controversial decision to support southern secessionists in the 1994 Yemen civil war.

Saudi-Yemeni relations saw another reversal after 9/11, the rise of al-Qaeda in the Arabian Peninsula (AQAP), and the beginning of the U.S.-led global war on terrorism. In addition to the threat of violent extremism (which specifically targeted Saudi interests as well as pursued a broader agenda of global jihad), the Saudis were increasingly concerned by the rise of militant Zaydi groups in the northern border area, especially the Houthi-led "Believing Youth" and "Ansar Allah." Zaydi militancy was fueled by the grievances of a population angered by the increase in Saudi-funded Wahhabi intrusions in traditionally Zaydi areas, perceived as marginalizing to Zaydi interests. The establishment of Dar al-Hadith Institute in Dammaj became a particular flashpoint for Zaydi militants. The Saudis predicted that the rise of Zaydi militancy could grow into a "Hezbollah-like" presence on their southern border. As a result, Riyadh supported Saleh's anti-Houthi agenda, which grew into a series of six armed confrontations, characterized as the Sa'dah wars. The Saudis themselves were briefly drawn into the sixth Sa'dah war when allegations that the Saudis were directly supporting the anti-Houthi agenda boiled over into a Houthi cross-border raid that resulted in the death of a Saudi border guard in 2009.

3.1. Qatar Mediates in the Sa'dah Wars

Qatar's proposal to mediate the conflict between the Saleh regime and the Houthis in May 2007 reflected a larger interest in the Qatari government to play a leadership role in regional mediation efforts. Consequently, it also marked the genesis of Saudi-Qatari competition in Yemen. Under the leadership of Sheikh Hamad bin Khalifa, Qatari foreign policy since the mid-1990s had evolved to promote its availability as a mediator in regional domestic conflicts. Sheikh Hamad's interest reflected his policy of raising Qatar's profile as an independent and pragmatic actor in regional affairs, one that was able to maintain balanced relations with a broad spectrum of foreign governments, ranging from the U.S. to Iran. In doing so, Sultan Barakat notes that Qatar fell into the category of small-state mediators that frame their engagement as "within a commitment to peace as part of a 'state branding' strategy that enhances their soft power or cultural influence."[4] But Barakat also makes clear that tensions with Saudi Arabia– which opposed Qatari autonomy in foreign policy–were among the drivers of Qatar's foreign policy reorientation.[5] In addition to its engagement in Yemen, Qatar also presented itself as a mediator in Lebanon, Palestine, Darfur, and between Eritrea and Ethiopia. Following a failed attempt by Libya's Moammar Qadafi to negotiate a resolution of the fourth Sa'dah war (February-June 2007), a Qatari mediation effort began to emerge. Sheikh Hamad personally led a senior Qatari delegation to Sana'a in May 2007. Ali Abdullah Saleh had just returned from Washington where Secretary of State Condoleezza Rice had reportedly pressed him to resolve the Houthi crisis over concerns that it was interfering with global efforts to confront al-Qaeda.[6] Qatar was a logical choice as a mediator in Yemen because of its financial resources as well as the fact that it did not have the historical baggage shared by other potential mediators like Saudi Arabia or Egypt.[7] Nevertheless, to avoid exacerbating Saudi suspicions Qatar's diplomatic initiative was kept under wraps until the negotiations were nearly completed.

After two months of mediation, the Saleh government and the Houthis announced that they had reached a ceasefire agreement. The "First Doha Agreement" as it came to be known included nine provisions. For their part, the Houthis committed to accept the legitimacy of the republican government, hand in their medium arms, and withdraw from their military positions. In exchange the government offered amnesty to the Houthi leadership and promised a Qatari-financed reconstruction program in the Houthi stronghold of Sa'dah, reportedly valued at $300-500 million.[8] Nevertheless, implementation of the agreement proved to be a challenge. Hardliners on both sides rejected the political agreement and continued to advocate for a military solution. One of the provisions, relocating the Houthi senior leadership to Doha, was impossible to implement as the Houthi leadership never demonstrated any commitment to depart Yemen. Meanwhile, the two sides jousted over their respective records in implementing other provisions. Consequently, fighting between the two sides, which had never fully come to a halt, resumed.

The Qatari mediation effort had failed. The International Crisis Group explained the failure as the result of a "lack of an effective follow-up mechanism to monitor implementation and adjudicate disputes."[9] In particular, the ICG noted that there were no regular contacts between the Doha Agreement's signatories and Qatari officials. Moreover, the agreement did not establish a mechanism for addressing disagreements.[10] In that regard, a Yemeni parliamentary committee issued a statement in July demanding Houthi compliance with the terms of the agreement within three days, while Abdulmalik al-Houthi complained that the implementation committee ignored the steps the Houthis had taken to fulfill their obligations. The Houthis later released a report documenting their performance, including the vacating of strongholds and the handing over of heavy weaponry that had been captured from the government. Additionally, the Houthis released some (but not all) of the prisoners they were holding.[11]

With both sides engaged in mutual recriminations, the Qataris suspended the financial reconstruction and development assistance for Sa'dah that had been contingent upon implementation of the Doha agreement. Finally, given these complications, that July the Qataris announced that they were recalling their delegation to Doha "for further consultation and evaluation of the situation."[12]

In addition to the structural deficiencies identified by the report, the International Crisis Group also alleged that competition between Saudi Arabia and Qatar was a secondary factor that contributed to the mediation effort's failure. "Qatari mediation in Sa'dah—a region that borders Saudi Arabia—appear[ed] to have prompted Riyadh to pour money into the Yemeni military and allied tribes" asserted the report. "At the same time, Saudi media portrayed the Qatari intercession as guided by Iran, suggesting that its timing reflected a joint bid to save the rebels from looming defeat."[13]

The damage done by these theories to Qatar's standing in Yemen has been long-lasting, leading to Saleh's 2009 declaration that Qatari mediation in Sa'dah was finished. In the face of this intensified Saudi criticism, according to Bernd Kaussler, Qatari Prime Minister Hamad bin Jassim (HbJ) insisted in public comments that Qatar had been a "fair broker in the conflict," while also advising Emir Sheikh Hamad bin Khalifa to discontinue Qatari involvement in Yemen.[14] Citing a leaked U.S. Embassy Doha cable, Kaussler reports that HbJ nevertheless told the U.S. Ambassador in the fall of 2009 that the Government of Qatar had been in contact with Saleh, inviting him to visit Doha for talks, despite Saleh's apparent "belie[f that] the Qataris are financing the Houthi rebels leading the Saada [sic] rebellion against his government."[15] In 2010, Qatar made one more attempt to resume its mediation role and implement ceasefire terms, according to the Chatham House report.[16] When press reports surfaced in January 2011 about the new Qatari reconciliation effort, Secretary of State Hillary Clinton asked Saleh for his views when she visited Sana'a.

Saleh exploded in response, repeating accusations that the Qataris were representing Iranian interests and supporting the Houthis. He made clear that further Qatari engagement would be unwelcome.[17] Saleh's ill will toward Qatar later influenced Doha's involvement in the GCC mediation effort that led to the "GCC Initiative and Implementing Mechanism."

4.1. The GCC Minus Qatar Negotiates Yemen's Political Transition

As a general principle, the GCC states did not respond to the 2011 Arab Spring movement in a coordinated fashion; each state pursued its own foreign policy priorities. Particularly, in regard to the anti-government uprisings in Tunisia and Egypt where Hosni Mubarak and Zine El Abidene Ben Ali enjoyed close relations with the Gulf, the GCC states were not supportive of the uprisings and were angered by international (especially U.S.) pressure on Mubarak to step down. Their views on the popular unrest sweeping the region were further complicated by their agitation over the role of the Muslim Brotherhood (MB), viewed broadly in the Gulf as at best a political threat, if not a full-fledged a terrorist organization. Qatar proved to be an exception to this consensus view among the GCC states, openly sympathizing with the MB. Qatar's position on political Islam, of course, antagonized the other GCC leaders and became one of the principal items cited in the "list of particulars" leveled at Qatar, and the subsequent intra-GCC crisis.[18]

In the case of Yemen, however, the GCC states were not committed to preserving Ali Abdullah Saleh's authoritarian rule and were thus able to arrive at a coordinated strategy in managing the political crisis. Saudi Arabia, the UAE, Kuwait, and Oman were all actively engaged in helping mediate the crisis and arranging for a peaceful, political transition in the country (Bahrain does not maintain an embassy in Sana'a and was therefore not involved in the GCC effort). The GCC Secretary General Abdul Latif al-Zayani and his team played a particularly substantive role in representing broader GCC interests. The differing approach to the 2011 Yemen crisis likely reflects several factors, including Yemen's geographical proximity to the GCC states which makes them more sensitive to instability on their borders.

Given the history of South Yemen's efforts to destabilize Oman in the 1960s and 1970s, the Omanis were perhaps the most sensitive among the GCC states to the threat posed by popular uprisings in their border regions. Perhaps influenced by that history, Oman sought to maintain the most positive relationship with Yemen out of all the GCC states.[19] Oman's ambassador of long-standing in Sana'a maintained a close relationship with Saleh and worked initially to promote reconciliation among the various parties (as did the US Embassy for reasons largely related to concerns over the counter-terrorism agenda). These efforts, however, were unsuccessful and the crisis continued to deepen.

Once Ali Abdullah Saleh eventually launched negotiations to find a political solution to the conflict, they remained largely confined to the Yemeni elite. However, the Yemenis did seek engagement from outsiders, both within and outside the region to assist with the talks. Ambassadors from the P5, the EU, and the UN itself each went on to play a supporting role in the negotiations. The GCC initiative, which formed the framework of the transition agreement, was key to the success of the negotiations. The genesis of the GCC's involvement also came primarily from within the Yemeni political elite. It was Yemeni Foreign Minister Abubakr al-Qirbi who proposed to the GCC Foreign Ministers in Abu Dhabi that the GCC mediate among the Yemeni factions. The ministers indicated a willingness to engage but only on the condition that Saleh agree, charging al-Qirbi with the responsibility of gaining Saleh's acquiescence. Qirbi convinced Saleh to accept a GCC mediation. Saudi Arabia's deeply experienced foreign minister, Prince Saud Al Faisal, took the lead in coordinating with his GCC counterparts and preparing a framework agreement. Qirbi had already worked with Omani Foreign Minister Yusuf bin Alawi and the Omani ambassador, Abdullah al-Badi, to draft the outline, which became the basis of the "GCC Initiative and Implementing Mechanism." GCC Secretary General al-Zayani presented the draft to Saleh, who initially resisted signing the agreement, accusing the GCC of conspiring against him.[20] However, after a near-fatal terror attack, Saleh signed the agreement in Riyadh in November 2011.

Despite their prominent role in the beginning phase of the political crisis, once the political negotiations began the Omanis reduced their presence in Sana'a and generally followed the Saudi and Emirati lead (along with the GCC Secretary General) in working out the details of the leadership away from Saleh.[21] Thus, even though the GCC engagement was officially billed as a consensus approach to the crisis, the Saudis unsurprisingly remained the dominant decision-makers within the bloc. As reflected by Saud Al Faisal's leadership within the foreign ministers' group, the Saudi position in support of the political transition was determinative.

Amidst this Saudi involvement appears a conundrum. Namely, having opposed similar transitions elsewhere among the countries affected by the Arab Spring, what could explain Saudi support for the anti-Saleh movement in Yemen? In part, Saudi willingness to cooperate on a change of leadership in Sana'a was probably a hangover from their continued unhappiness with the Yemeni leader. According to Ginny Hill, the Saudis were angry over Saleh's unwillingness to confront the threat from al-Qaeda as well as a residual sense that he had manipulated Riyadh over the Iranian role in supporting the Houthis.[22] Beyond those issues, traditional Saudi-Yemeni ties had been withering. The Saudi "brain trust" managing the Yemen account was in decline. The enfeeblement of Prince Sultan and Prince Nayef—for many years the dominant voices within the Saudi leadership on Yemen— reduced Saudi engagement with Yemen when the two rulers died in 2011 and 2012, respectively. On the Yemeni side, the 2007 death of Sheikh Abdullah al-Ahmar, the paramount sheikh of the Hashid federation and a key Yemeni interlocutor with the Saudi leadership, reduced Yemen's influence in Saudi councils. Finally, the split in Yemeni ranks amongst Saleh, his long-time partner General Ali Mohsen, and the sons of Sheikh Abdullah fractured Saudi Arabia's historic alliance in Yemen. As Hill notes, the Saudis were willing to accept Saleh's departure although their decision was delayed by their inability to identify a successor who they believed could be a reliable partner.[23]

As noted, the GCC member states were generally able to operate by consensus regarding Yemen policy throughout the Arab Spring. Aside from Bahrain, only Qatar refrained from engaging in the GCC mediation efforts, in part because of continuing sensitivities surrounding its unsuccessful involvement in mediating the Sa'dah wars. Saleh was particularly agitated by any indication that Qatar was playing a role in the spring 2011 negotiations. Al Jazeera's coverage (often provocative and misleading) of the anti-government demonstrations in Sana'a were a particular flashpoint for Saleh. Hamad Bin Jassim (HBJ) further incited Saleh's anger when, according to a Chatham House Report, he stated publicly that the GCC was working on a plan for Saleh to step down.[24] As a result of continued bilateral friction, Doha shuttered its embassy and recalled its ambassador for most of that spring. The Qataris played no further role in the GCC mediation, announcing publicly that they would not be a party to the negotiations. According to Dr. Abdullah Baabood, however, Qatar may have continued to influence the course of events in Sana'a from outside the GCC negotiating process. Baabood acknowledges that little is known about possible Qatari assistance to the Islah party (a Muslim Brotherhood affiliate in Yemen) but rumors swirl that Doha provided as much as $80 million to Islah during the unrest.[25]

5.1. The Political Transition Ends GCC Active Engagement and Its Consensus

Following the signing of the "GCC Initiative and Implementing Mechanism," involvement in Yemen's transition waned as the Gulf states largely ceded their oversight roles to the P-5 and the UN. In addition to the Omani ambassador, the Emirati ambassador (who had been one of the most active members of the diplomatic corps during the negotiations leading up to the transition agreement) departed from Sana'a and was not immediately replaced.

For their part, the Saudis grew increasingly frustrated with the performance of the Hadi-led transition government. Despite their co-leadership of the "Friends of Yemen group," (along with the UK) the Saudis were highly critical of the perceived corruption and incompetence of the transitional government, complaining about the government's inability to implement promised development projects. At the final Friends of Yemen session in New York prior to the outbreak of the civil war, an Arab News report claimed the Yemeni government had only spent about one-quarter of the funds pledged over the previous two years by international donors.[26] While at the meeting the Saudis reiterated their support for the Hadi government but, according to the article, became increasingly resistant to providing additional assistance. In response to US urgings that the Kingdom do more to help the transitional government address Yemen's economic collapse, on the eve of the conflict senior Saudis made clear they had lost confidence in Hadi and were reluctant to do more to help him.[27]

5.2. Saudi-Qatari Competition Persists

One exception to the general decline in GCC interest in Yemen has been the continuation of Saudi-Qatari tension over their respective Yemen policies. "Riyadh's accusations of Qatari meddling in Yemen only intensified after the Arab Spring in 2011," says Bernd Kaussler.

> Since then, Saudi and Qatari policy towards Yemen has been seen by both states largely through the prism of extending both hard and soft power over the country as well as the region as a whole. To Riyadh, Qatar's activist foreign policy in Yemen and beyond was seen as competing for control of the Gulf and patronage of Islamist groups.[43]

As the broader tension between Saudi Arabia and Qatar intensified in 2013, Saudi King Abdullah pressured the Qataris to sign an agreement that essentially demanded a complete reorientation of Qatari policy toward Yemen. When the Qataris rejected this Saudi pressure the Kuwaitis presented a re-drafted agreement in early 2014 containing a provision inter alia that Qatar would curtail its support for the Houthis in Yemen, which the Qataris did sign.[28]

5.3. The Hadi Government Collapses and the Saudis Intervene

Though frustrated with the Hadi government's performance and unwilling to engage directly in the political crisis unfolding in Sana'a through the fall of 2014, Saudi policy-makers were becoming increasingly alarmed by developments on their southern border. Quick moves by the Houthis to strengthen contacts with the Government of Iran, including the establishment of regular air service between Sana'a and Tehran, were coupled with aggressive statements by senior Houthi leaders perceived as threatening to Saudi security. The Houthis' threats went beyond verbal statements and even included plans to conduct military exercises on Saudi Arabia's southern border.

As noted previously, Saudi policy towards Yemen historically has been largely motivated by concerns about the potential spillover effects of Yemeni instability for its internal security. When Hadi was forced to flee Sana'a and the Houthis appeared to be on the verge of establishing complete control over the country, the Saudis determined that their interests compelled intervention. They were able to rapidly assemble a coalition, including their GCC partners (sans Oman) and several other Islamic states.

More than those of any other outside actor, Saudi interests in Yemen appear to be the most transparent: a secure southern border with Yemen, a friendly government in Sana'a, and confidence that Yemen will not become an Iranian foothold on the Arabian Peninsula harboring elements of the IRGC or Hezbollah.

6.1. Qatari Support Falls Victim to the Intra-GCC Dispute

Despite bilateral friction with Riyadh over competing policies in Yemen, the Qataris were formally included in the Saudi-led coalition that intervened in the Yemen Civil War in March 2015. According to the Emirates News Agency, the Qataris dispatched ten fighter jets to support the operation. Some 1,000 Qatari military personnel later joined the Coalition, resulting in many wounded and at least three Qatari casualties over the course of their engagement.

However, in spite of this contribution, Saudi Arabia and Yemen expelled Qatari military forces following the broad accusations leveled by the Quartet against the government of Qatar in May 2017. In Yemen, Qatar has been variously accused by the Coalition of supporting the Houthis, the Muslim Brotherhood, or both. Abdullah Baabood reported that allegations regarding Qatari support for the Houthis had persisted through the summer and fall of 2014 as the Houthis moved aggressively against the Hadi government in Sana'a.[29]

By 2018, the Southern Transitional Council (STC), closely aligned with the UAE, joined the coalition in accusing Qatar of supporting the Houthis. Emirati daily newspaper The National quoted Salem Thabet al-Awlaki, an STC spokesman, as alleging: "Qatar has played a very negative role in destabilizing the situation in Yemen by offering the Houthis and other terrorist groups (sic) all the support they needed to remain alive to serve Iranian agendas, which aim to destabilize the Arab world."[30] In May, as purported evidence of Qatari transgressions, coalition press reports alleged that a Qatari intelligence officer was arrested attempting to cross the Yemeni-Omani border. Coalition sources asserted that the officer was a Major in Qatari intelligence responsible for coordinating between the Houthis and the Government of Qatar.[31] A Qatari official statement responded that the individual, Mohsen al-Karbi, was a Qatari civilian merely trying to visit relatives in Yemen.[32]

Meanwhile, Coalition accusations of Qatari support for the Muslim Brotherhood and its Yemeni affiliate presented a complicated picture of a murky reality. As noted previously, Qatar is alleged to have provided support to Islah (the MB affiliate) during the Arab Spring. Islah, however, is represented in the ruling coalition that includes ROYG Vice President Ali Mohsen, who has maintained historically close ties to the Saudi government. Moreover, thousands of the fighters in the anti-Houthi campaign are members of Islah and work closely with the Saudi-led Coalition. For its part, the Qataris reject the Quartet's allegations, insisting that Qatar has adhered to the Gulf consensus on key regional issues, including Yemen. Qatar also denies that it supports the Muslim Brotherhood, despite its refusal to categorize the MB as a terrorist organization.[33]

7.1. Oman Maintains its Neutrality

As noted above, the Government of Oman reduced its engagement in the Yemeni political transition after the failure of its initial efforts to promote reconciliation among the political elites. Nevertheless, Omani foreign minister Yusuf bin Alawi was one of the architects of the GCC transition framework, with Muscat supporting the political arrangement that emerged from the negotiations. The Omani position was consistent with Sultan Qaboos' policy of non-alignment and his regular emphasis on dialogue to defuse crises and end conflicts.[34]

When the Yemen civil war erupted in early 2015, Oman declined to join the Saudi-led coalition. Beyond Oman's policy preference for peaceful resolutions of disputes, the conflict in Yemen presented Oman with strategic dilemmas. Oman too has been accused by its GCC partners of supporting the Houthis. Soon after fighting erupted in the spring of 2015, then-American Deputy Secretary of State Antony Blinken visited Muscat and met with Oman's Yemen team, where the Sultanate's sympathy for the Houthi position was made clear.[35] Ayman Abdulkareem cites a quote attributed to Foreign Minister bin Alawi that appeared on the Omani Foreign Ministry website,

> The media dressed the Houthis in a uniform that was not of their making, for they cannot control Yemen alone, so they formed alliances with others in Yemen after they got fed up with the situation, and that the Gulf states believed that the situation was under control and that the Gulf initiative was sufficient." This could not be further from the truth.[44]

The Coalition has attributed Oman's friendly stance toward the Houthis to its neutral policy towards Iran, accusing the Omanis of turning a blind eye to supposed Iranian use of Omani territory to smuggle weapons and personnel into Yemen for the Houthis, allegations the Omanis vehemently deny. However, Oman has long advocated a pragmatic approach to Tehran, with which it shares management of territorial waters, including the strategically vital Strait of Hormuz. Conversely, the Omanis fear that Salafi expansionism in the region can threaten Oman's social fabric, which is built around Ibadi Islam, a less commonly known "Third Branch" of Islam that is neither Sunni nor Shi'a.[36] In that regard, the development of new Wahhabi religious institutions in the Mahra governorate near the Oman-Yemeni border reinforces Oman's disquiet about possible Saudi and Emirati intentions in a post-conflict scenario.

In contrast to the Saudi-led coalition, the Omanis have continued to advance negotiations as the means to resolve the Yemeni political dispute. As a result of their stance, the Omanis enjoy the confidence of the Houthis, allowing Muscat to serve as the venue for Houthi meetings with outside parties, including the UN special envoy and former Secretary of State Kerry, who in an Omani-arranged meeting sat with a Houthi in December 2016 amidst a last-ditch U.S. effort to broker a peaceful resolution before the Obama administration left office.

The Omanis have also played an important role in resolving tangential issues with the Houthis. In February 2015, Oman played an essential role in facilitating the safe evacuation of U.S. and UK personnel from Sana'a, as well as in negotiating the safe return of Americans and other civilians held by the Houthis. In light of their central position, maintaining good relations with all of the key actors in the Yemen conflict, the Omanis are almost certainly going to be an essential partner in pursuing a peaceful resolution of the Yemen conflict despite coalition members' discontent with Sultan bin Qaboos' policy preferences.

8.1. Has the United Arab Emirates Gone Rogue?

Aside from the Saudis, no GCC government was more deeply engaged in the 2011 negotiations for a Yemeni political transition than the UAE. The Emirati ambassador to Sana'a, Abdulla al-Mazroui—widely respected by both the Yemeni political leadership and his diplomatic colleagues—was an active and highly effective participant in the negotiations, working especially closely with GCC Secretary General al-Zayani. Although the ambassador left soon after completion of the transition, the UAE embassy remained engaged in the agreement's implementation, including participation in discussions over the reorganization of the military and security force that had been called for in the GCC Initiative.[37]

When the security situation in Yemen deteriorated in early 2015 and the Saudis made the decision to intervene, the Emiratis became the second-largest force present within the Saudi-led coalition, providing air, sea, and land forces. In addition to its commitment to preserve the internationally recognized Hadi government, the Emirates also made clear their intention to demonstrate support for Saudi Arabia.

Over the course of the conflict, however, the Emiratis have reportedly become increasingly disillusioned with the performance of their Saudi partners, particularly due to the Kingdom's unwillingness to commit ground forces to the fighting in Yemen.[38] Additionally, alongside Emirati engagement with the coalition in the fight against the Houthi/Saleh forces, UAE forces have also sought to demonstrate their military capacity by establishing close coordination with US forces engaged in counter-terrorism efforts. Abu Dhabi's efforts in this capacity witnessed some victories, including the successful ejection of al-Qaeda elements from Mukalla in southeastern Yemen and the central al-Shabwa governorate.

Emirati dissatisfaction with Saudi Arabia's military performance has led to an increasing willingness to pursue objectives counter to Saudi goals. Since the outbreak of the conflict, while Qatari and Omani policies have been heavily criticized by the members of the coalition for their alleged tilt towards the Houthis or the Muslim Brotherhood, no other government has pursued objectives as opaque as those of the UAE. In part, the Emirati engagement in Yemen is, according to regional scholar Neil Partrick, an extension of its larger campaign against the Muslim Brotherhood and political Islam.[39] The UAE has pressed its Saudi partners to break with the Islah party because of its MB connections. So far, the Saudis have resisted, also according to Partrick, on the grounds that Islah's tribal factions make the group different from MB affiliates elsewhere in the region. Until Saleh's death in December 2017, the Emiratis were encouraging the Saudis to again turn to the former president as a potential unifier who could bring the conflict in Yemen to a conclusion.

By contrast, Saudi goals and objectives in Yemen appear relatively transparent, as demonstrated above, and are consistent with the terms of UN Security Council Resolution 2216, which calls to support Yemen's unity, territorial integrity, and sovereignty. However, Emirati actions, inadvertently or not, have ultimately weakened the Yemeni government and state. In particular, the concentration of Emirati forces in the south and east of Yemen has allowed the Emirates to extend its strategic reach, according to Abdulwahab al-Qassab.[40] The UAE's moves and its relations with southern political figures close to former South Yemen leader

Ali Salem al-Bidh have generated allegations that it is promoting plans to dominate southern Yemen in a federated republic or even to promote southern secessionism. In particular, Emirati support for the secessionist STC (including rumors that Abu Dhabi is financing the opening of an STC office in Washington, DC) has generated complaints from the Hadi government.

The Emiratis argue that their alliance with southern separatists is necessitated by the Hadi government's weakness and incompetence. Still, the UAE's actions have generated conflict with its Saudi coalition-partners. Early in 2017, Emirati allies battled Saudi-backed Yemeni forces for control of the Aden airport. More recently, Saudi negotiators were brought to the island of Socatra to resolve a dispute between Emirati forces and Hadi government representatives, including Prime Minister Ahmed bin Daghr, over control of the island.

The Emirati engagement in Yemen may also reflect a larger UAE strategy to become a dominant player in the broader Red Sea/Indian Ocean arena and compete with Turkey and Qatar. Within this context, Abdulwahab al-Qassab points to the growth of the Emirates' strategic position, as seen by its port at Berbera in Somaliland and a military facility at Assab in Eritrea.[41] The Emirates port management company DP World had also held contracts to manage the Aden port and the Doraleh Container Terminal in Djibouti, both of which it lost in legally contested decisions. Given this loss, the Emirates would then see their control of the Socotra archipelago as a strategic move to enhance their interests in the Indian Ocean and the Horn of Africa, offsetting their loss of access to Djibouti with gains elsewhere.

Against this backdrop of uncertain Emirati intentions in Yemen and the Red Sea region, which are also of vital strategic importance to Saudi Arabia, it appears that the potential for Saudi-Emirati competition is on the rise. While expressing a desire to quickly end the conflict in Yemen and withdraw their military forces, Emirati leaders have also expressed a determination to maintain a presence in Yemen well into the future. For their part, the Saudis may also be moving to stake out strong positions in the central and eastern regions of the country. In that regard, the Saudis announced in early August 2018 that they would be financing a number of development projects in the Mahra governorate, which borders Oman. In announcing the projects, President Hadi declared,

> The Kingdom of Saudi Arabia remains at the forefront in Yemen. Saudi Arabia was the first to realize the gravity of the danger and trouble in Yemen, and the Kingdom is the first to step forward to fulfill and champion the needs of Yemenis. Today, Saudi Arabia is the first, as usual, to build and construct. This is the Kingdom's destiny not only for the land and people of Yemen, but for humankind as a whole.

The Kingdom's interest in Mahra is significant not only because of its geographic importance, but also because of its historic alignment with Socotra as part of the Mahra Sultanate of Qishn and Socotra. However, these Saudi-Emirati efforts to expand their influence in Mahra may run afoul of its peoples' preferences. Given the history of Mahra's and Socotra's independence, Elisabeth Kendall observed there is little support within Mahra for further association with either the Republic of Yemen or a newly seceded South Yemen.[42] Moreover, most Mahris view with suspicion outside meddling in their governorate. (In fairness, Kendall also reports that most Socotrans don't support re-attaching the island to Mahra and were pleased when Socotra became its own governorate in 2013).

Conclusion

Yemen's neighbors have long been involved in the country's domestic political issues. This is especially true of Saudi Arabia and Oman. The former's fortunes have been closely linked with its southern neighbor since the 1930s, while the latter has similarly been challenged by developments in Yemen since the early days of Sultan Qaboos' rule. For the most part, the other states of the Arabian Peninsula have accepted Saudi primacy in determining regional approaches to Yemen, reflecting not only Saudi Arabia's proximity to Yemen and its long, shared border, but also Saudi political, financial, and tribal influence on Yemeni policy.

Nevertheless, divergent approaches to Yemen policy have emerged among the member states of the GCC. Qatar and Oman have both been outliers in their approaches to Yemen; Oman has historically been the friendliest of the GCC states to its western neighbor. The Omanis, ever mindful of South Yemen's efforts to destabilize Dhofar in the 1960s-1970s, have been the GCC state most supportive of bringing Yemen closer to the GCC fold. But Oman's global policy of positive neutrality has led it to reject participation in the Saudi-led Coalition against the Houthis, which has exacerbated tensions between Oman and its GCC partners who simplistically fail to see—or outright ignore—the Omani position as a reflection of its nuanced policy toward Iran. Omani engagement with the Houthis may also reflect sensitivities that the Ibadi majority Omani population shares with the Zaydi Shi'a Houthis over the rise of Salafism in Yemen and the threat this may pose to their traditional culture and social fabric. The introduction of Saudi-funded Salafi institutions in northern Oman underscores the potential risks for Muscat to their stability already posed by the increased Saudi and Emirati influence in eastern Yemen.

Tensions between Qatar and Saudi Arabia over Yemen policy emerged in the first decade of the twenty-first century, when Qatar's effort to promote itself as a regional mediator led to intervention in the Yemeni government's conflicts with the Houthis. Qatari involvement in Saudi Arabia's backyard raised Saudi suspicions and led to Riyadh's allegations, echoed by the Saleh government, that Doha was operating in tandem with the Houthis at the behest of Tehran. Subsequent accusations arising during the 2011 Arab Spring that the Qataris were also supporting the Muslim Brotherhood further deepened the confrontation between Qatar and its GCC partners. Saudi and Emirati efforts to rein in Qatar's independent foreign policy as early as 2013 became untenable in 2017 when the Quartet broke its ties with Doha and imposed an economic boycott on the country. Qatari support for the Saudi-led Coalition was collateral damage in the larger intra-GCC battle, even as the Qataris rejected allegations that their Yemen policy was at variance with their GCC partners.

The most significant differences that have emerged among GCC member states in the Yemen conflict involve the two states that have been closest in their approach to regional challenges: Saudi Arabia and the UAE. While the Emiratis quickly joined the Saudis in their decision to intervene in the Yemen civil war in March 2015 —primarily to demonstrate support for Saud Arabia's regional leadership—the Emiratis have made little effort to hide their frustration over the war's length or what they perceive as Saudi Arabia's wavering military performance. Beyond that frustration, however, the UAE's approach to the conflict, especially its emphasis on supporting elements in eastern and southern Yemen, including those advocating secession from a united Yemen, as well as their occupation of Socotra, have raised questions about the UAE's intentions.

In making clear that the Emirates intend to establish a long-term presence in Yemen, it would appear that the ambitious de facto ruler of the UAE, Crown Prince MbZ, sees Yemen as part of his strategy to establish the UAE as a dominant player in the larger Red Sea arena, stretching to the Horn of Africa. Emirati domination of eastern and southern Yemen, along with the Yemeni ports at Mukalla, Aden, Mocha, and, potentially, Hodeidah would ensure that the UAE would be able to establish a command presence in crucial shipping lanes that link the Arabian and Red Seas, as well as the Bab al-Mandeb, the Suez Canal and the African Red Sea coast. There is no evidence that the Saudis and Emiratis have coordinated this evolving UAE regional strategy, which holds clear implications for Saudi Arabia's own national security interests. Amid signs of a lack of communication between Riyadh and Abu Dhabi over the course of the Yemen conflict (as well as the larger strategic issues), the Saudis appear to be pushing back on the Emiratis' aggressive moves. The Kingdom forced the Emirates to back away from its support for the southern secessionists confronting the Hadi government in Aden earlier in 2018 and reduce its presence on Socotra when the island became a major friction point for the Yemeni political leadership. That the Saudis just announced a major expansion of their engagement in Mahra governorate appears to be a challenge to the UAE's efforts in establishing a dominant position in eastern Yemen. Thus, of all of the fracture lines within the GCC over Yemen policy, the Saudi-Emirati relationship calls for the closest scrutiny.

Endnotes

1. The republican rebellion against the Imamate in north Yemen lasted from 1962-1970. The internal YSP dispute in the PDRY inflicted an estimated 10,000 casualties among the civilian population of Aden in approximately two weeks of street battles.

2. Roby C. Barrett, *The Gulf and the Struggle for Hegemony: Arabs, Iranians, and the West in Conflict*, (Washington, DC.: Middle East Institute, 2016), 330.

3. Ginny Hill, and Gerd Nonneman, *Yemen, Saudi Arabia, and the Gulf States: Elite Politics, Street Protests and Regional diplomacy*, (London: Chatham House, 2011), 9.

4. Sultan Barakat, Qatari Mediation: Between Ambition and Achievement, (Doha: Brookings Institution, 2014), 10.

5. Barakat, 6

6. Marieke Brandt, T*ribes and Politics in Yemen: A History of the Houthi Conflict*, (New York: Oxford University Press, 2017), 238.

7. Brandt, 238

8. Brandt, 238

9. International Crisis Group, "Yemen: Defusing the Saada Time Bomb," May 27, 2009, 22.

10. International Crisis Group, 22

11. Marieke Brandt, Tribes and Politics in Yemen: A History of the Houthi Conflict.

12. Brandt, 242

13. International Crisis Group, "Yemen: Defusing the Saada Time Bomb"

14. Bernd Kaussler, Tracing Qatar's Foreign Policy and Its Impact on Regional Security, (Doha: Arab Center for Research and Policy Studies, 2015), 25.

15. Kaussler, 25

16. Ginny Hill, and Gerd Nonneman, *Yemen, Saudi Arabia, and the Gulf States: Elite Politics, Street Protests and Regional diplomacy*, 18.

17. Author was present in the discussion.

18. Abdullah Baabood, Gulf Countries and Arab Transitions: Role, Support and Effects, (Barcelona: IEMed, 2014), 42.

19. Ginny Hill and Gerd Nonneman, *Yemen, Saudi Arabia, and the Gulf States: Elite Politics, Street Protests and Regional diplomacy*, 11.

20. Author's communication with Abubakr al-Qirbi

21. Author engagement.

22. Ginny Hill, Y*emen Endures: Civil War, Saudi Adventurism and the Future of Arabia*, (New York: Oxford University Press, 2017), 238.

23. Ginny Hill, Y*emen Endures: Civil War, Saudi Adventurism and the Future of Arabia*, 239.

24. Ginny Hill and Gerd Nonneman, *Yemen, Saudi Arabia, and the Gulf States: Elite Politics, Street Protests and Regional diplomacy,* 12.

25. Abdullah Baabood, Gulf Countries and Arab Transitions: Role, Support and Effects, 46.

26. Ali Khan Ghazanfar, "Friends of Yemen to Hold Crucial Meeting," *Arab News* (Riyadh), September 22, 2014.

27. Author participated in discussions.

28. Author participated in discussions, 14.

29. Abdullah Baabood, Gulf Countries and Arab Transitions: Role, Support and Effects, 46.

30. Ali Mahmood, "Aden's STC says Qatar is Giving Houthis Financial Support," *The National* (Abu Dhabi), July 23, 2018.

31. Habib Toumi, "Qatar Intelligence Officer Arresated Over al-Houthi Links," *Gulf News* (Dubai), May 3, 2018.

32. "Qatar Complains After Citizen Held in Yemen," *Reuters* (London), May 3, 2018.

33. ACRPS Policy Analysis Unit, The Crisis in Gulf Relations: Old Rivalries, New Ambitions, (Washington, DC.: Arab Center, 2017), 3.

34. Ayman Abulkareem, Oman Positions on the Regional Crises, (Baghdad: al-Bayan Center for Planning and Studies, 2017), 8.

35. Author attended the meeting.

36. Author attended the meeting, 6.

37. Author observation.

38. Neil Partrick, The UAE's War Aims in Yemen, (Washington, DC.: Carnegie Endowment for International Peace, 2017), 2.

39. Partrick, 2.

40. Abdulwahab Al-Qassab, Strategic Considerations of the UAE Role in Yemen, (Washington, DC.: The Arab Center, 2018), 2.

41. Al-Qassab, 2.

42. Elisabeth Kendall, *The Mobilization of Yemen's Eastern Tribes: al-Mahra's Self-Organization Model*, (Oxford: University of Oxford Press), 76.

43. Bernd Kaussler, Tracing Qatar's Foreign Policy and Its Impact on Regional Security, 26.

44. Ayman Abulkareem, Oman Positions on the Regional Crises, 9

PART II

International Stakes and
the GCC Dispute

CHAPTER 7

Diplomacy behind Washington's Quest to Solve the Row

S I G U R D   N E U B A U E R

Introduction

The Gulf crisis erupted when US Secretaries of State and Defense, Rex Tillerson and James Mattis were travelling in Australia. Catching the world mostly by surprise, from the outset Tillerson engaged the disputing parties as he sought to quell the crisis while it was still in its infancy. However, in light of what appeared to be Tillerson's diminishing personal rapport with President Trump, in addition to strained relationships with White House Chief Strategist Stephen K. Bannon and Senior White House Advisor Jared Kushner, Tillerson sought to reach the president via Mattis in order to prevent further escalations. Marking Tillerson's resolve was a fear of military invasion, which loomed large during the first days of the crisis.

During the early stages of the crisis, as the dispute played out on social media replete with accusations, smears and innuendo against Gulf ruling families, it was unclear what constituted the supposed demands that were being asked of Qatar. Adding to the already tense media environment in the Gulf, the public relations war between Doha and the blockading states traveled to Washington, contributing to the confusion of US policymakers about what the crisis was really about.

Amid this lingering uncertainty, US State Department spokeswoman Heather Nauert issued a blistering statement in mid-June, requesting clarity about what the blockading countries were specifically asking from Qatar. Nauert comments:

> We see this as long-simmering tensions that have been going on for quite some time, and that is why we believe that this can be resolved peacefully among the parties without the United States having to step in in some sort of formal mediation role, that they can do this on their own, and we're asking them to 'Let's move this along.'[14]

She added that Tillerson had held more than twenty phone calls and meetings with leaders from the Gulf and elsewhere. Three days later the Quartet presented its thirteen demands to Qatar, giving the nation a ten-day deadline to comply with the matter.[1]

1.1. U.S.-Qatar Memorandum of Understanding

As part of Washington's efforts to defuse the crisis, the first steps taken by Tillerson aimed to reduce the dispute from one centering on terrorism-related matters (including allegations that Doha was a relaxed environment for terrorism financing issues) to one that focused on the two sides' differing foreign policy priorities in the immediate aftermath of the post-Arab Spring environment. Washington believed narrowing the scope of the dispute would better facilitate Kuwait's intra-GCC mediation.

With this objective in mind, in early July Washington accelerated a Doha-requested process that had begun in February 2017 to strengthen cooperation between the US Transportation Security Administration (TSA) and Qatar Airways in order to help the latter build up its security capacity. Padding Qatar's counterterrorism resume, the bilateral Memorandm of Understanding (MoU) expanded beyond its initial mandate to address issues pertaining to airport and aviation security, extending the comprehensiveness of the MoU towards cooperation in battling terrorist extremism.

Since the signing of the MoU, Washington and Doha have been moving forward on Counterterrorism Financing (CTF) cooperation, an issue not unique to Doha but to varying degrees a challenge for each of the GCC countries, including Qatar's detractors. Washington's principal objective with the MoU was to ensure that Doha would be competent to carry out the agreement's technical aspects and prevent Qatari citizens from being tempted to join extremist organizations.

The concept of a bilateral MoU on CTF was conceived in Washington weeks after the crisis erupted as part of an effort to demonstrate the US government's serious concern about issues related to terrorist financing. From a US perspective, the crisis presented an opportunity to expand its CTF cooperation with Qatar by formalizing it within an MoU, while at the same time demonstrating to the other side of the Gulf dispute that it was concerned about the allegations leveled against Doha.

The fact that the comprehensive scope of the MoU had no observable impact on the Quartet's positioning towards Qatar demonstrates that the crisis likely was never solely about terrorist financing. Just three days after Trump publicly rebuked Qatar, UAE Ambassador to the US Yousuf Al-Otaiba published an op-ed in the Wall Street Journal in early June calling for the relocation of the US's Al-Udeid Air Base from Qatar to the UAE, having the unintended consequence of helping to inform Trump about the seriousness of the crisis. Due to Doha's growing fear of its neighbors, it is widely understood that if the United States withdraws from either Al-Udeid or from Camp As Sayliyah, a second military facility in the country, Qatar would invite Russia to establish a military presence in the country.

Despite his initial positionings, by early July President Trump had a fuller understanding of what was at stake. Luckily for Qatar, at this point in Trump's presidency both Bannon and Gorka had left the White House, allowing Tillerson and Mattis to evolve into the primary voices advising the president on the Gulf crisis. However, despite Tillerson's repeated efforts to carry out shuttle diplomacy between Kuwait City, Riyadh and Doha, when his efforts did not succeed, Trump became personally involved.

Trump's personal involvement suggests that the standoff between Washington's key Gulf partners is disrupting the US regional agenda, thus necessitating intervention. Responding in kind to Trump's personal involvement to help solve the crisis as well as Tillerson's first round of shuttle diplomacy, in mid-July the Quartet distilled its initial thirteen demands into the so-called "Six Principles."[2] Amid these developments, what is less understood is that while Tillerson sought to narrow differences between the Quartet and Qatar, Washington never played any role in seeking to bridge the thirteen demands or use them as a basis of negotiations between the parties. This was also the case for the so-called Six Principles. Nonetheless, the morphing of thirteen demands into Six Principles had a stabilizing impact on Qatar as the reduced demands–as a theoretical matter–could provide the opposing parties with face saving mechanisms for negotiation purposes.

The diplomatic transformation of the thirteen demands to the Six Principles was directly attributed to Kuwait's mediating role within the crisis. Below are some brief statistics, outlining the extent to which Kuwait acted as a mediator amidst the crisis:

- Between June 5th and July 21st, Qatar had engaged with Kuwait twenty-three times.
- Saudi Arabia had engaged with Kuwait thirteen times.
- UAE had engaged with Kuwait seven times.
- Bahrain had engaged with Kuwait five times.
- Emir of Qatar, along with his foreign minister, met with the Kuwaiti Emir six times.
- King Salman of Saudi Arabia met with the Kuwaiti Emir twice.
- UAE's de-facto ruler MBZ met with the Kuwaiti Emir once.

For Qatar specifically, between June 5th and July 21st official meetings with Kuwait occurred on average twice a month, a figure that does not include the dozens of phone calls that occurred between the Qatari Emir, his foreign and defense ministers, and their Kuwaiti counterparts.

In late July, two days after the Quartet filtered its demands into the Six Principles, Emir Tamim delivered his first address to the Qatari nation since the crises had erupted. The Emir articulated his view that Qatar had been targeted by an unprecedented media smear campaign containing innuendo and fake news. He went on to express the high value he held for Kuwait's mediation and the support of the United States, Turkey and Germany in their efforts to resolve the crisis. The emir's speech became a turning point during the crisis, as it marked a consolidation of support amongst the people of Qatar.

Factors including the emir's unifying response to allegations leveled against the country, the distaste with how the oppositional media portrayed the nation and the royal family and the highly unpopular expulsion of Qatari citizens from Bahrain, UAE, and Saudi Arabia each motivated the Qatari population to close ranks behind their Emir. This amassing of support became even more vital given the Quartet's promotion of largely ahistorical Qatari royal lineages that led to "alternative emirs," in an attempt to threaten the legitimacy of the Al-Thani family's rule.

The emir's speech set the stage for Qatar's diplomatic engagement with its blockaders, where he articulated that Doha was open for dialogue with the blockading countries with the expected caveat that he would not allow the four nations to infringe upon Qatar's sovereignty. Perhaps addressing some of the Six Principles, the emir espoused his commitment that Qatar would "fight terrorism relentlessly without compromise" and reform its economy and public policy.

The emir's commitment to non-interference in the affairs of other Arab states can be read as an olive branch to the Quartet. In proclaiming as much, Qatar sought to dispel allegations that Doha had been meddling in their affairs, a key accusation of the original thirteen demands. Rejecting this accusation, the emir declared "Qatar does not try to impose its opinion on anyone."[3]

Arguably an additional olive branch, the Qatari emir appeared to acknowledge Qatar's past mistakes when he stated, "We are not afraid of identifying and correcting our error," alluding to an earlier fallout between Doha and some of its neighbors due to its foreign policy in the immediate aftermath of the Arab Spring.

Alternatively, the emir's speech and his acknowledgment of past "mistakes" in particular can be read as a token of appreciation for the Kuwaiti Emir's mediation efforts, allowing the Emir to give the embargoing states a tangible concession intended to grant Kuwait the leverage it needs in future mediations.

2.1. Impasse

Perhaps due to a perceived lack of sincerity, Qatar's so-called olive branches have done little to quell the crisis. The threat of an apparent escalation in August 2017 emerged when Saudi Arabia's Al Arabiya channel launched a simulation video depicting the shooting down of a Qatar Airways jet. Even when only simulated, such a threat was a red line for Washington and helped contribute to Trump's quest to accelerate the GCC reconciliation process.[4]

In early September, Trump hosted the Kuwaiti emir at the White House where he publicly–and unequivocally–reiterated Washington's support for GCC reconciliation through Kuwaiti mediation. From that point on, Trump has consistently called for an end to the dispute, while at the same time praising the U.S relationship with countries on all sides of the dispute.

Two days after the Trump-Sabah meeting, the former brokered a telephone call between Emir Tamim and Saudi Deputy Crown Prince Muhammad bin Salman al-Saud. The détente generated by the Trump-initiated phone call between Qatar and Saudi Arabia lasted for about an hour before it collapsed over the interpretation of a Qatari statement which gave Doha credit for the call, a position Riyadh undoubtedly found incorrect or incomplete. However, given that only a few days before the call the Quartet was believed to have been actively seeking regime change in Qatar, that the two sides were in direct communication was a welcome development. Also impeding the success of the call was an apparent disdain from the UAE, feeling that it had been skipped over in the resolution that had been formed.

In late September, President Trump and Emir Tamim met at the sidelines of the United Nations General Assembly (UNGA) in New York. While the two are believed to have discussed President Trump's proposed US-GCC Camp David Summit, the impetus for the impromptu encounter came after Saudi Arabia had threatened to bring Sheikh Abdullah Bin Ali Al-Thani (an obscure member of the Qatari royal family whom the Saudis were actively promoting as an "alternate emir" for Qatar) to join MbS at the UNGA. In spite of these threats, MbS was ultimately hesitant to make such a bold move, as the newly appointed Crown Prince had yet to leave

Saudi Arabia and was still in the midst of consolidating power domestically. In the end, Saudi Foreign Minister Adel Al-Jubair represented Saudi Arabia after the Trump-Tamim meeting signaled to the Riyadh that Washington would not tolerate any efforts to bring about regime change in Doha.

In a disputed correlation between the emerging relationship between President Trump and Emir Tamim, Saudi Arabia and UAE applied direct pressure on Bahrain to re-open territorial dispute claims with Qatar, despite such matters having been resolved in 2003.

Following the U.S. invasion of Iraq in 2003, and after the regime of Saddam Hussein had collapsed, Qatar and Bahrain negotiated a settlement to this long-standing territorial dispute. The diplomatic breakthrough was partially attributed to the fall of Saddam Hussein's regime, as he had been a supporter of Qatar amidst attempted coup d'état against Emir Hamad bin Khalifa Al Thani, that had been initiated by Bahrain, UAE and Saudi Arabia in 1996.

3.1. Military Isolation

In parallel with US and Kuwaiti diplomatic efforts to solve the crisis, the Quartet has attempted to isolate Qatar from various military exercises, with Washington pushing back against these measures as part of an effort to signal neutrality within the crisis. As part of that effort, Defense Secretary Mattis made an unannounced visit to Doha on September 28 where he met with Emir Tamim and his Qatari Defense counterpart at the Al-Udaid airbase.

Following his visit, the Associated Press reported on October 6 that the US military had halted some exercises with its Gulf partners due to the diplomatic crisis, specifically pausing an ongoing US-UAE exercise entitled "Iron Union 5."[5] It is also expected that the cutback will impact the annual Eagle Resolve Exercise in which the US and its GCC partners had traditionally worked together as a multinational force in a simulated battle. Washington's decision to cancel the joint exercises came as the parties had failed to respond to Tillerson's diplomatic initiatives (and to Trump's respective statements in particular) to negotiate an end to the crisis.

By scaling back military exercises with its Gulf partners, Washington signaled that it can- and is willing- to deliver tangible pressure on the various parties to bring an end to the standoff. If the opposing parties fail to engage in de-escalatory measures, it is conceivable that US intelligence and military cooperation with Saudi Arabia and the UAE on Yemen could be reduced next. Such a move would be considered an incremental escalation by Washington and could run in parallel with the suspension of future exercises.

Washington's clear message may also be the primary reason as to why Qatar was permitted to participate in the US-GCC multilateral Gulf Shield exercise, which took place from late March to early April in the eastern Saudi town of Ras Al Khair, north of Jubail.

A number of officers from the Qatari Armed Forces, led by Brigadier General Khamis Mohamed Deblan, participated in the exercise, along with land, sea and air forces from 25 other countries. The exercise featured a number of stages, including a command centers drill and field training. It concluded with the exercising of regular and non-regular fire with live ammunition, in addition to a military parade.[6]

4.1. GCC Summit in Kuwait

On the eve of the December 2017 GCC Summit in Kuwait, it was far from certain who among the respective monarchs would attend as only Emir Tamim had confirmed his presence. There were speculations until the last moment that Emir Sabah would not have pushed ahead with the summit without tacit approval from King Salman of Saudi Arabia, who was expected to arrive. At the time, it was well-understood that MbS would still refrain from foreign travel because of the Kingdom's precarious domestic stability. While Bahrain's king, Hamad bin Isa Al Khalifa, had declared in October that he would not attend the summit if Qatar was invited, his son, Crown Prince Salman, was believed to be attending the summit in his father's place.

As it pertains to the UAE, it was unclear who would attend. A consensus in Washington had emerged in early September—after the Tamim-MbS call—that it was UAE's Mohammed bin Zayed (MbZ) who is driving the crisis due to a grudge held over Qatar's past support for regional Islamist groups. It was therefore unlikely that MbZ would attend, with Dubai ruler Mohammed bin Rashid Al Maktoum expected to appear in his stead. From Oman, Sultan Qaboos Al-Said was represented by Deputy Prime Minister Fahd bin Mahmoud Al-Said. However, this move was unsurprising as he has represented the Omani ruler at GCC Summits and various other international fora for decades.

Going into the summit, it was clear that its success would hinge on the Saudi king's participation as neither Bahraini or Emirati heads of state hesitated to snub the summit by sending lower -ranking officials in their stead. During the planning stage, it was unclear whether the foreign ministers from the six GCC countries would even arrive to assist in preparing the summit's agenda. In the end, Bahrain, UAE, and Saudi each rebuffed the summit by dispatching lower ranking officials.

What was not publicly understood before the summit, however, was that the GCC crisis was never even to appear on the agenda. While the uninformed may have been looking to the summit as a platform for mediation, in order to simply reach an agreement about holding the conference in the first place Kuwait pledged to the holdouts that the ongoing crisis would not have appeared on the agenda.

The decisions of King Salman, along with the heads of state of Bahrain and the UAE, to skip the summit were apparently made at the last minute. Given that the meetings would likely have been broadcast live on GCC state television, there was a shared concern that Emir Sheikh Tamim would use the public platform to grandstand against his fellow monarchs. This, along with an apparent desire not to have the crisis between the leaders spill into the public, or to negotiate in public through competing state media outlets, were also likely factors influencing the decisions of the three abstaining rulers.[7]

Although his efforts failed, Kuwait's emir nonetheless sought to address the concerns by assuring the monarchs of Bahrain, the UAE, and Saudi Arabia that Emir Tamim would not use the occasion for a public pronouncement on the crisis. In the end, those assurances apparently were not enough to convince the three to attend.

It is unclear whether the discussions of what Emir Tamim might say in a public forum—or whether he would issue an official apology, as had been suggested by Saudi state media—led to the collapse of the talks during a GCC foreign ministers meeting held the day before the summit. Uncertainty over what to expect from Emir Tamim, coupled with renewed demands for Doha to sever diplomatic relations with Iran in exchange for resolving the crisis could help explain why Qatar's Foreign Minister Al-Thani chose not to attend a pre-scheduled luncheon with his Saudi and Omani counterparts and instead returned to Doha to brief Emir Tamim on the talks.

Another sticking point was that the Bahrain, Saudi Arabia, and the UAE insisted at the time that Egypt should also be part of the reconciliation process, despite the North African state not being a GCC member. Washington quickly rejected this stance, emphasizing that the United States wants the Gulf nations to resolve the standoff themselves.

During the immediate aftermath of the GCC Summit, Washington and Doha began preparations for the first US-Qatar Strategic Dialogue, built on the success of the 2016 US-Qatar Economic Dialogue, to take place on January 30 in Washington.

Qatar had sought to expand the Economic Dialogue months before the Gulf standoff commended and formally requested a bilateral Strategic Dialogue. However, the crisis coupled with the GCC's inability to solve the matter, Washington sought to frame the Strategic Dialogue as part of an effort to signal its commitment that the US-Qatar strategic partnership would not be influenced by the regional infighting amongst Washington's Arabian allies.

5.1. U.S.-Qatar Strategic Dialogue
The opening session of the US-Qatar Strategic Dialogue was jointly co-chaired by U.S. Secretary Tillerson and Secretary Mattis alongside Qatari Deputy Prime Minister and Minister of State for

Defense Khalid al-Attiyah and Qatari Deputy Prime Minister and Foreign Minister Mohammed bin Abdulrahman Al Thani.

During the Dialogue, the two countries signed four MoUs to enhance political cooperation, bolster defense, cooperate in counterterrorism, and increase trade and investment.

5.2. Political Cooperation

While the MoU on Political Cooperation was formally meant to signal to the blockading countries the US's support for each nation's sovereignty, it also reflected a broader reality—namely, that the bilateral US-Qatar relationship had strengthened throughout the crisis, including an increase in the personal rapport between Emir Tamim and President Trump. For instance, between July 2017 and the beginning of the Strategic Dialogue, President Trump and Emir Tamim held three phone calls, all of which focused on GCC reconciliation and appreciation for Qatar's counterterrorism policies.

Between July 2, 2017 and September 8, 2017, President Trump spoke separately with King Salman bin Abulaziz Al-Saud of Saudi Arabia, Crown Prince Muhammad bin Zayed Al-Nahyan of Abu Dhabi and Emir Tamim bin Hamad Al-Thani of Qatar imploring all three leaders to resolve the crisis.[8] On January 15, 2018 Trump called Tamim and reiterated his call for GCC unity. He also "thanked the Emir for Qatari action to counter terrorism and extremism in all forms."[9]

5.3. Defense Cooperation

The US-Qatar Defense Cooperation MoU reiterated Washington's support for Doha's sovereignty, while praising the emirate for expanding the Al-Udaid Air Base. "Qatari funding of capital expenditures and sustainment offers the possibility of an enduring presence, as with U.S. facilities in Europe and the Pacific. The two governments acknowledged the strong and lasting bilateral security partnership, and look forward to further discussions on the possibility of permanent basing," the US State Department said.

Washington's pronounced support for Al-Udaid was directly attributed to efforts by the UAE, its US representatives and various US pressure groups to wrest Al-Udaid away from Qatar during the peak of the Gulf crisis proxy war in Washington. The joint MoU on Counter Terrorism announced during the Dialogue sought to reconfirm the commitments from both countries as outlined in the initial MoU on Counter Terrorism signed in July of 2017.

5.4. Trade and Investment

Finally, the MoU on Trade and Investment builds on the initial US-Qatar Economic Dialogue of 2016, but includes expanded Qatari investments in the US, including the Qatar Investment Authority's previously committed investment of $45 billion in American firms, real estate, and jobs.

During the planning process of the dialogue, Secretaries Mnuchin and Perry traveled to Doha amidst Tillerson and Mattis' repeated engagements. Additionally, more U.S. cabinet secretaries traveled to Doha during the second half of 2017 then during the past several years combined. Also (Ret.) Anthony Zinni conducted additional shuttle diplomacy between Washington and the various Gulf capitals.

Altogether, the dialogue presents Doha with a diplomatic victory, effectively demonstrating that regardless of the veracity of the accusations leveled against it the embattled nation would work to either prove such accusations as false or take steps to address those that had some level of validity. Additionally, such US-GCC cooperation signals more broadly that Washington sees stability in the Gulf as a key national security interest.

The US-Qatar Strategic Dialogue is scheduled to become an annual event, but it is unclear for now whether hosting duties will alternate between Washington and Doha. A month after the inaugural dialogue, in late February 2018 Trump and Tamim discussed regional developments, including how to solve the crisis and deal with Iran.[10] The planning for Tamim's upcoming White House visit– and his second meeting with Trump– began.

These efforts came to fruition in early April when Trump hosted Tamim at the White House. During the meeting he praised the Qatari leader and announced that the US-Qatar relationship "works extremely well."[11] Washington, however, announced the following month that the proposed US-GCC Summit would be postponed until the fall, stopping short of attributing the delay to any party to the dispute.

Since then, the US-Qatar bilateral relationship appears to have slowed somewhat, although advisor to the president Jared Kushner visited Doha on June 25, 2015 to discuss Trump's peace plan. At Washington's request, Qatar has increased its cooperation with Israel on Gaza reconstruction efforts, which is consistent with its long-standing commitment to the Palestinian cause and is also meant to help Trump with advancing his peace plan.[12] In parallel with these efforts, Washington has sought to mediate between Saudi Arabia and Qatar regarding the Muslim hajj pilgrimage in order to ensure that the pilgrimage to Mecca does not become a politicized issue.

Conclusion

In light of these dynamics and coupled with a lingering uncertainty over the White House's official position, Doha's engagement with Washington during the initial phase of the crisis was spearheaded by a Qatari trifecta including Emir Tamim, Foreign Minister Al-Thani and Minister of State for Defense Al-Attiyah, each of whom led engagements with Tillerson and Mattis. Qatar also tapped its network of institutional relationships with the US Departments of Defense and State that he two nations had built over the decades since Qatari independence from Britain in 1971. Given that the early Trump White House was staffed by political outsiders and non-experts, including senior staffers Bannon and Sebastian Gorka– believed to have held negative views toward Qatar prior to joining the administration– connections with the career public servants at the departments of State and Defense became especially important.In parallel with these efforts, Kuwait (with the full backing of Washington) began its mediation attempts immediately after the crisis' onset. Emir Sabah Al-Ahmad Al-Jaber Al-Sabah of Kuwait acquired previous mediating experience during 2014 Gulf crisis, making him an obvious candidate to reassume the role.

What is less understood, however, is whether the proposed U.S.-GCC Summit scheduled for December 2018 will serve as an effective follow-up to last year's Riyadh Summit.

Once the Summit takes place, it will focus on regional issues, including economics, Iran, Syria, Yemen, Iraq and post-ISIS stabilization efforts, and not on the Gulf crisis perse. If the Gulf crisis is added to the agenda, it will only be on the sidelines because Washington has from the outset considered the various demands imposed on Qatar— whether the 13 Demands or the Six Principles—as illegitimate and the blockade of Qatar as a violation of international law.

Because the demands imposed on Doha are viewed in Washington as illegitimate, the US, since the crisis erupted, has sought to balance between protecting Qatar's sovereignty and preserving the long-term stability of Saudi Arabia during Crown Prince Muhammad Bin Salman's tumultuous rise to power, which explains why it continues to support Kuwait's mediation role.

Furthermore, Kuwaiti shuttle diplomacy—with active U.S. diplomatic support—is expected to continue as part of an effort to settle all differences between Qatar and the Quartet ahead of the US-GCC Summit.

It is also well-understood that the exact differences between the disputing parties will be hammered out prior to the proposed US-GCC Summit. In his repeated statements calling for GCC reconciliation, current U.S. Secretary of State Mike Pompeo has, "Emphasized the President's desire to see the Gulf dispute eased and eventually resolved, as it only benefits Iran." [13]

In practical terms, Pompeo's emphasis on "eased" can be interpreted as a U.S. call for the Quartet to lift the air, land and sea blockade imposed upon Qatar, a Qatari stipulation if the nation is to be convinced to begin serious talks with the blockaders concerning the nations' political differences. Furthermore, Kuwaiti shuttle diplomacy— with active U.S. diplomatic support— is expected to continue as part of an effort to settle all differences between Qatar and the Quartet ahead of the US-GCC Summit.

Fundamental to the crisis' evolution is an awareness that any conflict resolution must be accompanied by a newly constructed institutional infrastructure, most likely based on the 2014 principles in order to assure that such a crisis never again occurs.

According to CNN, which obtained leaked copies of the 2014 agreements,

The first agreement—handwritten and dated November 23, 2013—is signed by the King of Saudi Arabia, the Emir of Qatar and the Emir of Kuwait. It lays out commitments to avoid any interference in the internal affairs of other Gulf nations, including barring financial or political support to 'deviant' groups, a term used to describe anti-government activism The agreement, referred to as the Riyadh agreement, specifically mentions not supporting the Muslim Brotherhood, which the Gulf allies have repeatedly alleged of Qatar, as well as not backing opposition groups in Yemen that could threaten neighboring countries.[14]

A second agreement headlined as "top secret" and dated November 16, 2014, includes the King of Bahrain, the Crown Prince of Abu Dhabi and the Prime Minister of the UAE.[15] It specifically mentions the signatories' commitment to support Egypt's stability, including preventing Al Jazeera from being used as a platform for groups or figures challenging the Egyptian government. The second agreement specifically mentions Al Jazeera, tellingly excluding outlets such as the Saudi-owned Al Arabiya. After the agreement was signed, Al Jazeera had shut down, Aljazeera Mubashir Misr, an affiliate channel dedicated to covering Egypt.

A supplemental document to the 2013 agreement signed by the countries' foreign ministers discusses implementation of the agreement. It includes provisions barring support of the Muslim Brotherhood, as well as outside groups in Yemen and Saudi Arabia that pose a threat to security and stability of Gulf Cooperation Council as a whole.

Whether or not Washington will have to become a guarantor for a future Gulf truce remains to be seen. What is clear, however, is that any solution to the crisis is bound to impact Gulf dynamics for decades to come given that Crown Prince MbS of Saudi Arabia (32), Emir Tamim (37) and UAE's Crown Prince of Abu Dhabi and de-facto ruler Mohammed bin Zayed bin Sultan Al-Nahyan (56) are all young.

Unless the core issues of this crisis are dealt with accordingly – which center on the role of political Islam, political participation, and competing visions for a regional security architectural framework – tensions between Abu Dhabi and Doha in particular could once again trigger further hostilities.

Endnotes

1. Patrick Wintour, "Qatar given 10 days to meet 13 sweeping demands by Saudi Arabia," *The Guardian*, 23 June 2017.

2. Taimur Khan, "Arab countries' six principles for Qatar 'a measure to restart the negotiation process,'" *The National (UAE)*, July 19, 2017.

3. "Sheikh Tamim: Any talks must respect Qatar sovereignty," *Al Jazeera*, September, 22, 2018.

4. Alex Macheras, "Saudi News Channel Shows Simulated Downing of a Civilian Jet," *ThePointsGuy*, August 15, 2017.

5. Jon Gambrell, "US military halts exercises over Qatar crisis," *The Associated Press*, October 6, 2018.

6. "Qatari forces participate in Gulf shield drill in Saudi Arabia," *Al Jazeera*, April 19, 2018.

7. Sigurd Neubauer, "View: Despite Gulf Crisis over Qatar, GCC Pushes Ahead," *The Cipher Brief*, December 15, 2017.

8. "Readout of President Donald J. Trump's Calls with Gulf State Leaders," *The White House*, July 2, 2017.

9. "Readout of President Donald J. Trump's Call with Emir Tamim bin Hamad Al Thani of Qatar," *The White House*, January 15, 2018.

10. "Readout of President Donald J. Trump's Call with Emir Tamim bin Hamad Al Thani of Qatar," *The White House*, February 28, 2018.

11. "Trump: US-Qatar ties 'work extremely well,'" *Al Jazeera*, April 11, 2018.

12. Sigurd Neubauer, "Washington's Interest in Qatari-Israeli Relations," *International Policy Digest*, July, 17, 2018.

13. "Secretary Pompeo's Meeting With Qatari Foreign Minister Al Thani," *U.S. State Department*, July 26, 2018.

14. Jim Sciutto and Jeremy Herb, "Exclusive: The secret documents that help explain the Qatar crisis," *CNN*, July 11, 2017.

15. Gardiner Harris, "State Dept. Lashes Out at Gulf Countries Over Qatar Embargo," *The New York Times*, 20 June 2017.

CHAPTER 8

Exploring European and Russian Perspectives of the Gulf Crisis

COURTNEY FREER

Introduction

While a variety of public statements distributed in media outlets and through public relations campaigns have made the stances of the two opposing sides of the Gulf crisis abundantly clear, the positions taken by countries peripheral to the Middle East are much less self-evident. With strong alliances on both sides of the rift, countries of the European Union (including the UK at the time of writing) and Russia have struggled to react in a way that dually preserves critical interests on each side of the crisis and encourages swift mediation between all parties involved. In what follows, we break down by individual actor the countries most invested, and therefore most influential, in calculating and reacting to the Gulf crisis and the Quartet's efforts to isolate Qatar.

1.1. Europe
1.2. The European Union

As a whole, the European Union (like most of the international community) has repeatedly expressed strong support for Kuwaiti-led efforts to mediate the crisis. Europe's distrust in the Trump administration, along with its confidence in Kuwait's ability to understand and balance its neighbors' interests have fueled these efforts, particularly in light of Kuwait having effectively mediated a similar row in 2014.[1] Additionally, by finding a solution within the GCC, the EU hopes to prevent further internationalization of the conflict. However, aside from their rhetorical support for Kuwaiti efforts, little else has been expressed through official EU channels.

In May 2018, the EU reiterated the importance of resolving the GCC crisis and, to that end, is considering a new counterterrorism support package for the GCC countries.[2] The Head of the EU Delegation to Saudi Arabia, Bahrain, Kuwait, Oman, and Qatar, Michele Cervone d'Urso, told reporters that members of his office are engaging with Kuwait in particular to resolve the crisis.[3] He also suggested that "what is lacking is the political commitment," while insisting that "the GCC is very important."[4] On June 21 2018, just after the one-year anniversary of the crisis' onset, the European Parliament (EP) reaffirmed its support for Kuwaiti-led efforts to resolve the Gulf rift. In the words of David McAllister, Chair of the EP's Foreign Affairs Committee,

> [T]he European Union has good relations with all countries in the Gulf Cooperation Council including Qatar .... We support Kuwaiti mediation efforts in the Gulf crisis as GCC cohesion is critical to fostering cooperation and stability. We believe de-escalation is vital for regional stability. The crisis should be an opportunity for the GCC to emerge stronger.[5]

The EU certainly has major economic interests on both sides of the crisis. This conflict of interest has made it difficult for the organization as a whole to back a particular side, a tension unlikely to diminish in the future. In 2016, the total trade in EU-GCC goods amounted to $158.41 billion, with $115.2 billion exported from the EU to the Gulf, demonstrating how substantial the trade relationship is for European export markets.[6] Interestingly, in the past, some of the European exports that reached Qatar by way of Saudi Arabia have been lost since the crisis began in June 2017.[7]

In 2017, the EU, if counted as a single economy, was the largest trading partner of the GCC, with two-way trade amounting to over $163 billion in 2017.[8] The GCC is the EU's sixth-most important trading destination and fourth-most important export market, with exports and trade steadily growing fifty-four percent between 2007 and 2017.[9] After the global financial crisis of 2008, European economic ties to Gulf states became even more important, particularly as sovereign wealth funds (SWFs) in the region provided a welcome source of liquidity.

Gulf economies on both sides of the rift have been important for European trade. While the EU imported $5.8 billion from Qatar in 2016 and exported $10.75 billion, its export-import balance from Saudi Arabia amounted to a staggering $38 billion and $21.3 billion respectively.[10] It is important to keep in mind the structure of this trade, as Qatar's natural gas supply is particularly significant for increasingly reliant European markets. Demand for natural gas is set to increase in Europe: in 2015, it accounted for twenty-two percent of Europe's energy mix, a figure expected to reach twenty-eight percent by 2035.[11] The EU is more likely to turn to Qatar than Russia for its supply needs, especially as Europe's own resources diminish. In fact, in 2015 and 2016, Qatar was the largest exporter of liquefied natural gas (LNG) to Europe as well as the fourth largest natural gas provider in 2015, with a ten percent market share.[12] Among EU countries, the United Kingdom, Belgium, Spain, and Poland have each signed contracts with Qatar to import its LNG.[13] In terms of import share, Europe ranks second among Qatar's LNG customers.[14] In spite of the blockade, this trade has continued, with Egypt even allowing Qatar access to the Suez Canal despite their break in relations.

Beyond economics, the EU sees the GCC crisis as fundamentally threatening to its political interests in the Middle East. Indeed, after a meeting with Qatari Foreign Minister Sheikh Mohammed bin Abdulrahman al-Thani in June 2017, EU High Representative Federica Mogherini stated, "We see a clear risk of the situation escalating further and spreading in an unpleasant and dangerous manner beyond the region of the Gulf, be it in Africa, or in Southeast Asia or in the Middle East."[15] Further, the GCC states have worked alongside EU partners through the "Friends of Syria Group" and have been involved to varying degrees in efforts to contain the Iranian nuclear threat.

Unlike policies such as the European Neighborhood Policy or the Union of the Mediterranean, in which the EU has outlined collective policies towards extra-European regions, the body does not have a similarly specific regional policy towards the GCC. This lack of shared guidance makes it difficult for the union to agree on a unified approach.[16] As Christian Koch put it in a 2014 piece,

> The EU has always struggled to come up with a comprehensive structured approach towards the Middle East region as a whole, with the Gulf region most of the time finding itself being left out of direct EU policy instruments. Instead, relations are almost exclusively structured through the Cooperation Agreement signed between the two sides in 1988 with a focus on trade, overall economic relations, energy, investment promotion and technology.[17]

Although economic interests between the EU and GCC states are wide and varied, little exists in terms of institutional structure to encourage multilateralism in the relations between these states. Indeed, the most important talks aiming to better structure relations between the two regional bodies emerged in 1988 as the "Cooperation Agreement with the European Economic Community." The agreement, as Koch describes, created a joint council to meet annually and "was a fairly general document providing the institutional framework to 'promote overall co-operation between equal partners on mutually advantageous terms in all spheres between the two regions and further their economic development, taking into consideration the differences in development of the parties.'"[18] The accord therefore had both economic and political goals, including the sparking of trade and investment exchanges, the maintenance of the Gulf as an important supplier of hydrocarbons and a significant export market, in addition to working toward regional stability and security. Still, the deal's economic aspects have remained the focus of much discussion with particular effort having been put into developing an EU-GCC Free Trade Agreement (FTA), a project that has yet to materialize. The lack of progress on the latter agreement has arguably also hindered the enhancement of joint political cooperation in other domains, including in counterterrorism cooperation.[19]

FTA talks began in 1990, but only became realistic in 2003 when the GCC became a customs union, leading to accelerated talks four years later. Ultimately, the GCC halted formal negotiations in December 2008. Koch speculates that two reasons explain the failure to make progress on any type of FTA. First, there is the simple reality that the EU's petrochemical lobby opposed trade liberalization. Second, irregular human rights and migration clauses within the FTA—necessary in EU contracts with foreign countries—were seen as an attempt to interfere in domestic issues and were therefore rejected by the GCC states.[20] As Koch explains,

> The EU's view is that to some extent, the GCC countries' apparent aversion to the human rights clause disguises a more deep-rooted opposition to genuine liberalization–including in the services and investment sectors–and to the reduction of subsidies in their economies.[21]

The year 2003, which saw both the Iraq war as well as the GCC's implementation of its internal customs union, was arguably a turning point in EU-GCC economic and security cooperation. New regional dynamics also led the EU to create the "EU Strategic Partnership with the Mediterranean and the Middle East" in June 2004, which in actuality did not differ substantially from the recommendations put forward in 1995.[22] As noted above, Gulf SWFs became "an important source of liquidity" for European states during the 2009-2010 recession, with about one-third of emergency funding to European banks coming from the large GCC-based SWFs.[23]

A report issued by the European Parliament in March 2011 confirmed the new centrality of relations with the GCC, stating that "the Gulf region has to be seen today in terms of the emergence of a new global economic hub comprising the member states of the GCC" and that "the GCC member states play a key role in the global arena and thus have interests in common with the EU in relation to international stability and global economic governance."[24] Further, it dubbed the GCC "the only stable regional organization based on multilateralism and cooperation," in the Middle East, thus necessitating that "the EU...take a clear stand and maintain a lasting commitment in the Gulf region, thus guaranteeing itself greater visibility and a strategic presence in the area."[25] Ultimately, the EU failed to foster long-term cooperation with the GCC, making no progress on the FTA since 2008. A European Commission Delegation office was opened in Riyadh in 2004, with an announcement in 2013 that a second representative office would be opened in Abu Dhabi that year. Since then, no further delegations have been opened.[26] Perhaps reflecting current realities, the European Commission's more recent report on the Gulf highlights trade and investment almost exclusively–much of which is done bilaterally rather than with the GCC as a unit.

Indeed, Koch identifies the strength of bilateral ties between member states as hindering multilateralism between the EU and GCC.[27] Because decision-making in the GCC is largely done at the state level, bilateral agreements are often easier to forge than multilateral trade agreements. Rivalries among the individual states also come into play, not solely in the GCC but also in the EU. In 2010, progress appeared likely, with the EU and GCC agreeing on a Joint Action Program for 2010-2013. This program was meant to be followed by a document in 2014 that developed cooperation in fields such as higher education, trade, culture, and scientific research, yet such a document never emerged.[28] Further, because the EU's centrality to Gulf security is dwarfed by that of the United States, arranging a common policy for cooperation beyond economics is even more difficult.

The emergence of Iran has also undoubtedly colored GCC-EU relations over the past two years. The Joint Comprehensive Plan of Action (JCPOA), which came into force in 2016, was a watershed moment for EU-Iranian relations, especially considering the crucial involvement of European P5+1 actors (France, Germany, and the United Kingdom) that approved the deal. Following the imposition of the JCPOA, overall Iranian exports to the EU have increased 344.8%, while in the same time period EU exports have risen twenty-seven percent.[29] Further, European companies have made lucrative agreements in Iran, lending to the deal's importance on a bilateral level. These relationships, though they have undoubtedly become stronger, remain primarily limited to the economic rather than the political realm due to the general lack of trust among parties.[30] Regardless, engagement with Iran is more problematic for some European capitals than for others, leading to a variety of stances in lieu of a common EU position.[31]

Overall, we have seen what Koch dubs "quantitative," but not qualitative, improvement in EU-GCC ties, with much of the relationship being oriented around economics.[32] Indeed, although commonalities exist in terms of energy security, counterterrorism, and the desire for Israeli-Palestinian peace, exactly how to best contain Iran remains a major difference. Further, despite sharing many of the same concerns, the EU can by no means be seen as homogenous due to each member state having a distinct set of national interests. Below we consider the interests of three key EU actors in the GCC crisis: France, Germany, and the United Kingdom.

1.3. France: Seeking to Become a Mediator?

From the beginning, French leadership has been vocal in its concerns about the GCC crisis, with President Emmanuel Macron looking eager to solidify a place for France in Middle Eastern regional affairs. Indeed, following the outbreak of the GCC crisis, within the first forty-eight hours Macron flew to Morocco for discussions, urging GCC officials to quickly reconcile.[33] On June sixth, he spoke over the phone with the Qatari emir and the Turkish president, stressing the importance of finding a solution to the tensions. These were followed by similar talks with the Saudi king and Iranian president two days later.[34]

Macron's election in May 2017, less than a month before the start of the crisis, was helpful for the Gulf states, as he has shown himself interested in preserving the relationships with Saudi Arabia and Qatar that had been strengthened by his predecessor, President Nicholas Sarkozy. The relief felt by the GCC at Macron's election was made even more palpable by the risks presented by his challenger, far-right candidate Marine Le Pen.[35] Macron also appears more aligned with the GCC on Syria, having supported American airstrikes in the country in April 2017. Additionally,

Macron has demanded further international military intervention within a "diplomatic and political roadmap."[36] Macron also has stated that "the Syrian people have an enemy: Bashar al-Assad."[37] Still, tensions with Saudi Arabia in particular are likely to remain, due to France's commitment to the JCPOA.

As a whole, under Macron, it seems that "France is seeking to position itself as an indispensable mediator for all states in the Gulf, including Iran, as well as a bridge between Iran on one side and the US and Israel on the other."[38] France can also seek to fill a vacuum left by a Trump administration that has sent mixed signals on the crisis from the beginning. To this end, the French administration is also keen to maintain ties with Iran, with French oil giant Total having signed on for a $5 billion gas project in the country in late 2016.[39] In May 2018, Total announced that this project would be halted due to the new American sanctions on Iran expected in light of the US's announced withdrawal from the JCPOA.[40]

When it comes to the GCC crisis, the French message has consistently been that a solution must be found. French Foreign Minister Jean-Yves Le Drian in July 2017, during a trip to the Gulf, urged the Saudi/UAE-led coalition to end its blockade of Qatar: "France is calling for these measures to be lifted, especially ones that affect the [Qatari] population, specifically measures that impact bi-national families that have been separated."[41] He added that Paris hopes to serve as "a facilitator in the mediation" led by Kuwait.[42] In September 2017, the French foreign ministry chose former Ambassador to Saudi Arabia Bertrand Besancenot to serve as special envoy on the Gulf crisis to provide more focused French support.[43] In February 2018, he claimed that there were signs the crisis was reaching an end, highlighting Qatari efforts in particular to demonstrate their willingness to fight terrorism and to participate in dialogue. Even with this, no major developments have publicly emerged.[44]

France became unexpectedly central in the Gulf crisis due to developments between Lebanon and Saudi Arabia. The French President made an impromptu trip to Riyadh at which time Lebanese Prime Minister Saad Hariri, who citing concerns for his life, announced his resignation and accepted Macron's invitation to Paris.[45] Upon returning to Beirut after spending three days in the French capital, Hariri announced a revocation of his resignation, returning to his country for coalition talks in order to alienate Hezbollah from government.[46] Though France and Lebanon enjoy strong historic ties, the French government's decision to become involved in the Lebanese saga was surprising. Ultimately, this French intervention aided the Hariri government and diffused speculation from Lebanon that the Prime Minister was being held in Riyadh against his will. Macron thus helped to mediate between Lebanon, Iran, and Saudi Arabia at a time when the traditional hegemon, the United States, lacks ambassadors in both Beirut and Riyadh.[47]

Despite this greater French involvement in the Middle East, Macron still appears unwilling to choose sides when it comes to the GCC crisis. In a press conference in November, he stated that France intended to avoid "interfering in any national or regional divisions, or choosing one side against the other."[48] Following discussions with Egyptian President Sisi in November 2017, Macron made a point of not commenting on domestic affairs, such as human rights concerns, explaining that "I believe in the sovereignty of states, and therefore, just as I don't accept being lectured on how to govern my country, I don't lecture others."[49] This stance of preserving national sovereignty above all else has allowed France to continue its strong relationships with countries on both sides of the GCC crisis.

In April 2018, the French government signed a military agreement with Saudi Arabia, apparently in response to Crown Prince Mohammad bin Salman's complaints that previous arms trading between the countries had been handled through ODAS, a French weapons manufacturer, rather than through a direct intergovernmental agreement.[50] France is currently the third largest arms exporter in the world, having sold licenses worth potentially $22.1 billion to Saudi Arabia in 2016.[51] Continued arms trade with Saudi Arabia has spurred some domestic discontent inside France, particularly as these arms are used in an increasingly bloody campaign in Yemen. In fact, a group of twelve international NGOs urged President Macron to suspend arms sales until the blockade of Yemeni ports was lifted ahead of Saudi Crown Prince Mohammad bin Salman's visit to Paris in early 2018.[52] France has also sold arms to the Qatari side of the crisis. In December 2017, Macron, during a visit to Doha, secured deals worth $14.13 billion, including an agreement to sell twelve Rafele fighter jets and 490 armored vehicles.[53] Qatar and France additionally signed a $3.5 billion deal for the operation of the Doha Metro, which is currently under construction ahead of the 2022 World Cup.[54] In addition to assets within France worth some $10 billion, Qatar Airways has also placed a new order for Airbus 321neo aircrafts worth an extra $930 million.[55]

Thus, French military ties to the Gulf remain strong and have become more apparent through operations in Yemen and the Gulf of Aden.[56] Saudi and Emirati financing of the NATO-EU anti-piracy mission also remains important, and French support for the construction of a Saudi military base in Djibouti alongside French military installments "signal[s] a long-term shared interest in stabilizing Yemen and the Southern Red Sea."[57] Outside of the Middle East, a 2013 mission to stabilize Mali evidences French and Saudi Arabian cooperation in Sub-Saharan Africa.[58] For the first time since its colonial heyday, the French government in 2009 built a military base in the UAE, the first on foreign soil outside of a former French colony, housing 500 troops as well as major naval and air operations to protect shipping lanes.[59] Then-President Nicholas Sarkozy explained that "the base was the beginning of a long-term French engagement in the region, and not a question of 'targeting' a particular country but safeguarding France's 'friends' in the Emirates."[60]

French interests, both economic and military, are clearly at stake amidst a ceaseless GCC crisis, and President Macron is likely to continue his support for Kuwaiti-led mediation at arm's length in order to ensure preservation of the variety of French concerns in the Gulf and broader Middle East.

1.4. Germany: Isolating Saudi Arabia to Forge New Regional Partnerships?

Whereas France under Macron has sought to act as a mediator, Germany under Chancellor Angela Merkel has taken more of a definite stance on the crisis, appearing to formally take Qatar's side. In June, immediately at the start of the crisis, then-German Foreign Minister Sigmar Gabriel blamed the rift between Saudi Arabia and Qatar on what he called a dangerous "Trumpification" of relations in the Middle East.[61] Perhaps more controversially, he added that "[t]he latest gigantic military deals by US President Trump and the Gulf monarchies are exacerbating the risk of a new arms build-up. That is the completely wrong policy approach and certainly not that of Germany."[62] After meeting with Saudi Foreign Minister Adel al-Jubeir in Berlin in June, Gabriel again appeared sympathetic to Qatar, stating that the country "is being more or less completely isolated and existentially targeted [....] A further escalation serves no one."[63] After Qatar's Foreign Minister Sheikh Mohammed bin Abdulrahman Al Thani traveled to Germany to meet with him in June 2017, Gabriel called for "solutions, especially lifting the sea and air blockades."[64] For her part, Chancellor Merkel in June 2017 dubbed the situation "very unsettling" and called for Iran and Turkey to aid the GCC in reaching a solution.[65]

Germany also publicly decried the thirteen demands released to Qatar in July 2017 from the blockading quartet, with then-Foreign Minister Gabriel dubbing them "very provocative."[66] In an effort to end speculation about Qatari support for terrorist financing and end the rift, the German government encouraged Qatar to open its books to Germany's Federal Intelligence Service (BND)– a measure that unfortunately did not lead to any movement on the blockade.[67]

Relations between Germany and the Quartet experienced further deterioration after Saudi Arabia condemned remarks made by Gabriel that November in wake of Lebanese PM Saad Hariri's resignation, calling Lebanon a "pawn" of Saudi Arabia. Shortly after he made the comment, the Saudi government recalled its Ambassador to Germany for consultation where he still remains, having yet to return to Berlin.[68]

In March 2018, Foreign Minister Gabriel resigned from his position and was replaced by former Justice Minister Heiko Maas. To the consternation of the Saudi leadership, the new Foreign Minister has taken a position similar to that of his predecessor. In response, Saudi Arabia had begun blocking some German businesses from its market, with government agencies being told not to renew some non-essential contracts with German companies.[69] Given that Germany remains Saudi Arabia's top European trading partner and third-largest source of imports worldwide, this new policy could have a major effect.[70] Indeed, in 2017, Germany exported $7.5 billion worth of goods to the Kingdom.[71] In the same year, Siemens received an order for five gas turbines to be used in a gas extraction plant in Fadhili.[72] Thyssenkrupp AG, a major elevator and maritime division supplier, as well as Daimler, an auto-maker, are also likely to be affected.[73]

The stance taken by Germany towards the JCPOA has also likely worsened its already deteriorating relationship with Saudi Arabia. In fact, Germany, France, Russia, China, and the United States are set to meet in Vienna in summer 2018 to try to salvage the JCPOA after the American withdrawal last May.[74] After the American reversal, Qatar said that "its main priority is to ensure the Middle East region is clear from nuclear weapons, and to avoid a nuclear arms race which would have unspeakable consequences."[75] Saudi Arabia, on the other hand, said that it "supports and welcomes" Trump's withdrawal.[76]

Germany's relationship with the GCC as a whole has not been remarkably significant. In fact, in 1999, the German Foreign Office planned to shut down a number of diplomatic missions in the GCC, including its consulate in Jeddah.[77] Investment and trade between the two was also at low levels during that period. The attacks of 9/11, however, prompted greater German involvement in Gulf diplomatic missions and an increase in official visits to the region. In 2005, Gerard Schröder became the first German chancellor to visit Doha, during which the two parties reached a somewhat symbolic security agreement placing a German federal police official in Doha as a document and visa consultant.[78] It was around this time that the two nations also began to increase military cooperation, which included German training of the Qatari Coast Guard. Enhanced German-Qatari military cooperation was unpopular in Germany, with outrage expressed in parliament after Qatar's purchase of tanks from Germany became public in the early 2000s, apparently ignoring human rights violations as well as German legislation that requires approval from the national security council for all weapons sales to so-called "areas of tension."[79]

As Qatar began investing in its own infrastructure in the early 2000s (Qatar expects to invest some $200 billion in infrastructure by 2022 for the World Cup), Germany became more important as a trading partner. Coinciding with this increased infrastructure development, a German Business Council was created in Qatar in 2002 while an extension of the German Industry and Commerce Office opened around the same time.[80] The two countries also signed an Air Transport Agreement and Investment Promotion and Protection Agreement, and in 2007 created a German-Qatari joint economic commission.[81] Qatari investments in Germany are valued at more than $18 billion, with Qatar holding stakes in major German companies, including Volkswagen, Hochtief, Siemensand Deutsche Bank.[82] Since the 2013 Business and Investment in Qatar Forum in Berlin, attended by Chancellor Merkel and then-Qatari Prime Minister and head of Qatar Investment Authority (QIA) Hamad bin Jassim al-Thani, the QIA announced that it would invest more in Germany. Bilateral trade has increased to a high of $2.87 billion in 2015 and sixty-four German companies now operate in Qatar.[84] Bilateral relations between Qatar and Germany have thus steadily improved since 2005. However, a lack of security and energy cooperation remains a strategic obstacle to the countries' relations.

Despite strong military and economic ties to the Quartet, as a whole the German position seems aligned with Qatar. However, considering the Saudi reaction to German rhetoric about both the crisis and the JCPOA, the profile of the country's engagement in the GCC may change in the future.

1.5. The United Kingdom: Managing Gulf Allies Amidst Brexit Uncertainty

Preoccupied with the fallout from its decision to the leave the EU, the United Kingdom has remained rather absent amidst the Gulf crisis. UK annual trade with GCC countries seemed a potential means of salvaging the UK's trade profile, as it is worth an estimated $33.39 billion, a figure that does not include investments between the two countries.[85] The crisis has revealed the extent to which the UK is no longer a major player in the Gulf, with Gulf leaders pivoting toward American help in the matter long before seeking any aid from the UK. Like its neighbors, the British government has called for the boycotting states to de-escalate the situation, yet unlike France or Germany, the United Kingdom has avoided becoming deeply involved in a region once referred to as a "British Lake."

Where the UK has chosen to become involved, it has tried to foster mediation largely through Kuwaiti interlocutors, justifying its arm's-length approach to the conflict. British Prime Minister Theresa May has urged that all sides work to "deescalate" the situation. During a July 2017 phone call with Saudi Crown Prince Mohammad bin Salman, she is said to have highlighted that all sides should "take urgent steps to deescalate the situation and restore GCC unity."[86] That month, the UK and United States reportedly put together a plan to help resolve the standoff during then-American Secretary of State Rex Tillerson's trip to the Gulf, yet joint UK-US efforts at fostering mediation have thus far been unsuccessful.[87]

Ties on both sides of the Gulf rift are critical for the UK, especially in a post-Brexit environment. Discussions to foster GCC-UK trade arrangements for the post-Brexit era were put on hold in 2017 after the start of the crisis. Minister for Investment Graham Stuart said in May 2018 that talks are meant to resume "soon."[88] He also confirmed that the GCC is "near the top of our priority list" for post-Brexit trading options, yet due to the rift multilateral talks remain suspended.[89] In April 2018, the British Ambassador in Doha Ajay Sharma confirmed that the crisis is "an important issue [for the UK] that should be resolved because we would like to see a united GCC." He also voiced support for Kuwaiti mediation efforts in the crisis and stated, "This matters a lot for the UK and that is why it will continue to do whatever it can to bring about a resolution."[90]

In July 2017, Foreign Secretary Boris Johnson praised the Qatari Amir Sheikh Tamim bin Hamad al-Thani's "commitment to combat terrorism in all its manifestations, including terrorist financing."[91] The Qatari Emir had days earlier expressed his willingness to enter into dialogue to end the blockade leading

Johnson to communicate his hope that "in turn, Saudi Arabia, UAE, Egypt and Bahrain respond by taking steps towards lifting the embargo," and that "this will allow substantive discussions on remaining differences to begin."[92] Johnson said that the UK would continue working through its partners in the Gulf to help resolve the crisis, particularly through relations with Kuwait as it leads mediation efforts."[93] Remarkably little has been done, however, in terms of meetings or shuttle diplomacy, to provide concrete support for Kuwaiti-led mediation.

The GCC states continue to be important for British trade, accounting for over half of British arms sales globally in 2015.[94] Military sales have proceeded on both sides of the rift. In the first half of 2017, British sales to Saudi Arabia exceeded $1.28 billion, with $971.5 million in arms sold between April and June alone.[95] Saudi Arabia was also, as a major trading partner, one of the first states that Theresa May visited after the triggering of Brexit.[96] In September 2017, Saudi Arabia and the UK signed a military cooperation framework deal, and, since 2015, Saudi Arabia has ordered more than $5 billion worth of UK defense equipment.[97] Concurrent with these sales, in September 2017 the British government and BAE Systems announced a deal to supply Qatar with Eurofighter Typhoon jets, just one part of the over $160 million worth of arms that the UK has exported to Qatar since the 2017 election.[98]

Aside from their security relationship, Qatar provides nearly one-third of the UK's gas imports. Growing UK dependence on foreign energy sources has led some to argue that the UK should begin exploiting its own resources more fully, meaning that this market could be subject to change in the future.[99] Beyond the energy market, Qatar is the UK's third largest export market in the Middle East, with investments valued at over $40.67 billion within the UK, on top of a pledged $5.81 billion.[100] Given the risky future for an increasingly isolated Qatar, this level of investment has spurred fears in the UK about Qatar's potential need in the future to liquidate these assets in order to sustain a domestic economy.

Because the UK's strategy in the GCC crisis seems to be centered on Kuwaiti mediation efforts, news of potential expansion of ties between the UK and Kuwait makes sense. In February 2018, UK Ambassador to Kuwait Michael Davenport revealed that the UK is considering construction of a permanent military base in the country.[101] Military cooperation between the two has increased in recent years, with the Kuwaiti Ministry of Defense having invited British command personnel from the 51st Brigade to participate in military drills in 2017 to simulate an attack on Kuwait; these exercises are scheduled to again take place in 2019.[102] Further, in 2019 the Kuwaitis and the 2nd Battalion Princess of Wales's Royal Regiment will conduct a Land Overseas Training Exercise and in August 2017, the British Minister of Defense announced intentions to sign a new military cooperation agreement with Kuwait.[103]

In terms of a permanent military presence in the GCC, the UK signed agreements in 2017 with Oman that allow the Royal Navy to use facilities at the Port of Duqum, while a secret airbase exists in al-Minhad in the UAE.[104] With plans in place to host a permanent base in Kuwait, the UK seems eager to ramp up involvement in the region as the American hegemon looks poised to retreat. Nonetheless, when it comes to the GCC crisis, the UK leadership is hesitant to act beyond voicing support for ongoing Kuwaiti mediation efforts that have thus far been unsuccessful.

2.1. Russia's Role Beyond Investments

The division of the GCC does not appear to have dramatically altered the Gulf states' alignments vis-a-vis Moscow. At first glance, however, Russia and Qatar do appear to share more common interests, especially regarding the JCPOA and gas pricing. In fact, Russia volunteered to supply Qatar with food after the start of the blockade in June 2017. Nonetheless, when the crisis broke out, Foreign Minister Sergei Lavrov mentioned that Moscow's intention was to remain uninvolved. "These are bilateral relations of the states. We do not interfere in these decisions."[105]

Securing Gulf investments in Russia's economy is a high priority for Moscow, necessitating that Russia take a cautious approach to the crisis. Certainly, Russian interest in maintaining investments from countries on both sides of the Gulf crisis—namely Qatar, Saudi Arabia, and the UAE—has been one of the main factors driving Russia to maintain neutrality in the GCC's diplomatic row.

On the Qatari side, assets of its sovereign wealth fund (QIA) in Russia are valued at more than $2.5 billion, namely in large infrastructure projects.[106] QIA has a $500 million stake in VTB, a leading Russian bank, and a 25% stake in St. Petersburg's Pulkovo Airport. In March 2018, during Sheikh Tamim's official visit to Russia, Qatar Airways announced plans to buy a twenty-five percent stake in Vnukovo Airport in Moscow as well.[107] Additionally, QIA recently announced a staggering $11.3 billion investment in Rosneft, a Russian Petroleum refining company, to be used for upstream projects, and logistics, totaling one-fifth of Rosneft's privatization portfolio. Sheikh Hamad bin Jassim bin Jaber al-Thani, former Prime Minister, Foreign Minister and CEO of QIA, is also a board member of the Russian Direct Investment Fund (RDIF), Russia's sovereign wealth fund.[108] This arrangement suggests that investment decisions may go both ways.

Meanwhile, the largest sovereign wealth fund in the GCC, Abu Dhabi Investment Authority (ADIA), has invested billions in infrastructure and industry through the Russian Direct Investment Fund, (RDIF). DP World, a Dubai ports operator, has agreed to launch a joint venture with RDIF and, as of January 2018, is believed to be considering investing in a large port in Vladivostok.[109] In December 2017, Mubadala Investment Company also committed up to $6 billion of investments in renewable energy sources, infrastructure, and transport.[110]

For its part, Saudi Arabia's Public Investment Fund (PIF) agreed in 2015 to invest $10 billion in a general investment program with the RDIF in the areas of infrastructure, retail, logistics, and agriculture over five years.[111] This was the largest FDI in Russia at that time. In October 2017, at the Russian-Saudi Investment Forum, during King Salman's first visit to Russia, companies from each nation signed investment deals worth more than $3 billion.[112] These deals included the creation of a $1 billion fund to invest in energy projects, a deal to invest $150 million into Russia's Eurasia Drilling Company, and a $1.1 billion agreement for Russian petrochemical company Sibur to open a plant in the Kingdom. According to Russian statistics, in the first quarter of 2017, trade with Saudi Arabia amounted to $124 million, while trade with the UAE amounted to $296 million–impressive numbers, but ones that pale in comparison to Russian trade with Iran, which stood at $398 million.[113] Despite KSA and UAE outpacing Qatar in terms of dollars pledged, Russian academics have opined that Qatar differs from its neighbors in that it does not merely promise investments, but actually sees them through completion.[114]

Despite taking different stances in Syria, various GCC states have still expanded their military ties with Russia. In June 2018, Russia agreed to supply Qatar with an anti-aircraft system to counter what the Russian side has claimed were Saudi threats to escalate the conflict if the deal for the S-400 system went through.[115]

Also in June 2018, just three months after Sheikh Tamim's visit, President Putin received Abu Dhabi Crown Prince Sheikh Mohammed bin Zayed al-Nahyan in the Kremlin, where the two leaders agreed to increase cooperation in the fields of security and defense, aluminum and oil markets, as well as the economy more generally. Additionally, the two nations agreed to "coordinate efforts to convert the Middle East into a zone free of weapons of mass destruction."[116] Jointly, the two leaders called for an international counterterrorism coalition that would have "respect for the sovereignty of states" that had directly suffered terrorist attacks.[117] Nonetheless, even with this Russia-UAE cooperation, common interests between the Kremlin and Qatar, especially as it relates to oil and natural gas markets, remain.

For the first time in fifteen years, Russia collaborated with the Organization of Petroleum Exporting Countries (OPEC) on a joint oil production cut, agreed upon in December 2016. As of January 2018, Russia and OPEC confirmed that the cuts would last throughout 2018; Saudi Energy Minister Khalid al-Falih even suggesting that these cuts may continue into 2019. Regardless, Russia has indicated that it would cooperate with OPEC even after these reductions expired.[118]

Qatar, Russia, and Iran enjoy the world's largest natural gas reserves, making them natural energy partners, however unwittingly.[119] Indeed, the three nations are the main backers for the floated creation of a so-called "GASPEC," an idea opposed by Saudi Arabia, the UAE, and the United States.[120] Nonetheless, news surfaced in early 2018 that Russia and Saudi Arabia, encouraged by success gained through cooperating through OPEC, may reach a new energy agreement regarding the production of LNG.[121] Russian President Vladimir Putin has prioritized the expansion of Russia's LNG output, while Saudi Arabia also aims to double its domestic gas production in the next decade, potentially putting the Russians and Qataris at odds.[122]

Perhaps the most interesting and least discussed aspect of the GCC-Russia link is a shared interest in squelching Islamist influence, particularly between Moscow and Abu Dhabi. This comes despite the fact that the two have taken on opposing sides within the Syrian conflict. Although Russia publicly maintains neutrality in the Qatar crisis, the accusations levelled made by blockading countries insinuating Doha's support for Islamist movements were preceded by Moscow in the earlier stages of the Syrian crisis. Certainly, Doha's ties with various Islamist groups in the region was one of the major issues that fueled friction in Qatari-Russian relations prior to the Gulf dispute.

The Grozny Conference in September 2016, hosted by Chechen leader Ramzan Kadiroy, a self-proclaimed Sufi and friend of Putin, brought together some of Sunni Islam's most influential leaders to define what it means to be a Sunni. It was co-organized by the Abu Dhabi-based Tabah Foundation, the same sponsor of the Senior Scholars Council, which aims to recapture Saudi Arabia's near-monopoly over Islamic discourse, as well as to counter the Muslim Brotherhood ideologue Shaykh Yusuf al-Qaradawi's Doha-based International Union of Muslim Scholars.[123] James M. Dorsey aptly describes this event as demonstrating "successful behind-the-scenes maneuvering by the United Arab Emirates to counter Salafism despite the UAE's close collaboration with Saudi Arabia [....] It also shines a light on Russian efforts to cultivate Muslim religious leaders."[124] In attendance were the Imam of Al-Azhar Egyptian grand mufti, President Sisi's religious affairs advisor, the mufti of Damascus, and the influential Yemeni cleric and head of the Tabah Foundation Habib al-Jifri, who also has close ties with Abu Dhabi Crown Prince Mohammed bin Zayed. Interestingly, and quite tellingly, the conference excluded Wahhabism, Salafism, and Deobandism from its definition of Sunni Islam. Despite this oversight, just months after the conference, in November 2016, then-Deputy Crown Prince Mohammed bin Salman welcomed Kadirov to the kingdom, where he visited the Prophet's Mosque in Madinah.[125] All of these developments suggest that Russia shares sympathy with the Emirati and Saudi approach towards Sunni Islamists, who are considered a fundamental political danger.

However, despite this shared ideological approach, Russia has not wholeheartedly backed the Emirati and Saudi stance when it comes to isolating Qatar.

As far as multilateral communication, Moscow has held four strategic dialogues with the GCC since 2007—most recently in May 2016—suggesting that it aims to court the sub-regional organization as a collective. However, if the GCC crumbles, Russia may be forced to choose sides. In light of the power vacuum left by the US's relative retreat from the Middle East, states on both sides of the GCC's rift appear open to increased Russian involvement.

Conclusion

The overwhelming consensus among countries of the EU and Russia seems to be that Kuwait should manage mediation of the GCC crisis before it escalates any further. In terms of advancing the conversation about how exactly this can happen, states of the EU and Russia do not appear to have any concrete suggestions. Economically, relationships on either side of the rift appear to have been unchanged. However, politically the rift has led to a re-positioning on the part of Germany and has given France an opening to become a major player in the GCC rift.

Endnotes

1. Habib Toumi, "GCC Endured its Worst Diplomatic Crisis in 2014," *Gulf News*, 27 December 2014, https://gulfnews.com/news/gulf/saudi-arabia/gcc-endured-its-worst-diplomatic-crisis-in-2014-1.1432568

2. Santhosh V. Perumal, "EU Says Gulf Unity Crucial, But Won't Take Sides over Crisis," *Gulf Times*, 7 May 2018, http://studies.aljazeera.net/en/reports/2017/09/europe-gulf-crisis-170904124324515.html#a5.

3. Perumal.

4. Perumal.

5. "EP Reiterates Support to Kuwait Efforts to Resolve Gulf Crisis," *Kuwait News Agency*, 21 June 2018, https://www.kuna.net.kw/ArticleDetails.aspx?id=2733561&language=en.

6. Stasa Salacanin, "Europe and the Gulf Crisis," *Al Jazeera*, 4 September 2017, http://studies.aljazeera.net/en/reports/2017/09/europe-gulf-crisis-170904124324515.html#a5.

7. Salacanin.

8. "EU Becomes Largest Trading Partner of GCC with Two-Way Trade Exceeding €143 Billion," *Saudi Gazette*, 8 April 2018, http://saudigazette.com.sa/article/532289/BUSINESS/EU-becomes-largest-trading-partner-of-GCC-with-two-way-trade-exceeding-euro143-billion.

9. "EU Becomes Largest Trading Partner of GCC."

10. Przemysław Osiewicz, "Europe Seeks Peaceful End to Gulf Crisis," *The Middle East Institute*, June 28, 2017, http://www.mei.edu/content/article/europe-seeks-peaceful-end-gulf-crisis.

11. Osiewicz.

12. Osiewicz.

13. Osiewicz.

14. Amal A. Kandeel, "Regional Upheaval: The Stakes for the GCC," *Middle East Policy Council*, Vol. 20, no.4 (Winter 2017).

15. Osiewicz.

16. Christian Koch, "Constructing a Viable EU-GCC Partnership," (paper presented at the Research Paper, Kuwait Programme on Development, Governance and Globalisation in the Gulf States at the London School of Economics), January 3, 2014, http://eprints.lse.ac.uk/55282/1/Constructing-a-viable-U-GCC-relationship.pdf .

17. Koch, 3.

18. Koch, 4.

19. Koch, 6.

20. Koch, 7.

21. Koch, 7.

22. Koch, 6.

23. Koch, 7.

24. Koch, 8.

25. Koch, 8.

26. Koch, 9.

27. Koch, 8.

28. Koch, 11.

29. Silvia Colombo, "EU-GCC Relations and the Risk of Irrelevance," *Turkish Policy Quarterly*, December 14, 2017, http://turkishpolicy.com/article/880/eu-gcc-relations-and-the-risk-of-irrelevance.

30. Colombo.

31. Colombo.

32. Koch, 11.

33. Giorgio Cafiero, "Macron and the Qatar Crisis," *Lobe Log*, July 17, 2017, https://lobelog.com/macron-and-the-qatar-crisis/.

34. Cafiero.

35. Giorgio Cafiero and Theodore Karasik, "Macron's Victory is Welcome News for Saudi Arabia and Qatar," *Atlantic Council*, May 8, 2017, http://www.atlanticcouncil.org/blogs/new-atlanticist/macron-s-victory-is-welcome-news-for-saudi-arabia-and-qatar.

36. Cafiero and Karasik.

37. Cafiero and Karasik.

38. Giorgio Cafiero and Maya Yang, "French Ambitions in the Gulf," *TRT World*, January 25, 2018, https://www.trtworld.com/opinion/french-ambitions-in-the-gulf-14588.

39. J. Weston Phippen, "Iran Signs a $5 Billion Energy Deal with France's Total," *The Atlantic*, July 3, 2017, https://www.theatlantic.com/news/archive/2017/07/iran-total/532560/.

40 Alanna Petroff, "Total Halts $2 Billion Gas Project in Iran," *CNN Money*, May 16, 2018, http://money.cnn.com/2018/05/16/investing/iran-total-oil-gas-sanctions/index.html.

41. Cafiero.

42. "France Aims to be 'Facilitator' in Gulf Crisis Talks," *News24*, July 15, 2017, https://www.news24.com/World/News/france-aims-to-be-facilitator-in-gulf-crisis-talks-20170715.

43. "France Appoints Envoy to Mediate between Qatar, Arab States," *Reuters*, September 5, 2017, https://www.reuters.com/article/us-gulf-qatar-france/france-appoints-envoy-to-mediate-between-qatar-arab-states-idUSKCN1BG1KX.

44. "There are Calming Signs and Firm Desire to End Gulf Crisis: French Envoy to Gulf," *The Peninsula*, February 16, 2018, https://www.thepeninsulaqatar.com/article/18/02/2018/There-are-calming-signs-and-firm-desire-to-end-Gulf-crisis-French-Envoy-to-Gulf.

45. "France's Macron Makes Surprise Saudi Visit Amid Lebanon Crisis," *BBC News*, November 10, 2017, https://www.bbc.co.uk/news/world-middle-east-41937439.

46. Annabelle Timsit, "The Strange Case of Lebanon France, and a Prime Minister's Unresignation," *The Atlantic*, December 5, 2017, https://www.bbc.co.uk/news/world-middle-east-41937439.

https://www.theatlantic.com/international/archive/2017/12/macron-hariri-france-iran-saudi-arabia/547391/.

47. Timsit.

48. Timsit.

49. "Macron Avoids 'Lecturing' Egypt on Rights, Sisi Defends his Record," *Reuters*, October 24, 2017, https://www.reuters.com/article/us-france-egypt/macron-avoids-lecturing-egypt-on-rights-sisi-defends-his-record-idUSKBN1CT-2NT.

50. "France, Saudi Arabia Agree New Defense Contracts Strategy."

51. "France, Saudi Arabia Agree."

52. "France, Saudi Arabia Agree."

53. Hadeel Al Sayegh, "Qatar Flexes Financial Muscle with 12 Billion Euros of French Deals," *Reuters*, December 7, 2017, https://www.reuters.com/article/us-qatar-france-contracts/qatar-flexes-financial-muscle-with-12-billion-euros-of-french-deals-idUSKBN1E1162.

54. "Gulf Crisis Simmering Down Amid International Desire to End Dispute, Says France Special Envoy," *The New Arab*, February 18, 2018, https://www.alaraby.co.uk/english/news/2018/2/18/gulf-crisis-simmering-down-says-france-special-envoy-.

55. Al Sayegh.

56. "Macron's France and the Future of Franco-GCC Relations," SQ Law, https://sqlaw.com/macrons-france-future-franco-gcc-relations/.

57. "Macron's France."

58. "Macron's France."

59. Angelique Chrisafis, "France Opens Military Base in UAE Despite Iranian Concerns," *The Guardian*, May 26, 2009, https://www.theguardian.com/world/2009/may/26/france-military-base-uae.

60. Chrisafis.

61. Thomas Sigmund, Mathias Brüggmann, and Dieter Fockenbrock, "Foreign Minister Supports Qatar, Bashes Trump," *Handelsblatt Global*, June 6, 2017, https://global.handelsblatt.com/politics/german-foreign-minister-voices-support-for-qatar-bashes-trump-777208.

62. Sigmund.

63. "Germany Warns Gulf Crisis Exacerbates Middle East 'Powder Keg,'" *DW*, June 7, 2017, http://www.dw.com/en/germany-warns-gulf-crisis-exacerbates-middle-east-powder-keg/a-39153930.

64. Jeremias Kettner, "Germany and the Qatar Crisis," *International Policy Digest*, June 13, 2017, https://intpolicydigest.org/2017/06/13/germany-and-qatar-crisis/.

65. "Germany's Merkel Calls on Regional Power to Solve the Deepening GCC Crisis," *The New Arab*, June 10, 2017, https://www.alaraby.co.uk/english/news/2017/6/10/merkel-calls-on-iran-turkey-to-solve-gcc-crisis

66. Andrea Shalal, "Saudi Demands from Qatar 'Very Provocative,': Germany," *Reuters*, 26 June 2017, https://www.reuters.com/article/us-gulf-qatar-germany/saudi-demands-from-qatar-very-provocative-germany-idUSKBN19H2A3.

67. Ludovica Iaccino, "Qatar 'Opens its Books' to German Spies to Prove Doha Doesn't Support Terrorism," *International Business Times*, July 7, 2017, https://www.ibtimes.co.uk/qatar-opens-its-books-germanys-intelligence-agency-clear-terrorism-claims-1629260.

68. "Saudi Arabia Recalls Ambassador to Germany over Gabriel Comments," *Reuters*, November 18, 2017, https://www.reuters.com/article/us-saudi-germany-lebanon/saudi-arabia-recalls-ambassador-to-germany-over-gabriel-comments-idUSKBN1DI00V.

69. Vivian Nereim, Dinesh Nair, Matthew Martin, and Glen Carey, "Saudi Arabia Blocks Some Germany Business Over Rift," *Bloomberg*, March 15, 2018, https://www.bloomberg.com/news/articles/2018-03-15/saudi-arabia-is-said-to-block-some-german-business-over-rift.

70. Nereim, Nair, Martin, and Carey.

71. Matthias Brüggmann and Maike Telgheder, "Saudi Arabia Freezes Out German Companies," *Handelsblatt Global*, May 28, 2018, https://global.handelsblatt.com/politics/saudi-arabia-german-companies-boycott-928152.

72. Nereim, Nair, Martin, and Carey.

73. Nereim, Nair, Martin, and Carey.

74. "Germany to Meet with France, Britain, Russia and China to Save Iran Nuclear Deal," *DW*, May 20, 2018, https://www.dw.com/en/germany-to-meet-with-france-britain-russia-and-china-to-save-iran-nuclear-deal-report/a-43857576.

75. "Qatar Warns against Iran Escalation, Calls for Nuclear-Free Middle East," *The New Arab*, May 9, 2018, https://www.alaraby.co.uk/english/News/2018/5/9/Qatar-fears-escalation-calls-for-nuclear-free-Middle-East.

76. "Qatar Warns against Iran Escalation."

77. Kettner.

78. Kettner.

79. Kettner.

80. Kettner.

81. Kettner.

82. Kettner.

83. Kettner.

84. Kettner.

85. "Global Britain in the Gulf" Brexit and Relations with the GCC," Fondation pour la Recherche Stratégique, July 19, 2017, https://www.frstrategie.org/publications/notes/global-britain-in-the-gulf-brexit-and-relations-with-the-gcc-13-2017.

86. "British Prime Minister Calls for 'De-escalation' of Gulf Crisis in Call with Saudi Crown Prince," *The New Arab*, July 4, 2017, https://www.alaraby.co.uk/english/news/2017/7/4/uks-may-calls-for-de-escalation-of-gulf-diplomatic-crisis.

87. Salacanin.

88. Noor Nanji and Damien McElroy, "Post-Brexit Trade Talks between UK-GCC to Resume 'Soon,' Says Minister," *The National*, May 16, 2018, https://www.thenational.ae/world/europe/post-brexit-trade-talks-between-uk-gcc-to-resume-soon-says-minister-1.731161.

89. Nanji and McElroy.

90, Joey Aguilar, "UK Wants GCC Crisis Resolved 'as Quickly as Possible,'" *Gulf Times*, April 10, 2018, http://www.gulf-times.com/story/588512/UK-wants-GCC-crisis-resolved-as-quickly-as-possibl.

91. "UK Welcomes Qatar's Call for Gulf Crisis Talks," *Al Jazeera*, July 23, 2017, https://www.aljazeera.com/news/2017/07/uk-welcomes-qatar-call-gulf-crisis-talks-170723144805446.html.

92. "UK Welcomes Qatar's Call for Gulf Crisis Talks."

93. "UK Welcomes Qatar's Call for Gulf Crisis Talks."

94. Cafiero and Al Makahleh.

95. Jessica Elgot, "UK Sale of Arms and Military Kit to Saudi Arabia Hit £1.1bn in 2017," *The Guardian*, October 24, 2017, https://www.theguardian.com/world/2017/oct/24/uk-sales-of-arms-and-military-equipment-to-saudi-arabia-2017.

96. "Saudi Arabia and UK Sign Military Cooperation Deal," *The New Arab*, September 20, 2017, https://www.alaraby.co.uk/english/news/2017/9/20/saudi-arabia-and-uk-sign-military-cooperation-deal.

97. "Saudi Arabia and UK Sign Military Cooperation Deal."

98. Jamie Merrill, "UK to Supply Qatar with Eurofighter Jets in Billion-Dollar Deal," *Middle East Eye*, September 18, 2017, http://www.middleeasteye.net/news/uk-supply-qatar-eurofighter-jets-97038783.

99. Adam Vaughan, "Qatar Crisis Highlights Rising UK Energy Reliance on Imports," *The Guardian*, June 8, 2017, https://www.theguardian.com/business/2017/jun/08/qatar-crisis-highlights-rising-uk-energy-reliance-on-imports.

100. Ben Moshinsky, "The Crisis in Qatar Has Come at a Terrible Time for the UK," *Business Insider UK*, June, 12 2017, http://uk.businessinsider.com/qatar-ik-economic-trade-ties-2017-6.

101. Giorgio Cafiero and Shehab Al Makahleh, "Kuwait's Role in London's Return East of Suez," *Gulf International Forum*, February 27, 2018, https://gulfif.com/kuwaits-role-in-londons-return-east-of-suez-commentary/

102. Cafiero and Al Makahleh.

103. Cafiero and Al Makahleh.

104. Cafiero and Al Makahleh.

105. Leonid Issaev, "Russia and the GCC Crisis," *Al Jazeera*, June 13, 2017, https://www.aljazeera.com/indepth/opinion/2017/06/russia-gcc-crisis-170613073826800.html.

106. Theodore Karasik, "Why is Qatar Investing So Much in Russia?," *Middle East Institute*, March 8, 2017, http://www.mei.edu/content/article/why-qatar-investing-so-much-russia.

107. "Qatar Airways Plans to Buy Stake in Russian Airport as Emir Visits Morocco," *Reuters*, March 26, 2018, https://uk.reuters.com/article/us-russia-qatar-airport/qatar-airways-plans-to-buy-stake-in-russian-airport-as-emir-visits-moscow-idUKKBN1H211O.

108. Karasik.

109. Frank Kane, "'Reset' for Russian-GCC Trade Relations, but Still a Long Way to Go," *Arab News*, June 5, 2017, http://www.arabnews.com/node/1110241

110. Fareed Rahman, "RDIF in Talks with UAE Partners for Investments," *Gulf News*, December 3, 2017, https://gulfnews.com/business/sectors/investment/rdif-in-talks-with-uae-partners-for-investments-1.2134596.

111. Kathrin Hille, "Saudi Sovereign Fund to Invest $10bn in Russian," *Financial Times*, July 6, 2015, https://www.ft.com/content/0205a0d6-2412-11e5-bd83-71cb60e8f08c.

112. Henry Foy, "Saudi and Russia Line Up $3bn in Investment Deals," *Financial Times*, October 4, 2017, https://www.ft.com/content/3dbba10c-7a49-38ba-a7c5-59dc336fd196.

113. Kane.

114. "Discussion at Russian Strategy in the Middle East workshop," (RAND Corporation-LSE Middle East Centre), March 28, 2018.

115. "Russia Snubs Saudi Threats over Military Deal," Middle East Monitor, June 3, 2018, https://www.middleeastmonitor.com/20180603-russia-snubs-saudi-threats-over-qatar-military-deal/

116. Kirill Semenov, "UAE, Russia Leaders Affirm Common Ground in Moscow Meeting," *Al-Monitor*, June 4, 2018, https://www.al-monitor.com/pulse/originals/2018/06/russia-uae-privileged-partnership-nahyan-putin.html.

117. Semenov.

118. Elena Mazneva, Wael Mahdi, Grant Smith, and Annmarie Hordern, "OPEC, Russia Signal Global Oil Alliance May Endure Past 2018," *Bloomberg*, https://www.bloomberg.com/news/articles/2018-01-21/saudi-oil-minister-says-opec-allies-should-cooperate-past-2018.

119. Issaev.

120. Issaev.

121. Wael Mahdi and Elena Mazneva, "Russians, Saudis May Go Beyond Oil Alliance with LNG Project," *Bloomberg*, February 14, 2018, https://www.bloomberg.com/news/articles/2018-02-14/russia-saudis-may-go-beyond-their-oil-alliance-with-lng-deal.

122. Mahdi and Mazneva.

123. James M. Dorsey, "Fighting for the Soul of Islam: A Battle of the Paymasters," *Huffington Post*, September 30, 2016, https://www.huffingtonpost.com/james-dorsey/fighting-for-the-soul-of_b_12259312.html?guccounter=1

124. Dorsey.

125. "Saudi Deputy Crown Prince Meets with Chechen Leader," *Al Arabiya*, November 27 2016, https://english.alarabiya.net/en/News/gulf/2016/11/27/Saudi-Deputy-Crown-Prince-meets-with-Chechan-leader.html.

Conclusion

The new variables revealed by the Gulf Crisis reflects the transitional status of relations across the Middle East and North African region. Cracks and crises affecting the structure of the GCC's internal and external relations had existed under the surface for a long time and exploded in late 2010 amidst the outbreak of the so-called "Arab Spring," especially in Tunisia, Libya, Egypt, Syria, and Yemen. The Arab Gulf countries were not secure from this public outrage, and they reacted differently. Therefore, the question that has been asked over the past decades and is still being asked: Is this fissure simply the result of the divisions sowed by "Arab Spring," or is it symptomatic of much deeper problems involving the Gulf governments, institutions and societies?

It seems that the various domestic and external crises in this troubled region have not been properly contained or resolved. Rather than help, history shows that the ways in which Gulf monarchies confront these problems often lead to further complications. The current Gulf Crisis is a prominent example of negative Gulf-Arab political engagement with crises in times of uncertainty. The question on everyone's mind: Will this crisis be the final nail in the coffin for the Gulf Cooperation Council after its thirty-six year history?

While not being characterized by armed conflict, the Gulf Crisis is going against the interests of each of the GCC states with no rational steps being taken to resolve the feud. As many of the prior chapters have hinted, despite a consensus that the Gulf nations would only stand to benefit from increased centralization amongst GCC institutions, this regional entity has been characterized by an ineffective bureaucracy, and an unwillingness by member states to risk the appearance of conceding their respective regime interests.

Despite the body's espoused shortcomings, the economic and diplomatic benefits of the GCC have been widely experienced by each member nation. However, some current GCC leadership seems ready to ignore the benefits of this regional entity in order to inflict damage on other member states. The increasing tensions and differences on regional issues between Saudi Arabia, the UAE, and Bahrain on one hand, and Qatar on the other hand surfaced in the crisis we see today. The current crisis marks a clear dividing line in the GCC history reflecting a change in the political, economic, security, social, and media realities of the intra-GCC conflict.

As has been discussed, the current impasse in the Gulf is not a sudden development. Rather it is actually a result of years of internal differences in different policy realms. Distinguishing the Gulf crisis however, was the proliferation of these differences in the public arena, worsening the situation on every level.

The rift has cracked the institutions of the GCC, creating dissonance, fear, and concern for the future in place of what were once strong trans-Gulf social bonds. Given the crisis' consequences, it will be difficult to restore trust among GCC state members in the near future. This crisis has also revealed the political, economic and military weakness of the GCC, which was primarily established in 1981 because of security concerns related to the outbreak of the Iran-Iraq War (1980-88), the Islamic Revolution in Iran (1979), as well as the extension of the Arabian Peninsula as a proxy site of the Cold War (ending in 1989). As the twenty-first century brought with it continued crises (1991, 2003, 2011 and 2014) for the Gulf and non-Gulf nations, the pillars of this regional body are crumbling amidst security concerns and seemingly irreconcilable political difference. Case and point, the apparatus of the GCC has been largely and intentionally marginalized since the 2017 Gulf crisis. It has not had any role in neutralizing the crisis, let alone containing it. Tellingly absent has been the GCC Secretary General, whose lack of action has received widespread scorn.

The challenges presented by this crisis for the future of the GCC system are profound. They move us to change our frame of reference, from one focused on plans of cooperation, economic unity, integration, an open market and even a common currency, to the bitter reality that the GCC may not even survive, and if it does it may morph into something unrecognizable. Some parties pushing their respective states to build new alliances with regional or international powers could would lead to a further minimization of the GCC's influence, leaving the body equally irrelevant as the Arab League, or perhaps even discarded into history à la Arab Maghreb Union.

As with most developments in international affairs, future conflict scenarios are likely to be more complex than they initially seem. While this book seemingly focused on the relationship of high-level diplomats and regional decisionmakers, a topic for further research undoubtedly should focus on the societal impacts for Gulf citizens and residents, whose voices and experiences are usually excluded within traditional analyses of international affairs. Additionally, the ongoing crisis certainly calls for a comparative approach, perhaps looking to the histories of other transnational bodies such as the European Union or the Association of Southeast Asian Nations in order locate a framework for how regional organizations can reemerge after periods of internal fragmentation. For now, however, it is helpful to remember the mantra introduced by Dr. Mohammed Al-Rumaihi in the beginning of this work, "the whole is greater than the sum of its parts."

The Editors

Biographies of Contributors

Dr. Mohammed Al-Rumaihi is a Professor of Sociology at the University of Kuwait. Dr Rumaihi holds a PhD from Durham University where he researched Social and Political Change in Bahrain (1920-1970). Dr. Rumaihi has published more than 20 books about the social and political changes in the Arab Gulf states. He has served as Editor-in-Chief for prominent newspapers and magazines in Kuwait and other Arab Gulf states. He was Secretary General of the National Council for Culture, Arts and Literature during 1998-2002. Dr. Rumaihi has served as a member on several committees in the Kuwaiti government and as a board member at several universities and development organizations in the Gulf and Arab world. Dr. Rumaihi is also a frequent lecturer in Cairo, Qatar, Bahrain, UK and Saudi Arabia.

Giorgio Cafiero is the CEO of Gulf State Analytics. He is a frequent contributor to Middle East Institute, Atlantic Council, Carnegie Endowment for International Peace, Middle East Policy Council, Al Jazeera, New Arab, Qatar Peninsula, Al Arabiya, Gulf Daily News, Al Monitor, TRT World, and LobeLog. Throughout Cafiero's career, he has spoken at international conferences and participated in closed door meetings with high-ranking government officials, diplomats, scholars, businessmen, and journalists in GCC states, Iran, Turkey, and Egypt. From 2014-2015, he worked as analyst at Kroll. Cafiero holds an M.A. in International Relations from the University of San Diego. Follow him on Twitter @GiorgioCafiero.

Professor David B. Des Roches is Professor at the Near East South Asia Center for Strategic Studies. Prof. Des Roches served as the Defense Department director responsible for policy concerning Saudi Arabia, Kuwait, Qatar, Bahrain, Oman, the UAE and Yemen. He also served in the Office of the Secretary of Defense as Liaison to the Department of Homeland Security, as senior Country Director for Pakistan, as NATO Operations Director, and as deputy director for peacekeeping. He graduated from the United States Military Academy and obtained advanced degrees in Arab Politics from the University of London School of Oriental and African Studies, in War Studies from Kings College London, and Strategic Studies from the US Army War College.

Dr. Kristian Coates Ulrichsen is a Fellow for the Middle East at James A. Baker III Institute for Public Policy, Rice University. He works across the disciplines of political science, international relations and international political economy. His research examines the changing position of Persian Gulf states in the global order, as well as the emergence of longer-term, nonmilitary challenges to regional security. Previously, he worked as senior Gulf analyst at the Gulf Center for Strategic Studies between 2006 and 2008 and as co-director of the Kuwait Program on Development, Governance and Globalization in the Gulf States at the London School of Economics (LSE) from 2008 until 2013.

Dr. Khalid Al-Jaber is Director of MENA Institute in Washington DC. Previously, he served as Editor-in-Chief of The Peninsula, Qatar's leading English language daily newspaper, and Deputy Editor-in-Chief of Al Sharq ("The East"), the sister Arabic daily of The Peninsula. Dr. Al-Jaber is also a visiting Assistant Professor of Political Communication in the Gulf Studies Program (GSP) at Qatar University, and a visiting Assistant Professor at Northwestern University in Doha. Al-Jaber has published a number of books and academic articles on GCC foreign relations, Gulf–US relations, and political communication in the Middle East and North Africa region

Amb. (ret.) Gerald Feierstein is the director for Gulf Affairs and Government Relations at Middle East Institute. He retired from the US Foreign Service in May 2016 after a 41-year career with the personal rank of Career Minister. As a diplomat he served in nine overseas postings, including three tours of duty in Pakistan, as well as assignments in Saudi Arabia, Oman, Lebanon, Jerusalem, and Tunisia. In 2010, President Obama appointed Amb. Feierstein US Ambassador to Yemen, where he served until 2013. From 2013 until his retirement, Amb. Feierstein was Principal Deputy Assistant Secretary of State for Near Eastern Affairs.

Sigurd Neubauer is a non-Resident Fellow at Gulf International Forum and a columnist for Arab News. Neubauer's expertise includes Oman; Qatar, Saudi Arabia, Yemen, Persian Gulf security, inter-Gulf Cooperation Council dynamics, Arab-Israeli relations, and Afghanistan. His work has also been translated into Arabic and Farsi. Neubauer has nine years experience from the US defense industry. From 2015-2017, Neubauer was a Non-Resident Fellow at the Arab Gulf States Institute in Washington and a columnist for Al Arabiya English. Fluent in seven languages, Neubauer is a graduate of Yeshiva University in New York where he studied Jewish History (MA), Political Science (BA) and French Literature (BA).

Courtney Freer is a Research Officer at Middle East Centre at the London School of Economics and Political Science. Dr. Freer's work focuses on domestic politics of the Gulf states, with interest in Islamism and tribalism. She previously served as Research Assistant at the Brookings Doha Center, and a researcher at the US–Saudi Arabian Business Council. She holds MA in Middle Eastern Studies from George Washington University, and PhD from University of Oxford.; her book *Rentier Islamism: The Influence of the Muslim Brotherhood in Gulf Monarchies* was released in 2018 with Oxford University Press.

Bibliography

Abdelfattah, Mohammed. "In the Middle East, Two-Thirds Get News on Social Media; Less than Half Trust it." *Northwestern University*, September 17, 2017 https://news.northwestern.edu/stories/2017/september/middle-east-news-social-media-trust/

"A Century of Lawmaking for a New Nation: U.S. Congressional Documents and Debates, 1774-1875," *Annals of Congress*, Senate, 18th Congress, 1st Session, Dec 1823. https://memory.loc.gov/ammem/amlaw/

Adel bin Ahmed al-Jubeir, "Saudi Arabia – Minister for Foreign Affairs Addresses General Debate, 72nd Session," Filmed 23 September 2017, 00:11:00. United Nations Audio/Visual Library. Posted 25 September 2017. http://webtv.un.org/meetings-events/conferencessummits/un-alliance-of-civilizations-5th-global-forum-27-28-february-2013-vienna/watch/saudi-arabia-minister-for-foreign-affairs-addresses-general-debate-72nd-session/5584856257001/?term=?lanarabic&sort=date

Aftandilian, Gregory. "The Future of Iraq-Kuwaiti Relations: Overcoming a Troubled History." *Arab Center Washington DC*, July 10, 2018.

Aguilar, Joey. "UK Wants GCC Crisis Resolved 'as Quickly as Possible.'" *Gulf Times*, April 10, 2018. https://www.gulf-times.com/story/588512/UK-wants-GCC-crisis-resolved-as-quickly-as-possibl

Al Jaber, Khalid and Giorgio Cafiero. "The GCC's Worst Summit." *Al Jazeera*, December 9, 2017. https://www.aljazeera.com/indepth/opinion/gcc-worst-summit-171208133340270.html

Al Sayegh, Hadeel. "Qatar Flexes Financial Muscle with 12 Billion Euros of French Deals." *Reuters*, December 7, 2017. https://www.reuters.com/article/us-qatar-france-contracts/qatar-flexes-financial-muscle-with-12-billion-euros-of-french-deals-idUSKBN1E1162

Al Shaibany, Saleh and Taimur Khan. "Kuwait Emir and King Salman Meet Over Qatar Crisis as Trump Backs UAE and Saudi." *The National*, June 6, 2017. https://www.thenational.ae/world/kuwaiti-emir-and-king-salman-meet-over-qatar-crisis-as-trump-backs-uae-and-saudi-1.82485

Alan Jangian, "The Cypriot-Turkish Conflict and NATO-EU Cooperation," MA diss., Naval Post Graduate School, 2017.

"Arab States Issue 13 Demands to End Qatar-Gulf Crisis." *Al Jazeera*, July 12, 2017. https://www.aljazeera.com/news/2017/06/arab-states-issue-list-demands-qatar-crisis-170623022133024.html

Al-Enezi, Mohammad. "Bahrain Welcomes Kuwaiti Naval Forces." *Kuwait News Agency*, March 21, 2011. https://www.kuna.net.kw/ArticleDetails.aspx?id=2154115&language=en

Baabood, Abdullah. "Oman and the Gulf Diplomatic Crisis." *OXGAPS*, Autumn 2017.

"Bahrain Independent Commission of Inquiry Excerpts." *BBC*, November 23, 2011. https://www.bbc.com/news/world-middle-east-15861353

"Bahrain's Foreign Minister Says Putting Al-Jazeera on Trial is Gulf Demand."
Bahrain Mirror, April 23, 2018. http://bahrainmirror.com/en/news/46725.
html

"Blockade against Qatar 'hindering' planning for long-term operation: Pentagon." *Reuters*, June 9, 2017 https://www.reuters.com/article/us-gulf-qa-
tar-usa-military-idUSKBN1902R2

Ben Ibrahim, Abdullah. "Khalifa Haftar's War on Opponents Gets Religious
Boost From Radical Salafists." *The Libya Observer*, February 5, 2018.
https://www.libyaobserver.ly/news/khalifa-haftar%E2%80%99s-war-op-
ponents-gets-religious-boost-radical-salafists

"Bombs Explode Near Egyptian and UAE Embassies in Libyan Capital." *Reuters*,
November 13, 2014. https://www.reuters.com/article/us-libya-secu-
rity/bomb-explodes-near-egyptian-embassy-in-libyan-capital-witness-
es-idUSKCN0IX0CO20141113

Bowman, Dylan. "GCC Common Market Comes into Effect." *Reuters*, January 1,
2008.

"British Prime Minister Calls for 'De-escalation' of Gulf Crisis in Call with Saudi
Crown Prince." *The New Arab*, July 4, 2017. https://www.alaraby.co.uk/
english/news/2017/7/4/uks-may-calls-for-de-escalation-of-gulf-diplomat-
ic-crisis

Browne, Ryan."US announces sale of F-15 fighter jets to Qatar," *CNN*, December 22, 2017. https://www.cnn.com/2017/12/22/politics/us-qatar-f-15-
fighter-jets-sale/index.html

Browning, Noah. "Yemen Combatants Not Ready for Talks, Says Neighbor
Oman." *Reuters*, April 2, 2015. https://www.reuters.com/article/us-ye-
men-security-oman/yemen-combatants-not-ready-for-talks-says-neigh-
bor-oman-idUSKBN0MT22Q20150402

Brüggmann, Matthias and Maike Telgheder. "Saudi Arabia Freezes Out German
Companies." *Handelsblatt Global*, May 28, 2018. https://global.handels-
blatt.com/politics/saudi-arabia-german-companies-boycott-928152

"Building the Panama Canal, 1903-1914," *United States Department of State*.
https://history.state.gov/milestones/1899-1913/panama-canal.

Cafiero, Giorgio and Cinzia Miotto. "Kuwaiti-Iranian Relations: The Energy
Angle." *Atlantic Council,* September 29, 2016. http://www.atlanticcouncil.
org/blogs/menasource/kuwaiti-iranian-relations-the-energy-angle

Cafiero, Giorgio and Maya Yang. "French Ambitions in the Gulf." *TRT World*,
January 25, 2018. https://www.trtworld.com/opinion/french-ambitions-
in-the-gulf-14588

Cafiero, Giorgio and Shehab Al Makahleh. "Kuwait's Role in London's Return
East of Suez." *Gulf International Forum*, February 27, 2018. https://gulfif.
com/kuwaits-role-in-londons-return-east-of-suez-commentary/

Cafiero, Giorgio and Theodore Karasik. "Macron's Victory is Welcome News
for Saudi Arabia and Qatar." *Atlantic Council*, May 8, 2017. http://www.
atlanticcouncil.org/blogs/new-atlanticist/macron-s-victory-is-welcome-
news-for-saudi-arabia-and-qatar

Cafiero, Giorgio. "Macron and the Qatar Crisis." *Lobe Log*, July 17, 2017.
https://lobelog.com/macron-and-the-qatar-crisis/

Carter, Jimmy. "1980 – The Carter Doctrine Announced." Filmed 1980. YouTube
Video, 00:01:05. Posted August 5, 2014. https://www.youtube.com/
watch?v=jjcMXKmW28E

Chandrasekaren, Rajiv. "In the UAE, the United States has a Quiet, Potent Ally Nicknamed 'Little Sparta.'" *The Washington Post*, November 9, 2014. https://www.washingtonpost.com/world/national-security/in-the-uae-the-united-states-has-a-quiet-potent-ally-nicknamed-little-sparta/2014/11/08/3fc6a50c-643a-11e4-836c-83bc4f26eb67_story.html?utm_term=.9064f344422d

"Charter of the Organization of American States," *Organization of American States*. http://www.oas.org/en/sla/dil/inter_american_treaties_A-41_charter_OAS.asp.

Chrisafis, Angelique. "France Opens Military Base in UAE Despite Iranian Concerns." *The Guardian*, May 26, 2009. https://www.theguardian.com/world/2009/may/26/france-military-base-uae

Chuter, Andrew. "Qatar to buy 24 Typhoon fighters from UK," *Defense News*, September 18, 2017. https://www.defensenews.com/air/2017/09/18/qatar-to-buy-24-typhoon-fighters-from-uk/

Cochrane, Paul. "Revealed: Secret Details of Turkey's New Military Pact with Qatar." *Middle East Eye*, January 27, 2016. https://www.middleeasteye.net/news/turkey-qatar-military-agreement-940298365

Cohen, Jordan. "America Must Actively Seek an End to the Qatar Crisis." *The National Interest*, November 26, 2017 https://nationalinterest.org/feature/america-must-actively-seek-end-the-qatar-crisis-23353

Cole, Juan. "David and Goliath: How Qatar Defeated the Saudi and UAE Annexation Plot." *The Nation*, February 16, 2018. https://www.thenation.com/article/david-and-goliath-how-qatar-defeated-the-saudi-and-uae-annexation-plot/

Colombo, Silvia. "EU-GCC Relations and the Risk of Irrelevance." *Turkish Policy Quarterly*, December 14, 2017.

"Country Ratings," *Gallup*. https://news.gallup.com/poll/1624/perceptions-foreign-countries.aspx

Critchlow, Andy. "Saudis Demand Say in Emirates Pipeline." *International Herald Tribune*, July 12, 2006. https://www.nytimes.com/2006/07/12/business/worldbusiness/12iht-pipe.2180611.html

Dargin, Justin. "Qatar's Natural Gas: The Foreign-Policy Driver." *Middle East Policy*, 14(3), 2007. https://www.mepc.org/journal/qatars-natural-gas-foreign-policy-driver

Dargin, Justin. "The Dolphin Project: The Development of a Gulf Gas Initiative." Oxford Institute for Energy Studies, NG 22, 2008.

Des Roches, David. "A Base is More Than Buildings." *War on the Rocks*, June 8, 2017. https://warontherocks.com/2017/06/a-base-is-more-than-buildings-the-military-implications-of-the-qatar-crisis/

Dionne Sinclair, "US Military Interventions in the Caribbean, 1898-1998," (MA diss., US Army Command and General Staff College, 2012.)

"Discussion at Russian Strategy in the Middle East workshop." (RAND Corporation-LSE Middle East Centre), March 28, 2018.

Diwan, Kristin. "Kuwait: Finding Balance in a Maximalist Gulf," (Report by The Arab Gulf States Institute in Washington), June 29, 2018. https://agsiw.org/kuwait-finding-balance-maximalist-gulf/.

Doha Center for Media Freedom, Second Annual Report 2013. http://www.dc4mf.org/wp-content/uploads/2017/12/english_for_web.pdf

Donaghy, Rori. "Saudi Arabia Shift Closer to Change in Policy Toward Muslim Brotherhood." *Middle East Eye*, February 13, 2015. https://www.middlee-asteye.net/news/saudi-arabia-shift-closer-change-policy-toward-mus-lim-brotherhood-994741112

Dorsey, James M. "Fighting for the Soul of Islam: A Battle of the Paymasters." *Huffington Post*, September 30, 2016. https://www.huffingtonpost.com/james-dorsey/fighting-for-the-soul-of_b_12259312.html

Dudley, Dominic. "As Qatar Prepares to Mark a Year Under the Saudi Embargo, it Looks Like the Winner in the Dispute." *Forbes*, May 17, 2018. https://www.forbes.com/sites/dominicdudley/2018/05/17/as-qatar-prepares-to-mark-a-year-under-the-saudi-embargo-it-looks-like-the-winner-in-the-dis-pute/#640f26697720

"Egypt blocks 21 websites including Al Jazeera- security sources." *Reuters*, May 24, 2017 https://af.reuters.com/article/egyptNews/idAFL8N1IQ758

Elgot, Jessica. "UK Sale of Arms and Military Kit to Saudi Arabia Hit £1.1bn in 2017." *The Guardian*, October 24, 2017. https://www.theguardian.com/world/2017/oct/24/uk-sales-of-arms-and-military-equipment-to-saudi-arabia-2017

Emmons, Alex. "Saudi Arabia Planned to Invade Qatar Last Summer. Rex Tiller-son's Efforts to Stop It May Have Cost Him his Job." *The Intercept*, August 1, 2018. https://theintercept.com/2018/08/01/rex-tillerson-qatar-sau-di-uae/

"EP Reiterates Support to Kuwait Efforts to Resolve Gulf Crisis." *Kuwait News Agency*, June 21, 2018. https://www.kuna.net.kw/ArticleDetails.aspx-?id=2733561&language=en

Estebari, Amir Hossein. "Conflict with Qatar and Unforeseen Consequences for Saudi Arabia – Analysis." *Iran Review*, July 30, 2017. http://www.iranre-view.org/content/Documents/Conflict-with-Qatar-And-Unforeseen-Con-sequences-for-Saudi-Arabia.htm

"EU Becomes Largest Trading Partner of GCC with Two-Way Trade Exceeding €143 Billion." *Saudi Gazette*, April 8, 2018. http://saudigazette.com.sa/article/532289/BUSINESS/EU-becomes-largest-trading-partner-of-GCC-with-two-way-trade-exceeding-euro143-billion

Filkins, Dexter. "A Saudi Prince's Quest to Remake the Middle East." *The New Yorker*, April 9, 2018. https://www.newyorker.com/magazine/2018/04/09/a-saudi-princes-quest-to-remake-the-middle-east

"Final Deal on Oman, Iran Gas Pipeline Soon." *Oman Observer*, April 21, 2018. http://www.omanobserver.om/final-deal-on-oman-iran-gas-pipeline-soon/

Fornaji, Hadi. "Faiez Serraj Arrives in Muscat For Two-Day Visit to Oman." *Libya Herald*, November 8, 2017. https://www.libyaherald.com/2017/11/08/faiez-serraj-arrives-in-muscat-for-two-day-visit-to-oman/

Foy, Henry. "Saudi and Russia Line Up $3bn in Investment Deals." *Financial Times*, October 4, 2017. https://www.ft.com/content/3dbba10c-7a49-38ba-a7c5-59dc336fd196

"France Aims to be 'Facilitator' in Gulf Crisis Talks." *News24*, July 15, 2017. https://www.news24.com/World/News/france-aims-to-be-facilitator-in-gulf-crisis-talks-20170715

"France Appoints Envoy to Mediate between Qatar, Arab States." *Reuters*, September 5, 2017. https://www.reuters.com/article/us-gulf-qatar-france/france-appoints-envoy-to-mediate-between-qatar-arab-states-idUSKCN-1BG1KX

"France, Saudi Arabia Agree New Defense Contracts Strategy." *Reuters*, April 8, 2018. https://www.reuters.com/article/us-france-saudi-defence/france-saudi-arabia-agree-new-defense-contracts-strategy-idUSKBN-1HF0DN

"France's Macron Makes Surprise Saudi Visit Amid Lebanon Crisis." *BBC News*, November 10, 2017. https://www.bbc.com/news/world-middle-east-41937439

Freedom House, Freedom in the World 2017. https://freedomhouse.org/sites/default/files/FH_FIW_2017_Report_Final.pdf

Gambrell, Jon. "US military halts exercises over Qatar crisis." *The Associated Press*, October 6, 2018.

Gates, Dr. Robert. "Welcome Remarks by Cliff May with Dr. Robert Gates," 00:50:00, YouTube Video, Published May 23, 2017. https://www.youtube.com/watch?v=bT6ypHHH9JA

"GCC Rail Project Delayed Over 'Technical Problems." *Trade Arabia*, March 30, 2017. http://www.tradearabia.com/news/CONS_322680.html

"Germany to Meet with France, Britain, Russia and China to Save Iran Nuclear Deal." *DW*, May 20, 2018. https://www.dw.com/en/germany-to-meet-with-france-britain-russia-and-china-to-save-iran-nuclear-deal-report/a-43857576

"Germany Warns Gulf Crisis Exacerbates Middle East 'Powder Keg.'" *DW*, June 7, 2017. https://www.dw.com/en/germany-warns-gulf-crisis-exacerbates-middle-east-powder-keg/a-39153930

"Germany's Merkel Calls on Regional Power to Solve the Deepening GCC Crisis." *The New Arab*, June 10, 2017. https://www.alaraby.co.uk/english/news/2017/6/10/merkel-calls-on-iran-turkey-to-solve-gcc-crisis

"Global Britain in the Gulf: Brexit and Relations with the GCC." *Fondation pour la Recherche Stratégique*, July 19, 2017. https://www.frstrategie.org/publications/notes/global-britain-in-the-gulf-brexit-and-relations-with-the-gcc-13-2017.

Gould, Joe. "Qatar rift sets back Trump's 'Arab NATO.'" *Defense News*, June 6, 2017 https://www.defensenews.com/global/2017/06/06/qatar-rift-sets-back-trump-s-arab-nato/

Grant, Will. "Cuba Concerns over Venezuela's Economic Woes." *BBC*, March 11, 2016. https://www.bbc.com/news/world-latin-america-35686683

Grieveson, Chris and Mads Odeskaug. "What Does the Qatar Embargo Mean for Shipping?" *The Maritime Executive*, July 21, 2017. https://www.maritime-executive.com/editorials/what-does-the-qatar-embargo-mean-for-shipping

Griffing, Alexander. "How the Saudi-led Blockade of Qatar Actually Made the Tiny Emirate Stronger." *Ha'aretz*, May 30, 2018. https://newstral.com/en/article/en/1096601424/how-the-saudi-led-blockade-of-qatar-actually-made-the-tiny-emirate-stronger

Grim, Ryan. "Gulf government gave secret $20 million gift to D.C. think tank." *The Intercept*, August 9, 2017 https://theintercept.com/2017/08/09/gulf-government-gave-secret-20-million-gift-to-d-c-think-tank/

Grim, Ryan and Akbar Shahid Ahmed. "His Town." *The Huffington Post*. https:// highline.huffingtonpost.com/articles/en/his-town/

"Gulf Crisis Simmering Down Amid International Desire to End Dispute, Says France Special Envoy." *The New Arab*, February 18, 2018. https://www. alaraby.co.uk/english/news/2018/2/18/gulf-crisis-simmering-down-says-france-special-envoy-

"Gulf Crisis: Six Months On, Families Still Bearing the Brunt of Qatar Political Dispute." *Amnesty International*, December 14, 2017. https://www. amnestyusa.org/press-releases/gulf-crisis-six-months-on-families-still-bearing-brunt-of-qatar-political-dispute/

"Gulf States Prepare for VAT in Time of Crisis." *AFP*, June 21, 2017.

Hannah, John. "It's Time for the Trump Administration to Step Up in the Qatar Crisis." *Foreign Policy*, June 27, 2017 https://foreignpolicy. com/2017/06/27/its-time-for-the-trump-administration-to-step-up-in-the-qatar-crisis/

Harris, Gardiner. "State Dept. Lashes Out at Gulf Countries Over Qatar Embargo." *The New York Times*, June 20, 2017. https://www.nytimes. com/2017/06/20/world/middleeast/qatar-saudi-arabia-trump-tillerson. html

Harvey, Jonathan-Fenton. "Saudi Arabia and UAE's Dangerous Rivalry Over Yemen." *The New Arab*, May 31, 2018. https://www.alaraby.co.uk/english/ indepth/2018/5/31/saudi-arabia-and-uaes-dangerous-rivalry-over-yemen

Henderson, Simon. "Meet the Two Princes Reshaping the Middle East." *Politico*, June 13, 2017. https://www.politico.com/magazine/story/2017/06/13/saudi-arabia-middle-east-donald-trump-215254

Herman, Edward and Noam Chomsky. *Manufacturing Consent: The Political Economy of Mass Media*. New York: Pantheon Books, 1988.

Hille, Kathrin. "Saudi Sovereign Fund to Invest $10bn in Russia." *Financial Times*, July 6, 2015. https://www.ft.com/content/0205a0d6-2412-11e5-bd83-71cb60e8f08c

"Hitler Fought Way to Power Unique in Modern History." *The New York Times*, May 2, 1945 https://archive.nytimes.com/www.nytimes.com/learning/ general/onthisday/bday/0420.html

Hollingsworth, Julia. "Why Qatar Matters to China, in Spite of Gulf Isolation." *South China Morning Post*, June 7, 2017; Giorgio Cafiero and Elaine Miao

Howard, Newton. "Nuclear Power for the Gulf States." Center for Advanced Defense Studies, Defense Concepts Series, April 2007. https://www.files. ethz.ch/isn/31170/24_arabnuclear_apr07.pdf.

Iaccino, Ludovica. "Qatar 'Opens its Books' to German Spies to Prove Doha Doesn't Support Terrorism." *International Business Times*, July 7, 2017. https://www.ibtimes.co.uk/qatar-opens-its-books-germanys-intelligence-agency-clear-terrorism-claims-1629260

"India's Role in Qatar's Food Security Crisis." *TRT World*, September 15, 2017. https://www.scmp.com/news/china/diplomacy-defence/article/2097206/ why-qatar-matters-china-spite-gulf-isolation

Issaev, Leonid. "Russia and the GCC Crisis." *Al Jazeera*, June 13, 2017. https://www.aljazeera.com/indepth/opinion/2017/06/russia-gcc-crisis-170613073826800.html

Jacobs, Jennifer. "Trump Warned Saudis Off Military Move on Qatar." *Bloomberg*, September 19, 2017 https://www.bloomberg.com/news/articles/2017-09-19/trump-is-said-to-have-warned-saudis-off-military-move-on-qatar

Jansen, Bart. "U.S., Qatar Reach Agreement in Long-running Dispute Involving Qatar Airways." *USA Today*, January 30, 2018. https://www.usatoday.com/story/travel/flights/todayinthesky/2018/01/30/us-qatar-reach-agreement-airline-finances/1079830001/

Johnston, Suzanne C. *An American Legacy in Panama: A Brief History of Department of Defense Installations and Properties in the Former Canal Zone of Panama* (Panama City, Panama: United States Army South, n.d.). http://ufdc.ufl.edu/AA00022175/00001.

Jivraj, Hassan. "Qatar: A Year on From the Boycott." *DebtWire*, July 28, 2018. http://www.debtwire.com/pdf/Qatar-SpecialFeature.pdf

Kabbani, Nader. "The High Cost of High Stakes: Economic Implications of the 2017 Gulf Crisis." *Brookings*, June 15, 2017. https://www.brookings.edu/blog/markaz/2017/06/15/the-high-cost-of-high-stakes-economic-implications-of-the-2017-gulf-crisis/

Kandeel, Amal A. "Regional Upheaval: The Stakes for the GCC." *Middle East Policy Council*, Vol. 20, no.4 (Winter 2017). https://www.mepc.org/regional-upheaval-stakes-gcc

Kane, Frank. "'Reset' for Russian-GCC Trade Relations, but Still a Long Way to Go." *Arab News*, June 5, 2017. http://www.arabnews.com/node/1110241

Karasik, Theodore and Giorgio Cafiero. "Why China Sold Qatar the SY-400 Ballistic Missile System." *LobeLog*, December 21, 2017. https://lobelog.com/why-china-sold-qatar-the-sy-400-ballistic-missile-system/

Karasik, Theodore. "Why is Qatar Investing So Much in Russia?" *Middle East Institute*, March 8, 2017. http://www.mei.edu/content/article/why-qatar-investing-so-much-russia

Kerr, Simeon. "UAE and Saudi Arabia Forge Economic and Military Alliance." *Financial Times,* December 5, 2017. https://www.ft.com/content/f2306d1c-d99a-11e7-a039-c64b1c09b482.

Kettner, Jeremias. "Germany and the Qatar Crisis." *International Policy Digest*, June 13, 2017. https://intpolicydigest.org/2017/06/13/germany-and-qatar-crisis/

Khan, Taimur. "Arab countries' six principles for Qatar 'a measure to restart the negotiation process.'" *The National*, July 19, 2017. https://www.thenational.ae/world/gcc/arab-countries-six-principles-for-qatar-a-measure-to-restart-the-negotiation-process-1.610314

Kirkpatrick, David. "Emirati Prince Flees to Qatar, Exposing Tensions in UAE." *New York Times*, July 14, 2018. https://www.thenational.ae/world/gcc/arab-countries-six-principles-for-qatar-a-measure-to-restart-the-negotiation-process-1.610314

Koch, Christian. "Constructing a Viable EU-GCC Partnership," (paper presented at the Research Paper, Kuwait Programme on Development, Governance and Globalisation in the Gulf States at the London School of Economics), January 2014.

Koch, Christian. "GCC Confronted by Dichotomy." *Gulf News*, December 22, 2012. https://gulfnews.com/opinion/thinkers/gcc-confronted-by-dichotomy-1.1122050

Kosmas Tsokhas, "The Political Economy of Cuban Dependence on the Soviet Union," Theory and Society 9, no. 2 (March 1980).

Kumar, Sachin. "Surge in Qatar-Oman Trade." *The Peninsula*, January 30, 2018; Hafsa Adli, "Turkey, Iran, Pakistan See Big Trade Boost with Qatar." *Al Jazeera*, December 3, 2017.

"Kuwait Recalls Ambassador to Iran as Row Escalates." *Reuters*, January 5, 2016. https://www.aljazeera.com/news/2016/01/kuwait-recalls-ambassador-iran-rising-tensions-160105090603667.html.

"Kuwait to Send Troops to Saudi Arabia to Fight Yemen Rebels – Newspaper." *Reuters*, December 29, 2015. https://uk.reuters.com/article/uk-kuwait-yemen-security-idUKKBN0UC0I520151229

Landler, Mark. "Trump Takes Credit for Saudi Move Against Qatar, a U.S Military Partner." *The New York Times,* June 6, 2017. https://www.thepeninsulaqatar.com/article/30/01/2018/Surge-in-Qatar-Oman-trade

Lenderking, Timothy, Perry Cammack, Ali Shihabi, David Des Roches. "The GCC Rift: Regional and Global Implications," *Middle East Policy* 24, no. 4 (Winter 2017). https://www.mepc.org/journal/gcc-rift-regional-and-global-implications

Lons, Camille. "Oman: Between Iran and a Hard Place." *European Council on Foreign Relations*, May 3, 2018. https://www.ecfr.eu/article/commentary_oman_between_iran_and_a_hard_place1

Luomi, Mari. "Abu Dhabi's Alternative-Energy Initiatives: Seizing Climate-Change Opportunities." *Middle East Policy*, 16(4), 2009. https://www.mepc.org/abu-dhabis-alternative-energy-initiatives-seizing-climate-change-opportunities

Lynch, Marc. *The Arab Uprising: The Unfinished Revolutions of the New Middle East*. New York City: Public Affairs Books, 2013.

Macheras, Alex. "Saudi News Channel Shows Simulated Downing of a Civilian Jet." *The Points Guy*, August 15, 2017. https://thepointsguy.com/2017/08/saudi-channel-simulation-downing-jet/

"Macron Avoids 'Lecturing' Egypt on Rights, Sisi Defends his Record." *Reuters*, October 24, 2017. https://www.reuters.com/article/us-france-egypt/macron-avoids-lecturing-egypt-on-rights-sisi-defends-his-record-idUSKBN1CT2NT

"Macron's France and the Future of Franco-GCC Relations." *SQ Law*. https://sqlaw.com/macrons-france-future-franco-gcc-relations/

Mahdi, Wael and Elena Mazneva. "Russians, Saudis May Go Beyond Oil Alliance with LNG Project." *Bloomberg*, February 14, 2018. https://www.bloomberg.com/news/articles/2018-02-14/russia-saudis-may-go-beyond-their-oil-alliance-with-lng-deal

Mazneva, Elena, Wael Mahdi, Grant Smith, and Annmarie Hordern. "OPEC, Russia Signal Global Oil Alliance May Endure Past 2018." *Bloomberg*, January 21, 2018. https://www.bloomberg.com/news/articles/2018-01-21/saudi-oil-minister-says-opec-allies-should-cooperate-past-2018

Merrill, Jamie. "UK to Supply Qatar with Eurofighter Jets in Billion-Dollar Deal." *Middle East Eye*, September 18, 2017. https://www.middleeasteye.net/news/uk-supply-qatar-eurofighter-jets-97038783

Miller, Rory. "GCC Meeting in Riyadh Points the Way Forward." *The National*, November 22, 2016. https://www.thenational.ae/opinion/gcc-meeting-in-riyadh-points-the-way-forward-1.217761

Mountachaf, Chirine. "A Huge Military Build-up is Underway in Qatar. But Who Will Man the Systems?" *Defense News*, December 15, 2017. https://www. defensenews.com/global/mideast-africa/2017/12/15/a-huge-military-buildup-is-underway-in-qatar-but-who-will-man-the-systems/

Mortimer, Caroline. "UAE Crown Prince asked US to bomb Al Jazeera during war on terror," *The Independent*, June 29, 2017 https://www.indepen-dent.co.uk/news/world/middle-east/uae-crown-prince-us-bomb-al-ja-zeera-mohammed-bin-zayed-al-nahyan-wikileaks-qatar-a7814691.html

Moshinsky, Ben. "The Crisis in Qatar Has Come at a Terrible Time for the UK." *Business Insider,* June 12, 2017. https://www.businessinsider.com/qatar-ik-economic-trade-ties-2017-6

Nanji, Noor and Damien McElroy. "Post-Brexit Trade Talks between UK-GCC to Resume 'Soon,' Says Minister." *The National*, May 16, 2018. https://www. thenational.ae/world/europe/post-brexit-trade-talks-between-uk-gcc-to-resume-soon-says-minister-1.731161

Nereim, Vivian, Dinesh Nair, Matthew Martin, and Glen Carey. "Saudi Arabia Blocks Some Germany Business Over Rift." *Bloomberg*, March 15, 2018. https://www.bloomberg.com/news/articles/2018-03-15/saudi-arabia-is-said-to-block-some-german-business-over-rift

Neubauer, Sigurd. "Washington's Interest in Qatari-Israeli Relations." *International Policy Digest*, July 17, 2018. https://intpolicydigest. org/2018/07/17/washington-s-interest-in-qatari-israeli-relations/

Neubauer, Sigurd."View: Despite Gulf Crisis over Qatar, GCC Pushes Ahead." *The Cipher Brief*, December 15, 2017. https://www.thecipherbrief.com/ view-despite-gulf-crisis-qatar-gcc-pushes-ahead

"New Mega Projects to Boost Self-Sufficiency in Food Production." *The Peninsula*, April 20, 2018. https://www.thepeninsulaqatar.com/arti-cle/20/04/2018/New-mega-projects-to-boost-self-sufficiency-in-food-pro-duction

"New Qatar-India Shipping Line Launched." *Gulf Times*, June 15, 2017. https:// www.gulf-times.com/story/553366/New-Qatar-India-shipping-line-launched

"No Military Solution to Yemen Crisis." *Kuwait News Agency*, March 8, 2018. https://www.kuna.net.kw/ArticleDetails.aspx?id=2739796&language=en

"Oman Joins Saudi-Led Islamic Alliance: Gulf Sources." *Reuters*, December 28, 2016. https://www.reuters.com/article/us-saudi-oman-coalition-idUSKB-N14H1L4

"Oman Says Busts UAE Spy Network, UAE Denies Role." *Reuters*, January 30, 2011.

"Oman's Role in a Turbulent Region." (Presented at Middle East Institute Event, Washington D.C, April 30, 2018). http://www.mei.edu/events/oman-s-role-turbulent-region.

Osiewicz, Przemysław. "Europe Seeks Peaceful End to Gulf Crisis." *The Middle East Institute*, June 28, 2017. http://www.mei.edu/content/article/eu-rope-seeks-peaceful-end-gulf-crisis

Pacheco, Filipe. "Qatar Stocks Erase Losses Suffered Since Embargo Began Last Year." *Bloomberg*, August 1, 2018. https://www.bloomberg.com/news/articles/2018-08-01/qatar-stocks-erase-losses-suffered-since-embargo-began-last-year

Paraskova, Tsvetana. "Qatar's LNG Exports to the UK Plunge." *Oilprice.com*, April 12, 2018.

Perumal, Santhosh V. "EU Says Gulf Unity Crucial, But Won't Take Sides over Crisis." *Gulf Times*, May 7, 2018. http://www.gulf-times.com/story/591912/EU-says-Gulf-unity-crucial-but-won-t-takes-sides-o.

Petroff, Alanna. "Total Halts $2 Billion Gas Project in Iran." *CNN Money*, May 16, 2018. https://money.cnn.com/2018/05/16/investing/iran-total-oil-gas-sanctions/index.html

Phippen, J. Weston. "Iran Signs a $5 Billion Energy Deal with France's Total." *The Atlantic*, July 3, 2017. https://www.theatlantic.com/news/archive/2017/07/iran-total/532560/

"Proof that Qatar News Agency was not hacked." *Al-Arabiya English*, May 24, 2017 https://english.alarabiya.net/en/media/digital/2017/05/24/Proof-that-Qatar-News-Agency-was-not-hacked.html

"Qatar Airways Plans to Buy Stake in Russian Airport as Emir Visits Morocco." *Reuters*, March 26, 2018. https://www.reuters.com/article/us-russia-qatar-airport/qatar-airways-plans-to-buy-stake-in-russian-airport-as-emir-visits-moscow-idUSKBN1H211O

"Qatar Mulls Buying Russia's Su-35 Fighter Jets." *Tass*, March 1, 2018. http://tass.com/defense/992351

"Qatar state news agency 'hacked with fake positive story about Israel and Iran.'" *The Telegraph*, May 24, 2017 https://www.telegraph.co.uk/news/2017/05/24/qatar-state-news-agency-hacked-fake-positive-story-israel-iran/

"Qatar Warns against Iran Escalation, Calls for Nuclear-Free Middle East." *The New Arab*, May 9, 2018. https://www.alaraby.co.uk/english/news/2018/5/9/qatar-fears-escalation-calls-for-nuclear-free-middle-east

"Qatari forces participate in Gulf shield drill in Saudi Arabia." *Al Jazeera*, April 19, 2018. https://www.aljazeera.com/news/2018/04/qatari-forces-participate-gulf-shield-drill-saudi-arabia-180419053305193.html

"Qatar-Oman Trade Volume Increases." *The Peninsula*, September 20, 2017. https://www.thepeninsulaqatar.com/article/10/09/2017/Qatar-Oman-trade-volume-increases

"Qatar-U.S Strategic Dialogue Stresses Two Countries Need to Remain Close Allies." *Ministry of Foreign Affairs- Qatar*, February 4, 2018. https://www.mofa.gov.qa/en/all-mofa-news/details/2018/02/04/qatar-us-strategic-dialogue'-stresses-two-countries'-need-to-remain-close-allies

Qiblawi, Tamara. "UAE social media users 'showing sympathy' for Qatar could face jail time." *CNN*, July 27, 2017 https://www.cnn.com/2017/06/07/middleeast/uae-social-media-qatar/index.html

Rahman, Fareed. "RDIF in Talks with UAE Partners for Investments." *Gulf News*, December 3, 2017. https://gulfnews.com/business/sectors/investment/rdif-in-talks-with-uae-partners-for-investments-1.2134596

Ramani, Samuel. "China's Growing Security Relationship with Qatar." *The Diplomat*, November 16, 2017. https://thediplomat.com/2017/11/chinas-growing-security-relationship-with-qatar/

"Readout of President Donald J. Trump's Call with Emir Tamim bin Hamad Al Thani of Qatar." The White House, January 15, 2018. https://www.whitehouse.gov/briefings-statements/readout-president-donald-j-trumps-call-emir-tamim-bin-hamad-al-thani-qatar-4/.

"Readout of President Donald J. Trump's Call with Emir Tamim bin Hamad Al Thani of Qatar." The White House, February 28, 2018. https://www.whitehouse.gov/briefings-statements/readout-president-donald-j-trumps-call-emir-tamim-bin-hamad-al-thani-qatar-2/

"Readout of President Donald J. Trump's Calls with Gulf State Leaders." The White House, July 2, 2017. https://www.whitehouse.gov/briefings-statements/readout-president-donald-j-trumps-calls-gulf-state-leaders/

"Remarks by President Trump and Emir Sabah al-Ahmed al-Jaber Al-Sabah of Kuwait in Joint Press Conference." The White House, September 7, 2017. https://www.whitehouse.gov/briefings-statements/remarks-president-trump-emir-sabah-al-ahmed-al-jaber-al-sabah-kuwait-joint-press-conference/

"Report: Saudi-UAE Coalition 'Cut Deals' With Al-Qaeda in Yemen." Al Jazeera, August 6, 2018. https://www.aljazeera.com/news/2018/08/report-saudi-uae-coalition-cut-deals-al-qaeda-yemen-180806074659521.html

"Responding to Iraqi Aggression in the Gulf, National Security Directive 54," The White House, August 20, 1990. https://fas.org/irp/offdocs/nsd/nsd_54.htm.

Riedel, Bruce. "Is the GCC Dead?" Al-Monitor, June 18, 2018. https://www.al-monitor.com/pulse/originals/2018/06/gcc-dead-saudi-arabia-qatar-dispute-salman-mbs.html

Roberts, David. Qatar: Securing the Global Ambitions of a City-State. London: Oxford University Press, 2017.

"Russia Snubs Saudi Threats over Military Deal." Middle East Monitor, June 3, 2018. https://www.middleeastmonitor.com/20180603-russia-snubs-saudi-threats-over-qatar-military-deal/

Sailer, Matthias. "UAE Foreign Policy and the Crown Prince of Abu Dhabi: Hardly a Ruler in Waiting." Qantara, March 23, 2018. https://en.qantara.de/content/uae-foreign-policy-and-the-crown-prince-of-abu-dhabi-hardly-a-ruler-in-waiting

Salacanin, Stasa. "Europe and the Gulf Crisis." Al Jazeera, September 4, 2017. http://studies.aljazeera.net/en/reports/2017/09/europe-gulf-crisis-170904124324515.html

"Saudi Arabia and UK Sign Military Cooperation Deal." The New Arab, September 20, 2017. https://www.alaraby.co.uk/english/news/2017/9/20/saudi-arabia-and-uk-sign-military-cooperation-deal

"Saudi Arabia Recalls Ambassador to Germany over Gabriel Comments." Reuters, November 18, 2017. https://www.reuters.com/article/us-saudi-germany-lebanon/saudi-arabia-recalls-ambassador-to-germany-over-gabriel-comments-idUSKBN1DI00V

"Saudi Deputy Crown Prince Meets with Chechen Leader." Al Arabiya, November 27, 2016. https://english.alarabiya.net/en/News/gulf/2016/11/27/Saudi-Deputy-Crown-Prince-meets-with-Chechan-leader.html

"Saudi Soldiers Sent Into Bahrain." Al Jazeera, March 15, 2011. https://www.aljazeera.com/news/middleeast/2011/03/2011314124928850647.html

"Secretary Pompeo's Meeting With Qatari Foreign Minister Al Thani." U.S. State Department, July 26, 2018. https://www.state.gov/r/pa/prs/ps/2018/08/285315.htm

Semenov, Kirill. "UAE, Russia Leaders Affirm Common Ground in Moscow Meeting." *Al-Monitor*, June 4, 2018. https://www.al-monitor.com/pulse/originals/2018/06/russia-uae-privileged-partnership-nahyan-putin.html

Sergie, Mohammed. "Embattled Qatar is Rich Enough to Get By for Another 100 Years." *Bloomberg Businessweek*, June 6, 2018. https://www.bloombergquint.com/businessweek/2018/06/06/a-year-later-iran-is-the-big-winner-of-the-qatar-embargo#gs.INMrYtc

Sezer, Murad. "Qatar Airways Confirms 'Substantial' Annual Loss, Blames Regional Row." *Reuters*, April 25, 2018. https://uk.reuters.com/article/uk-qatar-airlines-qatar-airways/qatar-airways-confirms-substantial-annual-loss-blames-regional-row-idUKKBN1HW1YW

"Sheikh Tamim: Any talks must respect Qatar sovereignty." *Al Jazeera*, September 22, 2018. https://www.aljazeera.com/news/2017/07/sheikh-tamim-talks-respect-qatar-sovereignty-170721184815998.html

"Special Interest Lobbies – Ethnic Lobbies," *Encyclopedia of the New American Nation*. http://www.americanforeignrelations.com/O-W/Special-Interest-Lobbies-Ethnic-lobbies.html

Shalal, Andrea. "Saudi Demands from Qatar 'Very Provocative': Germany." *Reuters*, June 26, 2017. https://www.reuters.com/article/us-gulf-qatar-germany/saudi-demands-from-qatar-very-provocative-germany-idUSKBN19H2A3

Shennib, Ghaith and Marie-Louise Gumuchian. "UAE Embassy Compound Attacked in Libyan Capital." *Reuters*, July 25, 2013. https://www.reuters.com/article/us-libya-uae-attack/uae-embassy-compound-attacked-in-libyan-capital-idUSBRE96O04J20130725

Shoeb, Mohammad. "Number of Factories in Qatar Doubled During Blockade: Minister." *Al Bawaba*, December 18, 2017. https://www.albawaba.com/business/number-factories-qatar-doubled-during-blockade-minister-1062998

Sigmund, Thomas, Mathias Brüggmann, and Dieter Fockenbrock. "Foreign Minister Supports Qatar, Bashes Trump." *Handelsblatt Global*, June 6, 2017. https://global.handelsblatt.com/politics/german-foreign-minister-voices-support-for-qatar-bashes-trump-777208

Stancati, Margherita. "Saudi Crown Prince and U.A.E Heir Forge Pivotal Ties." *The Wall Street Journal*, August 6, 2017. https://www.wsj.com/articles/saudi-crown-prince-and-u-a-e-heir-forge-pivotal-ties-1502017202

Suchliki, James. "Why Cuba Will Still be Anti-American After Castro." *The Atlantic*, March 4, 2013. https://www.theatlantic.com/international/archive/2013/03/why-cuba-will-still-be-anti-american-after-castro/273680/

"Syria's Top Diplomat Visits Oman on Rare Gulf Mission." *Yahoo!*, March 26, 2018. https://www.yahoo.com/news/syrias-top-diplomat-visits-oman-rare-gulf-mission-174311992.html

"The Hard Man of the Hills." *The Economist*, July 15, 2017. https://www.economist.com/briefing/2017/07/15/paul-kagame-feted-and-feared?fsrc=scn/tw/te/bl/ed/paulkagamefetedandfeared

"There are Calming Signs and Firm Desire to End Gulf Crisis: French Envoy to Gulf." *The Peninsula*, February 16, 2018. https://www.thepeninsulaqatar. com/article/18/02/2018/There-are-calming-signs-and-firm-desire-to-end-Gulf-crisis-French-Envoy-to-Gulf

Timsit, Annabelle. "The Strange Case of Lebanon France, and a Prime Minister's Unresignation." *The Atlantic*, December 5, 2017. https://www. theatlantic.com/international/archive/2017/12/macron-hariri-france-iran-saudi-arabia/547391/

"Top UN Court Rules UAE Blockade Violated Qataris' Rights." *Al Jazeera*, July 23, 2018. https://www.aljazeera.com/news/2018/07/top-court-rules-uae-blockade-violated-qataris-rights-180723131444047.html

Torchia, Andrew, Agnieszka Barteczko, and Oleg Vukmanovic, "Qatargas Agrees to Double LNG Supplies to Poland." *Reuters*, March 14, 2017. https:// www.reuters.com/article/qatar-poland-lng-idUSL5N1GR1AO

Toumi, Habib. "GCC Endured its Worst Diplomatic Crisis in 2014." *Gulf News*, December 27, 2014. https://gulfnews.com/news/gulf/saudi-arabia/gcc-endured-its-worst-diplomatic-crisis-in-2014-1.1432568

Toumi, Habib. "Saudi Grand Mufti rejects Brotherhood accusations." *The Gulf News*, June 15, 2017 https://gulfnews.com/news/gulf/qatar/sau-di-grand-mufti-rejects-brotherhood-accusations-1.2044068

Tran, Pierre. "Qatar moves to buy more Rafale jets, order infantry fighting vehicles." *Defense News*, December 7, 2017. https://www.defensenews. com/global/mideast-africa/2017/12/07/qatar-moves-to-buy-more-rafale-jets-order-infantry-fighting-vehicles/

Trump, Donald (@realDonaldTrump). "During my recent trip to the Middle East I stated that there can no longer be funding of Radical Ideology. Leaders pointed to Qatar- look!" June 6, 2017. https://twitter.com/realdon-aldtrump/status/872062159789985792?lang=en

Trump, Donald (@realDonaldTrump). "So good to see the Saudi Arabia visit with the King and 50 countries already paying off. They said they would take a hard line on funding..." June 6, 2017 https://twitter.com/realdon-aldtrump/status/872084870620520448?lang=en and "...extremism, and all reference was pointing to Qatar. Perhaps this will be the beginning of the end of the horror of terrorism!" June 6, 2017. https://twitter.com/realdonaldtrump/status/872086906804240384?lang=en

"Trump: US-Qatar ties 'work extremely well.'" *Al Jazeera*, April 11, 2018. https://www.aljazeera.com/news/2018/04/trump-qatar-ties-work-ex-tremely-180410135820276.html

"Turkey and Qatar: Behind the Strategic Alliance." *Al Jazeera*, February 1, 2018. https://www.aljazeera.com/news/2017/10/turkey-qatar-strategic-alli-ance-171024133518768.html

"Turkey Marches Ahead with its Military Plans in Qatar." *Stratfor,* June 16, 2017. https://worldview.stratfor.com/article/turkey-marches-ahead-its-military-plans-qatar

"UAE crown prince asked US to bomb al Jazeera, WikiLeaks claims." *Daily Sabah*, June 29 2017 https://www.dailysabah.com/mideast/2017/06/29/uae-crown-prince-asked-us-to-bomb-al-jazeera-wikileaks-claims

"UAE Denies Pro-Hezbollah Newspaper Claims Of Oman Pressure." *The National*, July 23, 2018. https://www.thenational.ae/world/mena/uae-denies-pro-hezbollah-newspaper-claims-of-oman-pressure-1.753249

"UK Welcomes Qatar's Call for Gulf Crisis Talks." *Al Jazeera*, July 23, 2017. https://www.aljazeera.com/news/2017/07/uk-welcomes-qatar-call-gulf-crisis-talks-170723144805446.html

Ulrichsen, Kristian Coates, ed. *The Changing Security Dynamics of the Persian Gulf*. Oxford: Oxford University Press, 2018.

Ulrichsen, Kristian Coates. "Crown Prince of Disorder." *Foreign Policy*, March 21, 2018. https://foreignpolicy.com/2018/03/21/crown-prince-of-disorder/

Ulrichsen, Kristian Coates. "The Needless Crisis in the Arabian Gulf." *Arab Center Washington DC*, June 5, 2018. http://arabcenterdc.org/policy_analyses/the-needless-crisis-in-the-arabian-gulf/

Ulrichsen, Kristian Coates. "Trump's Transactional Relationship with Saudi Arabia." *Arab Center Washington DC,* March 22, 2018. http://arabcenterdc.org/viewpoint/trumps-transactional-relationship-with-saudi-arabia/

Ulrichsen, Kristian Coates. *The Gulf States in International Political Economy*. Basingstoke: Palgrave Macmillan, 2016.

Umar, Baba. "Yemen's War Wounded Find Comfort in 'Brotherly' Oman." *Al Jazeera*, December 16, 2018. https://www.aljazeera.com/news/2016/11/yemen-war-wounded-find-comfort-brotherly-oman-161120065419274.html

"US and UAE Hold Talks on Security and Iran." *The New Arab*, May 17, 2017. https://www.alaraby.co.uk/english/news/2017/5/17/us-and-uae-hold-talks-on-security-and-iran

"US Invasion and Occupation of Haiti, 1915-34," United States Department of State. https://history.state.gov/milestones/1914-1920/haiti

"U.S.-Qatari Military-to-Military Relations," Filmed January 29, 2018 00:49:13, The Heritage Foundation. https://www.heritage.org/defense/event/us-qatari-military-military-relations

Vaughan, Adam. "Qatar Crisis Highlights Rising UK Energy Reliance on Imports." *The Guardian*, June 8, 2017. https://www.theguardian.com/business/2017/jun/08/qatar-crisis-highlights-rising-uk-energy-reliance-on-imports

Venna, Srivani. "Qatar Petroleum Delivers 500th LNG Cargo to South Hook LNG Terminal in the UK." *Hydrocarbons Technology*, March 27, 2016.

"War 'stopped' between Qatar, blockading Arab nations." *Al Jazeera*, September 7, 2017 https://www.aljazeera.com/news/2017/09/war-stopped-qatar-blockading-arab-nations-170908012658804.html

"Websites of Al Jazeera, Qatari newspapers blocked in Saudi Arabia and UAE." *Al-Arabiya English*, May 24, 2017 https://english.alarabiya.net/en/media/digital/2017/05/24/Websites-of-Al-Jazeera-Qatari-newspapers-blocked-in-Saudi-Arabia.html

Wehrey, Frederic M. *Sectarian Politics in the Gulf: From the Iraq War To the Arab Uprisings,* New York: Columbia University Press, 2016.

Wehrey, Frederic. "Quiet No More?" *Carnegie Middle East Center*, October 13, 2016. http://carnegie-mec.org/diwan/64846

Wintour, Patrick. "Qatar given 10 days to meet 13 sweeping demands by Saudi Arabia." *The Guardian*, June 23, 2017. https://www.theguardian.com/world/2017/jun/23/close-al-jazeera-saudi-arabia-issues-qatar-with-13-demands-to-end-blockade

"Yemen Peace Talks in Kuwait End Amid Fighting." *Reuters*, August 7, 2016. https://www.aljazeera.com/news/2016/08/yemen-peace-talks-collapse-fighting-intensifies-160807042106210.html

"Yemen, Houthis and Saudi Arabia in Secret Talks to End War – Sources." *Reuters*, March 15, 2018. https://www.reuters.com/article/yemen-security-saudi-talks/yemens-houthis-and-saudi-arabia-in-secret-talks-to-end-war-sources-idUSL8N1QX1FK

"Yemen's Rebels 'Attack' Abu Dhabi Airport Using a Drone." *Reuters*, July 27, 2018. https://www.aljazeera.com/news/2018/07/yemen-rebels-attack-abu-dhabi-airport-drone-180726155103669.html

Zhdannikov, Dmitry. "Qatar Sees Stampede for Gas Projects to Help Beat Crisis." *Reuters*, January 24, 2018. https://www.reuters.com/article/us-davos-meeting-qatar-energy/qatar-sees-stampede-for-gas-projects-to-help-beat-crisis-idUSKBN1FD0R6

Glossary

AQAP: Al-Qaeda in the Arabian Peninsula
ASEAN: Association of Southeast Asian Nations (Thailand, Laos, Vietnam, Myanmar, Cambodia, Indonesia, Malaysia, Singapore, Brunei & Philippines).
Quartet: (Saudi Arabia, Bahrain, The United Arab Emirates & Egypt)
CTF: Counterterrorism Financing
EP: European Parliament
EU: European Union
FTA: Free Trade Agreement
GCC: Gulf Cooperation Council (Saudi Arabia, Kuwait, Qatar, Bahrain, Oman & The United Arab Emirates)
IRGC: Islamic Revolutionary Guard Corps
HbJ: Former Qatari Prime Minister Hamad bin Jasim
JCPOA: Joint Comprehensive Plan of Action
KSA: Kingdom of Saudi Arabia
LNG: Liquified Natural Gas
MB: Muslim Brotherhood
MbS: Mohammed bin Salman
MbN: Mohammed bin Nayef
MbZ: Mohammed bin Zayed
MENA: Middle East and North Africa
MoU: Memorandum of Understanding
NGO: Non-Governmental Organization
OPEC: Organization of Petroleum Exporting Countries
PIF: Saudi Arabian Public Investment Fund
PDRY: Peoples Democratic Republic of Yemen
P5+1: United States, United Kingdom, France, Russia, China and Germany
QNA: Qatar News Agency
STC: Southern Transitional Council
SWF: Sovereign Wealth Fund
UAE: United Arab Emirates
UK: United Kingdom
UN: United Nations